A Measure Filled

Lisa Sergio

A Measure Filled

the life of

Lena Madesin Phillips

drawn from her

autobiography

Robert B. Luce, Inc.   New York – Washington

Copyright © 1972 by Lisa Sergio

Library of Congress Catalog Card Number 71-190073

To the memory

of

MARJORY LACEY-BAKER

Contents

Introduction

This book is dedicated to the memory of Marjory Lacey-Baker not merely in recognition of the devoted friendship which bound her to Lena Madesin Phillips for some thirty-five years of her life, but also because of her eagerness to see a book emerge from the voluminous collection of papers of which she had become custodian upon the death of her friend in 1955.

When Dr. Phillips set off on her trip to the Middle East in May of that year, the baggage placed in her cabin aboard the *S.S. Excambion* included a great deal of the material she expected to use in writing the history of the International Federation of Business and Professional Women. She had carefully planned her itinerary abroad to provide her with several stretches of time, free from all obligations, to be devoted to the task she was never able to 'plunge into, body and soul' as she said, when she was at home. The material returned to Westport, untouched.

Towards the end of 1957, when Miss Lacey-Baker had finished the basic sorting and classifying of an entire roomful of paper covering well over half a century of Dr. Phillips' ceaseless and varied activities, she sought the help of Emma Gelders Sterne. A distinguished author and a sensitive person, in sympathy with many of Lena Madesin Phillips' causes, she undertook to complete the history and did so with perception and skill. However, by the time she considered her assignment fulfilled, Miss Lacey-Baker, having come upon more documentation, decided to embark on a major revision of the manuscript on her own. Interrupted by ill-health and other unforseen difficulties, the work was held up while a growing international membership pressed its demand for a history of the organization.

Finally, in 1969, the International Federation itself brought out such a history, prepared from the official records and written by Phyllis A. Deakin, noted English journalist and an officer of her country's BPW Federation. A succinct and effective review of thirty-eight years of endeavor by the International Federation, it extends a decade beyond its founder's lifetime. When Marjory Lacey-Baker died in March 1971, the personal story of Lena Madesin Phillips still remained to be extracted from, literally, a mountain of material scarcely touched in the unfinished history, and

1

destined by Dr. Phillips' will to the Women's Archives at Radcliffe where it is now to be found. Miss Lacey-Baker's will, however, requested that the papers be first utilized for a biography of Dr. Phillips, if no longer for a Federation history.

It was at this point that I was privileged to receive an invitation from Mrs. Boynton Schmitt, a niece of Miss Lacey-Baker and the executrix of her Estate, to examine the material and consider writing the biography. My first view of filing cabinets, folders, boxes and envelopes assembled in one room in the Westport house where Miss Lacey-Baker had lived after Dr. Phillips' death was discouraging on a very warm day at the end of June. However, thanks chiefly to the wisdom and enthusiasm of Isabelle Claridge Taylor who accompanied me on that excursion and helped in that initial research, I decided to take on the triple challenge: examining all the material, meeting a short deadline imposed by my other professional commitments and, most important of all, trying to do justice to the subject. The first two have been safely met. Only the readers can return a verdict on the third.

My first meeting with Lena Madesin Phillips goes back to her visit to Rome in 1936 when that was still my home. After I came to the United States, in 1937, I worked with her and for her on many a cause. Very soon I came to admire her well-honed mind, her sense of humor and her extraordinary sense of fairness. A friendship developed which I now treasure in memory after enjoying it in action for nearly twenty years, but which made it more rather than less difficult to produce this book.

Lena Madesin Phillips had thought of writing an autobiography and, in a style all her own, occasionally put some of it on paper, most of which I have used. Limitations of space prevented me from including some of her editorials, written for *Pictorial Review* in the 30's and still as timely as today's news, or her political speeches which were prophetic. The original manuscript by Emma Gelders Sterne, which she generously authorized me to use as I pleased, proved most valuable. The title, *A Measure Filled,* taken from a quotation Madesin liked but which I have failed to track to its source, was Mrs. Sterne's idea. I regard it as a gift from her and wish she were still living so that I could thank her for it.

Miss Marjorie Smith, former Dean of Women at Syracuse University, a leading BPW and a friend of Lena Madesin Phillips, most generously read the manuscript and made excellent suggestions for its improvement. Mrs. Boynton Schmitt has cooperated in more ways that I could hope to list and Mrs. Virginia Boyd, Marjory Lacey-Baker's attorney, has been most helpful. Mrs. Lucille Shriver, Executive Director of the U.S. Federation of Business and Professional Women, serving as a bridge to Federation Officers, Board members and, on occasion, to her staff, has me greatly in her debt, as does Mr. Joseph Binns, my unprocrastinating editor at Robert B. Luce, Inc.

Lena Madesin Phillips at the head of her "Maine Avengers," Nicholasville, Kentucky, 1898

1.   A Vision Takes Form

"A pleasant place in which to be born, Kentucky" Lena Madesin Phillips liked to say. Yet, no matter how pleasant, the little town of Nicholasville, where her roots were, must have seemed even to her a most unlikely place to have brought forth the confirmed internationalist and active feminist which she was now recognized to be. This 'unlikeliness' may well have come into her mind on a certain evening of August 1930 in Switzerland when, having become a successful lawyer and turning fifty, she stood before an international gathering in Geneva to deliver one of the most significant speeches of her career.

The International Federation of Business and Professional Women, fruit of her vision and hard work, had just been created and some two hundred prominent women from sixteen countries, as well as a number of government officials, were holding a banquet to mark the event. More important, however, they had assembled to pledge their support to the new organization and to its founder, Dr. Phillips, who that day had also been elected its first president.

At that time at least half a dozen international associations of women were already militating for the political, educational and social equality of the sexes, but Lena Madesin Phillips had long been convinced that no form of equality could endure, or prove effective once achieved, unless it had a sound economic base. Thus, for nearly fifteen years she had centered her efforts on organizing women who earned their living in business or a profession, starting in her own country, the United States, where she had attained her objective in 1919. In August 1930 she had drawn into the same pattern the business and professional women of sixteen countries, hoping that, some day, the working women of the entire world would be able to join forces likewise.

When she rose to speak a great burst of applause kept her standing almost motionless, silhouetting her in dramatic fashion against a huge window that framed the myriad lights around Geneva's lake and the snow-capped Alps towering in the background. Not markedly tall, but striking in appearance, Lena Madesin Phillips cut a commanding figure.

5

Her head carried erect above straight shoulders and the thick, well-groomed silver hair framing a high forehead, added much to her stature. Her brilliant grey eyes traveled over the hall, looking out from a strong face, animated by the smile that so frequently served to reveal her sense of humor. A repeated gesture of her hands, which was at once acknowledgment of the tribute and a plea for its conclusion, finally brought enough silence among the crowd to let her begin her say. Her voice, low-pitched and enormously persuasive, immediately created stillness all around, as if a spell were holding even those who would have to wait for the translation of her speech into other languages before they could fully understand the meaning of her words.

"The women in this room tonight," she said, "will face new opportunities but also great new responsibilities. But I must warn you that those who build organizations must also know how to stand against the doubters and the questioners who say, not only, 'What are you accomplishing?', but also, 'What do *I* get out of it?' Indeed, we shall have to be able to stand against harsher criticism than this, but if our motive is right, if we have faith, vision and courage, accomplishment must come. After tonight we shall be going back to our countries as pioneers. We must know how to share with the women at home the long vision of the future without which 'the people perish.' "

Had Lena Madesin Phillips been able to peer forty years into that future, she would have seen that what she was saying so forcefully and yet so quietly in the 1930's would be shouted angrily in the streets in the 1970's by thousands of young and impatient women demanding not merely an economic equality that continued to elude them but, with ever greater vehemence, a whole new set of freedoms defined as women's liberation. Not that the force she had set in motion in 1919 among the working women of America and in 1920 among those of many other lands had failed to advance towards its goal—far from it. At her death, in 1955, well over a quarter of a million women, respected in their various fields, had joined the federation in more than a score of countries and were beginning to make themselves heard. But, even in the fifties, only a minority shared Madesin's conviction that equality had to rest on a sound economic foundation and that women needed to gain full and free access to every field of endeavor before they could claim to be the equals of man in human society. Twenty years later, in the seventies, this view, finally accepted, was generating waves of feminine protest that became increasingly vociferous and on occasion even dangerously overactive. Although Lena Madesin Phillips had an innate abhorrence of unruliness and confusion, not to speak of violence, it is not impossible that, in the secrecy of her being, she might have looked upon the Women's Liberation Movement as a victory, obviously not yet for the equal status of women but

6

for the principle which had finally achieved recognition on the world scene.

In Geneva, that August evening of 1930, the women who had responded to her call were only a handful as compared to the hundreds upon hundreds of thousands who stood to gain from her appeal for unity, but they were, unquestionably, the cream of the crop. Lawyers, doctors, writers, university professors, owners or managers of businesses, musicians, government officials, chemists, bankers, farmers and at least one labor leader, each of the two hundred in that hall was as determined as Madesin herself to find the means of drawing together an enormous feminine force whose economic impact could not be shrugged off by a man-ruled society. The sincerity of their unspoken pledge to carry on the effort which Madesin had launched pervaded the gathering as powerfully as if every woman present had shouted it to the rafters. "It was a deeply rewarding moment," Madesin later told a friend, "but as I looked back on the long pull it had been, up from Nicholasville, Kentucky, to that banquet hall in Geneva across the Atlantic, the strongest feeling in me seems to have been one of humility rather than any other that I could identify."

Sudden humility in the face of her own achievements seemed to spring spontaneously out of Madesin's intrinsic makeup, even though she was never one to discount the validity or minimize the cost of her own goals. That evening she may well have asked herself who, in that small, self-contained, sometimes smug, rural town of Nicholasville where she was raised, had ever dared to mention such outlandish ideas as women's rights or equality of the sexes, let alone consider them acceptable. But the fact was, however, that Judge Phillips' small daughter had begun in childhood to notice, long before she could understand it, a wide gap between what her elders persistently said was right and proper for her to be when she grew up, and what a voice speaking within her told her she ought to be. Very soon she had decided she wanted to be a 'person,' independent, imaginative and heeded as was her father. She would not be, like other girls in town, a puppet cast from a common mold and forever subservient to the decisions of the males around them. The gap became wider and its nature clearer as the child became an adolescent, as the adolescent discovered herself to have become a woman.

At the age of eleven Madesin, the child, scored her first victory over parental determination. Rejecting her given name—Anna Lena—which she detested, she invented another and called herself Madesin. This adaptation of the French words 'médecin' was an admiring tribute to her half-brother, then studying medicine in Paris. Thanks to her perseverance, one of her strongest traits, the new name prevailed and finally Anna was erased from everyone's memory. Lena Madesin Phillips became officially her own. To her friends and close associates, as to herself, she was always, simply, Madesin.

This name was the symbol of personal independence. She carried it out of Kentucky, to live with her through an era of history fraught with the tragedy of two World Wars and the advent of nuclear power, and to play a part in some of its challenging moments. It was the name worn by a 'real person' who, having decided early to break out of a stultifying predestined mold, was willing to face whatever came her way from that decision. And, of course, it is the name that goes with the story of her life.

Judge William Henry Phillips, 1899

Alice Phillips, 1907

2.　　　　Rooted in Kentucky

On September 15, 1881, when Anna Lena Phillips was born, Nicholasville was still little more than a village crossroads. In eighty-three years of existence the town had scarcely changed, even though it had always been the county seat, proud of its Court House which served a vast rural area known as Jessamine County. The baby's father, William Henry Phillips, was the County Judge.

Founded by the Reverend John Metcalf, Nicholasville was named after Colonel George Nicholas, an important figure in early Kentucky history. The Colonel had been advised of the honor in a letter written to him by the preacher in 1778: "I must inform you that I have named our county seat Nicholasville in honor of you. I was all day laying off three streets today and my nerves are very much affected by the severe labors in wet weather." Two years later, the marriage of Madesin's great-grandparents, William Phillips, and Elizabeth Moss, was one of the first to be recorded in Jessamine County. The groom had come to Kentucky from Maryland, his bride from Virginia. She was serious-minded and intensely religious; he a dashing young man given to fox hunting and horse racing.

"In 1800 when my great-grandfather came to Jessamine County," Madesin writes, "he could, of course, have had his choice of the rich productive land now known as the Bluegrass. Instead, he bought a thin, rocky farm which lay on the high cliffs bordering the Kentucky River because, as it was told me, it afforded the best fox hunting. The log cabin he built was at the bottom of a slope facing a wilderness. Here he brought his bride, and here, little changed through the years, my grandfather and father were born.

"I wish that I knew more about my great-grandmother, Elizabeth, who, at the age of thirty-three, after twelve years of married life, was left a widow with six children to raise on that rocky farm along the river cliffs.

"Fortunately, Elizabeth Moss was of fighting stock. In 1760 her English born grandfather had been captain of the Goochland County Mili-

9

tia in Virginia and commissioned a major in 1770. He had fought the British in the Revolutionary War and died from wounds received in battle. As a girl, Elizabeth had traveled with her family by covered wagon, on horseback and afoot, the seven hundred miles which lay between Goochland County, Virginia, and Fayette County, Kentucky.

"Now that her man was gone, she was a lone woman against the primeval. It is not surprising that she grew stern and sometimes sharp of speech. Nor is it strange that to her the Lord was an ever-present help. My father loved to tell how, when a child, she would take him with her when she went into the woods to pray. There, he said, she would kneel down and pray aloud, long and fervently. She would pray until she shouted triumphantly or sometimes could only weep."

Madesin's childhood memories of her paternal grandfather were vividly clear and also very pleasant: "My kindly grandfather, a tall, thin old man, had whiskers like Abraham Lincoln, although in Kentucky in those days nobody would dare to say so. My part-Dutch, part-Irish grandmother, her head surrounded by curls, her plump, unhampered body in starched gingham or calico dress, always sat in the same worn rocking chair with pink roses painted on the head and arm rests. She said funny things that made us laugh.

"My grandparents were important to me chiefly because they were attached to the farm, the rugged land I knew instinctively and loved. The thickets of redbud, paw-paws, maple and hickory trees, with cardinals and mocking birds nesting in them, the rock-strewn fields cut by deep gullies, the split-rail fences, wild flowers in springtime, nuts and grapes in autumn—to these I belonged and they to me."

Judge Phillips, a widower, was forty-three years old when Anna Lena was born. The four children by his first marriage already had homes of their own. His second wife, who came from Versailles, Indiana, was a staunch Methodist, educated in a Roman Catholic convent, a gifted musician and already thirty-five when her child came into the world.

Although it was with her father that Madesin learned to enjoy the wilderness as well as some of his favorite pursuits—"we were of the same stuff, alike in temperament and taste"—she knew that his world was not her world. She was a girl and her status was predetermined. "Thus," she notes, "it was not his, but my mother's favor and approval which I anxiously sought. She was the yardstick by which I measured everything, hers the regulating power of thought and deed, the dynamic force that drove me on. . . . She was of medium height with serious grey-blue eyes and firmly set lips. Her heavy brown hair was coiled in a soft knot on the top of her head. Her domain was the house and on Sundays, at prayer meeting or revival time, the Church. An excellent housekeeper, she dealt with dirt and disorder as with an enemy to be

10

kept under at any cost, yet she loved arranging the flowers my father brought her from the garden."

Miss Alice, as her mother was always called, was practical, precise, with "a passion for goodness" and an equally passionate hatred of sin as defined by the codes of the Southern Methodist Church. Conforming in every respect to the conventions of Nicholasville society, she was the opposite, in many ways, to her easy-going, indulgent husband. "My father gave me his personality," writes Madesin, "but my mother impressed it with her character and ideals. She was positive, where he was passive. Yet his character was as fine as hers. But he never seemed aspiring, striving, or even conscious of what he was or was not. If ever there was one, my father was a 'natural.' He just grew.

"My strong-willed mother was the potter's wheel on which my resistant Phillips clay was turned. Like most other mothers, mine, too, wanted to see her dreams come true in her daughter. But, probably more than anything else, she wanted me to be 'good,' that is, religious. God and Church came first, at least theoretically, in our community. But she also wanted me to be highly educated—the phrase then in general use—far beyond her own convent schooling. Like every mother, she wanted me to be beautiful, or at least 'pretty.' In this her reach far exceeded her grasp and she compromised on 'stylish' and 'attractively dressed.' And since all girls were created primarily for the purpose of getting married, naturally she wanted me to be a good housekeeper.

"To scale these heights she did her best and I think I, too, did mine, but alas, her program was a lost cause from the beginning. However, under the spur of her will and ambition I obtained an excellent educational foundation. During the school year, practically all my waking hours were devoted to study. I practiced on the piano from five until seven each morning before breakfast. Now I realize that the laurels really go to my father, for not every man would have suffered the *Gradus ad Parnassum*, Bach and Chopin, to be thumped out daily under his bed.

"My mother wanted me to be religious and I was violently so. No one attended Church more regularly, sang in the choir at a more tender age, testified and prayed in public more earnestly, sought salvation, at least outwardly, more continuously than that good little Methodist, Lena Phillips. But the 'inner me' saw the situation even then. I knew I could conform, but not condemn. For the Methodist church, dancing, card playing and the like was all sin. Therefore my mother did not wish me to dance or play cards. Very well, for her sake, I would not, but I had my own secret pleasures which could be comfortably indulged in at home and about which one heard little at Church. For instance, I slipped into some corner to read dangerous books by George Eliot and Thomas

11

Hardy, or I helped myself to a glass of wine or a swallow of bourbon from the jug in the hall closet . . . and I mentioned nothing about this when I testified at Church or helped sinners to repentance.

"Time has dulled the edge of many memories, but looking back after some sixty years, I see that what I really wanted was only that for which human beings have struggled through countless generations: I wanted to be myself. Yet, that was what I could not be. The price exacted by society was too great, the cost to my conventional mother too high. Thus in the very depths of me, the child, there was always a sullen resentment that things must be as they were—a resentment beyond my comprehension but not beyond pain. Nevertheless, I did my best to conform."

While she did manage to conform, Madesin never forgot the maddening restrictions that had been imposed upon her only because she was a girl, and in the course of time did something about it which helped to change the life of many a woman and lessen the frustrations of many a little girl. Indeed, to understand Madesin Phillips' early environment is also to perceive how long, and at times bitter, has been America's inner struggle to advance from frontier isolationism to leadership in the family of nations.

When Madesin was born, the two thousand inhabitants of the County seat were still of the same stock that had first settled there. Nicholasville had not even been touched by the fresh waves of immigration that in the last decades of the nineteenth century were beginning to link America with the rest of the world. Since no newcomers of different cultures came to this borderland of South, North, East and West, there were almost no strangers while fellow Americans, unless they came from Virginia, were 'outsiders.' A person born in a foreign land was an oddity. "Nowhere in that town," writes Madesin, "was to be found the belief that all human beings, whatever their nationality or sex, possessed the same basic desires and needs. As for women in professions or business . . . the very word 'woman' was strange and out of place. 'Ladies' was the accepted term and our *milieu* was the front porch, the parlor, the church." This narrowness seems to have affected her and what caused it began to shape the rebel long before she knew enough to identify it, but she was also able to say: "Love of nature, faith in a Supreme Being, faith in myself— these things bestowed upon me in the little town of my birth nourished me through my life." Indeed the memory of Silver Hill, the old house where she was born, and of everything connected with it, was forever etched on her mind. "The place was nearly a century old when my father bought it," she writes. "It stood on Main Street at the top of the hill where town and country met. Like the houses of its time it had thick walls and an irregular floor level. You went up or down one short step

12

in entering almost any room. From a center hall the stairway, with its polished cherry rail and white rungs, led to three rooms on the second floor. One of these belonged to me when, as a child, I attained the dignity of a room of my own. It was long and narrow, unheated in winter, hot in summer, and later used as a passageway to the bathroom, when that modern luxury was installed. Made of brick without much foundation, it was damp and cold. The open fireplaces could not cope with the situation, but the big hardcoal stove in the living room could.

"The house was surrounded by several acres of land which my father had made beautiful. There were cedar, maple, linden, locust and many kinds of fruit trees. Beside the house was a broad flower bed, a riotous conglomeration of almost every annual known to the community.

"In the yard were old-fashioned white and yellow roses, snowballs, calicanthus, and a hedge of purple lilacs shutting off the yard from the street. On the southern slope of the hill, overlooking the carriage drive, was the pit where plants were kept during the winter. This was my father's 'greenhouse,' beneath whose frosted glass the fragrant Maréchal Niel provided yellow rosebuds for a little girl to take to a favorite teacher. And there were Parma violets grown in a smaller pit nearby.

"To the Phillips family, flowers were important. They were everywhere, crowding against a sunny window in the wintertime, scattered along the driveway and throughout the vegetable garden during the summer. There were, of course, beds of strawberries and asparagus, a raspberry patch, and a long row of celery, dirt-covered to the very head until it came glistening white for winter use. The vegetable garden lay back of the house, toward town.

"On the country side were the outbuildings: the hen house, where it was fun to gather the eggs, the backhouse, screened from inquiring eyes by blue morning glories on a trellis, the carriage house, the coal house and the barn, ending up with the room where the buckboard was kept. The barn offered endless delights. I brushed, curried and scrubbed the horses, braiding their manes and tails. The very air, dust-laden, heavy with hay and horse, pleased me. A back door led to the big horse lot, where I rode, played with the dogs and dreamed. It lent itself to daring deeds. In the center of the horse lot was the pond in which my father had planted water lilies and the stately Egyptian lotus, a strange sight in our community. There was a frame building we called 'the cellar' with a carpenter's work bench and tools. I learned early to use hammer, saw and lathe. I knew the chisel and the awl. My father was a good carpenter and he let me help him. I also did much target shooting and I soon learned to 'drive a tack' with my rifle.

"The long broad driveway from the street was the scene of my first business, when I was very small. On County Court day farmers hitched their horses to the stone wall along our driveway because the public hitching-rail was crowded and the livery stable 'charged for putting up' a horse. My father gladly shared anything he had, but I, instead, saw this as a chance to make money—for more licorice sticks or lemon drops. One day, when two farmers rode up, I told them that it cost five cents to hitch there. The men paid and my prospects seemed bright until they laughingly told my father. He returned the nickels declaring, in no uncertain terms, that the driveway was free to his friends. My market was at an early end.

"Best of all I liked the visits to the farm of my grandfather. The greatest treat was the customary walk after dinner, when the ladies retired to the front porch to talk about church and the neighbors. I, instead, joined the men on their walk. Wherever my father went, I was taken for granted. Our destination was always a high cliff overlooking the Kentucky River. There we rested, while the men told tales of Indians, wildcats, birds and fish. Few pilgrimages do I remember with such unblemished joy. Could it be that, cropping up in me even then, was the impulse that drove old William Phillips to flee from the conformity of Maryland to the freedom of Kentucky's wilderness?"

The answer could well have been 'yes,' for Madesin had within her something of each of the several strains in her ancestry. Anyone who, having known her at the height of her multi-faceted career, had tried to match the pieces of that ethnic mosaic with her personality might have wondered: Did the Irish grandmother provide the imagination Madesin used in planning, plus the wit and drama that made her speeches so stirring? Did the charm of manner come from her French Huguenot ancestors, while the sturdy Pennsylvania Dutch had made her down to earth, in her step-by-step way of approaching problems? Fairness and integrity, two traits which often got her into hot water, and usually also got her out of it, were probably an English legacy, while the ability to make the most of very little and a healthy respect for making and having money certainly came to her from the Scots!

Quite naturally, the idea of sending Lena to public school was never even considered by her family. The school had to be private and select. Nicholasville had just such a place. On the hill beyond the Phillips home, a large frame building surrounded by heavily wooded landscaping housed the Jessamine Female Institute. Run by a "highborn" Southern lady, though it was in the town of Nicholasville, it was never of it, for most of the students and teachers came from other states. Both a boarding and a day school, it had been "finishing" fashionable young ladies since 1854.

But the 1880's were no longer the 1850's. The struggles of such women as Mary Lyon and Emma Willard had borne fruit and the arguments for the existence of intellectual capacity in the female brain had been partially won. By 1885 the prophecies of brain fever, physical breakdown and general demoralization if females had access to the world's learning, had been, to some degree, disproved. Colleges for women— Elmira, Vassar, Smith, Mount Holyoke, Wellesley, Radcliffe and Bryn Mawr—had been established. Courses in Latin, Greek, mathematics and philosophy, identical with those required for academic degrees in men's colleges, had been mastered by young women without producing the ill effects predicted by the prophets of gloom. The trend toward equal education had spread as far south as Maryland where, in 1888, the Women's College of Baltimore had received a charter, and even the Jessamine Female Institute in Nicholasville was offering girls a thorough grounding in the classics if they wished it.

"At the age of seven I entered the Institute. The student body ranged from a few day pupils of my age to boarders of sixteen years or older. Two teachers were from Germany, and several were Yankees.

"School began each morning with a hymn, reading of the scriptures, prayer, often a sermon. We always recited Bible verses from memory. For me, Jehovah was an ever-present ruler of His subjects. He determined the rightness of even the smallest incident in a little girl's daily doings. He had a heaven about which we thought a good deal. I clearly recall my idea of it. There were streets of gold upon which people wandered leisurely, waving palms, and always a hot breeze blowing. At the far right-hand side was the abyss. There one could stand and safely look down upon the sinners writhing in the torments of hell. But the very heart of heaven was the throne. The great chair stood upon a raised marble platform which somewhat resembled, although much cleaner and far more magnificent, Fountain Square in Cincinnati, Ohio, then to me the height of grandeur. Most important of all, on the top step leading to the throne sat little Lena Phillips—always eating a large, never diminishing, dish of ice cream.

"Our deportment and learning were furthered by a system of rules and rewards. The record kept was as important to me as The Big Book I visualized for Judgment Day. Not only were we watched by the teacher in charge of study hall, but we were required to report upon our own behavior. When the daily roll was called, each of us answered for her conduct: Perfect if no rule had been broken, no word spoken, no note written, no lunch secretly nibbled; otherwise, we were expected to 'give in' as we called it.

"Doubtless some of the pupils accepted these strict regulations with a grain of salt, feeling themselves entitled to ignore what had not been detected. But I took them seriously. In my eyes, rules were rules and to be obeyed. The discipline of my mother and the teachings of the church dominated me. Sin was real to me. I had to tell the truth.

Therefore to answer 'perfect' one must be well-nigh perfect. What a system for encouraging cheats and prigs!

"Merit was rewarded with small badges of ribbon—blue for scholarship, white for conduct, pink for attendance. For the glory of wearing this bit of ribbon, one inch wide and four long, small children toiled and worried and usually lied all year.

"A small gold star, the Three-Roll Medal, was our reward for a year of perfect attendance, perfect conduct and an average of ninety or more in all studies. Then there was the Thousand Medal. That called for complete perfection. I received several of the Three-Roll Medals but the Thousand only once. For that I sacrificed playtime, parties and occasionally a trip. I went to school with all sorts of aches and pains, coughs and colds, carrying my germs with me. Each evening my mother heard my lessons. She would even follow me to school sometimes and call me into the cloak room to make certain of my spelling or of my answer to a problem in arithmetic.

"To fail near the close of such an endurance test was a major catastrophe. I have never forgotten the year in which I tried for the Thousand Medal a second time and missed a word in spelling, in the spring. It was a simple word. The teacher pronounced it: 'Pillow.' I was uncertain. Panic seized me. What if—my heart stood still, my mind blocked—go on, Lena, everyone is waiting, looking. You must try. At last I guessed—and missed. I felt overwhelmed as I neared home that afternoon. I had failed my mother, and shattered a year of hopes and endeavors. I cried my heart out, my head buried in my mother's lap.

"As a child I began the study of Latin and gave it eight hard profitable years. To me, it was a reasonable language; it could be analyzed, understood and mastered. Then a new teacher convinced me that if Latin was good, Greek was better. And so I also studied Greek. But years later, standing on the steps of the Parthenon, I could recall nothing of the language which had once meant much to me. As for French, I acquired only a halting, incorrect pronunciation which further study and countless visits to France failed to improve.

"No girl today can understand what piano playing meant in feminine life half a century ago. It was a means of embellishment. Not to understand music, but to perform was the ideal. If she could play her piece through to the end, preferably from memory, nothing more was asked. Children without interest or talent must each day serve just so much time on the piano bench. Parents made financial sacrifices so that their girls might become 'accomplished.' Teachers who knew little and cared less went from house to house to give lessons. At annual commencements each pupil must take part, otherwise no small-town music teacher could expect a class next year.

"My situation was somewhat different because my mother really loved music. She was a brilliant technician and played the flamboyant compositions of the day with commanding fire and skill. She took it for granted that I would also have a talent for music, and early gave me my first piano lessons. Afterwards I fell into the capable hands of two thorough-going Germans, both excellent teachers. If they made it difficult for me—and they did—I probably repaid them in kind.

"That I was the best musician among all the girls in our circle may not say much, but the consciousness of this fact stimulated my ambition and had its influence on my character. The others easily surpassed me in such desirable things as personal appearance, beaux and charm. But I could play the piano. Music helped me through many a trying time."

Madesin's perennial interest in politics was already well established when, at the age of fifteen, she went to visit her mother's family in Indiana. It was 1896, a presidential election year. The Democratic candidate was the "silver-tongued orator," William Jennings Bryan, running on a free-silver platform and making a tremendous appeal to the South and the West where it was thought that all economic life was dominated by Wall Street. Opposing Bryan was the ultimate victor, William McKinley.

During this visit, Madesin wrote a letter to the *Jessamine Journal*. The editor published it with the heading: "A Spicy Letter from a Nicholasville Damsel who Talks Politics." It said, in part:

"As I came through Cincinnati I noticed that the political feelings of a great many people were made public through these little buttons and badges, and I became a little downhearted as I noticed that almost everyone felt wrong. I asked at one place for a Bryan button and the gentleman laughed and said, 'We don't keep them, only McKinleys.' . . . When I reached Versailles, a place that was once the heart of Republicanism, I found that it had improved greatly . . . and now I think the Democrats will be victorious. The party lines, however, have mostly gone under and it is no longer a question of Democrat or Republican, but of silver or gold. . . .

"As I have told you how the people feel here politically, I will bring this to a close. If anyone who reads this far enough to see the name attached and thinks it is uncalled for and improper for me to talk, write or argue politics, being as I'm a girl, please let them remember that it is born and bred in me, and that I couldn't well help it, as I am so very closely related to my father. Whether there is credit or discredit in this, don't give any of it to my mother. She hasn't much to say politically, and sometimes stops me from

17

talking free silver. I think she is inclined the wrong way. She is not as enthusiastic about silver as Papa and myself.

Sincerely yours,
Lena Madesin Phillips"

"Being as I'm a girl" was a limitation she encountered on whatever path her inquiring mind chose to travel. Her envy of the larger life open to men was never stilled. Boys knew what their education would lead to, but so far as she could see, her own studies would take her merely to a dead-end, despite a diploma and some medals earned with hard work from the Jessamine Female Institute.

Her rebellion took various forms. She went fishing and camping with her father and listened attentively when the men talked politics. She teased her father into persuading her mother to let her have a bicycle. With a skirt to her ankles and pigtails flying, she broke precedent riding to school. At seventeen, during the Spanish-American War of 1898, she electrified the countryside by organizing twenty-one of her schoolmates into a military company. A young militiaman taught her to drill them. "We called ourselves the 'Maine Avengers.' We wore percale uniforms— white blouses, blue skirts, zouave jackets, and peaked caps. We carried wooden swords wrapped in tinfoil, but as captain, I carried a real one. We were invited to exhibit our drills at community celebrations. I suppose we believed we were helping to win the war by reminding people about the blowing up of the U.S. battleship *Maine* in Havana harbor."

Church affairs held an important place in Nicholasville and from time to time religious dignitaries came to Madesin's home. One of these was Miss Belle Bennett, leader of the women of the Southern Methodist Church, founder of Scarritt College for Christian Workers, and a woman who, in later years, was to be instrumental in changing the course of Madesin's life.

Religion was connected with Madesin's first proposal of marriage, when she was barely sixteen. "The Annual Conference of the Southern Methodist Church being held in Nicholasville," she writes. "Our home was selected as the appropriate stopping place for the Bishop who held his Cabinet Meetings in our parlor. I hung around chiefly out of curiosity, but also with a degree of interest and ostensibly a desire to be helpful. Among the Presiding Elders was a widower, of considerable charm. Between Cabinet Meetings we had little talks together, and after the Conference adjourned, he asked me to marry him. I refused.

"This troubled me, but I felt no urge to become his wife, even though I did cherish the romantic memory of this dear, stricken man whose lonely heart was presumably yearning for me. At next year's Conference, however, my would-be suitor brought with him a plain, middle-aged woman, his newly wedded wife. Secretly humiliated by the

18

sympathy I had wasted, I resolved then never to be so gullible again. Later, a gentle, lovable young man came a-wooing and I took him to the garden to cut asparagus for the family dinner. When I refused to marry him, his pleas left me wholly unmoved."

At seventeen, Lena Phillips was graduated *Magna Cum Laude* from the Jessamine Female Institute and gave the class oration. In spite of the school's narrow traditionalism, which at times had made her want to run away, she was always grateful that the schooling had been so thorough, that she had learned the necessity of disciplined thinking and had been led to "discover the wonderful world of the intellect."

Lena Madesin Phillips at the age of 9 and, below, a graduation picture taken in 1899

3.   Brush With Adversity

On a September day in 1899, two young women stepped off a trolley car in Baltimore, Maryland, and waited while the conductor handed down their luggage. Fashionably dressed in long skirts, jackets with leg-o-mutton sleeves and high-necked shirtwaists, their sailor hats, perched on birdnest pompadours, were anchored with pins and veils against the breezes. One of them, tall, willowy, Martha Land, flicked out her bustle and smoothed her gloves, assuming the posture of the popular Gibson Girl, but the other, Lena Phillips (she would not be allowed to register as Madesin), gave no thought to her appearance. Madesin's eyes were fixed on her destination across the street: The Woman's College of Baltimore.

College had been Miss Alice's idea for a daughter who had no apparent interest in matrimony, and the idea was without precedent in Nicholasville. Judge Phillips had demurred a little—he would miss his faithful companion. But as usual, Miss Alice had her way after explaining that The Woman's College of Baltimore (later to be known as Goucher College) was the jewel of the Southern Methodist Conference, and that Lena's close friend, Martha Land, would be her roommate.

While Madesin had been poring over the catalog to select her courses, Miss Alice had read with approval the College's statement of purpose: "The formation of womanly character for womanly ends." The rules of deportment had given her an added sense of security:

> Residents are not permitted to attend the theatre or the opera, or card parties, or to indulge in card playing in their own rooms or anywhere upon the college premises. Dancing is not allowed at the college receptions whether held in the Homes or in the Halls, nor have residents the privilege of participating in dancing elsewhere at public receptions or on similar occasions when they may be allowed to accept invitations. . . . Occasional calls from lady friends may be received. Gentlemen friends, not near relatives, are not permitted to call. It will not be conceded that any relation is possible between the young ladies in the Homes and young

20

gentlemen of the city that would bring calls from the latter within the limits of propriety. At the same time it is neither desired nor deemed wise to debar residents all intercourse with gentlemen. At the monthly At Home and the various receptions they are invited to meet their own and each other's friends under conditions to which no exception can be taken. . . . Residents of the Homes are expected to attend Divine Service on Sunday morning at some place of worship. Each resident must hand in a signed slip on Monday morning giving the name of the church she had attended the day before.

Entering with half a credit from the Jessamine Institute, Madesin hoped to complete her college courses in three years, with music her main interest and concern. Like the child who had twice struggled to attain the Thousand Medal, she set goals for herself far beyond her strength. Elected almost at once to membership in the College's Southern Club, she was soon involved in countless extracurricular activities. Without forgoing her piano, she took organ lessons in a neighboring church, sang contralto in the Glee Club, wrote several songs for the Glee Club concerts, played *Dazzle* in a public performance of *London Assurance,* became college correspondent for the *Baltimore Sun,* and in the spring gave an organ recital at Baltimore's Episcopal Church.

The academic program she had elected to carry left her so exhausted at the end of her first year, that when September came around she was not well enough to return to Baltimore. During a spell of comparative inactivity at home, music became the chief outlet for her tense emotional condition. Her second and third years at college were largely a repetition of the overloaded schedules of the first, with more piano and organ and evergrowing participation in college affairs. Her mother's letters were filled with anxious warnings about her health "but I did not learn then or ever after," she admitted, "to gauge my limitations. Spendthrift in energy, I shot all I had, often regardless of the importance of the target. When the firing became too incessant my only safeguard was to stop altogether, let the nerves quiver and wait for the smoke to clear."

"At the close of the second semester of my third year, I knew I was not able to meet the increasing demands of both study and music. My love for the latter dominated my decision and I have always regretted that I did not finish my college education."

Forty years later, invited to address Goucher's graduating class of '42, she said: "Goucher did its best for me and I must ever be grateful for its teaching. But deeper by far is my gratitude that it pointed the way to greater satisfaction in books, in drama, art and people—that it opened wider the door through which I caught visions of unending truth and beauty."

21

However, in her private notes Madesin made a far more intimate appraisal of what two and a half years of college had done for her, saying: "What I learned in books never seemed to stay in place. It went through a process of assimilation to appear again not as a detached fact, but reflected in opinion and judgment. Therefore I often knew the answers to knotty problems without quite realizing just how I knew them. College was neither sufficiently exacting nor sufficiently generous to bring out my best. Competition was keener than it had been at home and my grades were just average. The wonder is that they were as good as they were.

"In social life I did not have a 'set' or a clique, and of close friends, only a few. Intuitively I felt myself on the fringe of things. The examining physician considered me not strong enough for regular work in the gymnasium or strenuous sports and I did not have this opportunity for companionship. Nor was I pulled toward normalcy by association with other girls in a college sorority. I was not outstanding in scholarship, wealth, appearance or sports, but sororities usually encourage their members to win their place in the college sun and I was sufficiently talented in several lines to have achieved this. But I remained aloof from these activities and indifferent to such things. My real interest was in another kind of world."

Having decided to enter the Peabody Conservatory of Music in Baltimore, she had Harold Randolph, its director, for her teacher. "I was flattered," she writes, "that he, who took only a few pupils, would accept me. Now, at last, my future seemed to be clear—a career as a concert pianist. By mid-winter, at a public concert, I played a Beethoven quintet with stringed instruments from the Peabody orchestra. Next, I was to play the Schumann *Concerto in A Minor* with full orchestra."

Suddenly the first major frustration of her life—indeed, a tragedy for her at the time—was upon her:

"Returning home one night, I slipped on the icy pavement, taking the full weight of the fall on my right elbow as it struck the ground. But no bones seemed broken and the next morning found me practicing vigorously. What was a little pain when the concerto called for so much practice? The pain would gradually go away, whereas any time lost could never be regained. But the pain did not go away. It grew worse. A doctor was consulted. He ordered all practice to cease, not for a few days or weeks, but indefinitely. The nerve had been seriously injured. It would be a long, long time before it was strong again.

"My right arm in a sling, I returned to Kentucky. Weeks became months, and with the leaden tread of pain and helplessness, months gathered into a threat to hope. Spring stirred, then blossomed. The petals of peach and quince, syringa and bluebell laid a rainbow on the young grass. Then the green leaves thickened against the southern sun and it was summer. So, too, did physicians and treatments follow each other in a never ending succession: medical doctors, osteopaths, liniments, salves, antiphlogistine, more exercise, less exercise. I found that piano selections for the left hand became a new kind of curiosity because of the music which one hand could produce.

"By autumn it was clear that I could not return to Peabody for the coming year, if ever. My despondency and apathy were a source of anxiety to my family. The Judge and Miss Alice surely must also have grown tired of this helpless, self pitying person who could do nothing but play the piano with the left hand and grieve. Such behavior was too melodramatic for the Phillips family."

It was her father's wisdom that changed the situation. Without her knowledge, he arranged with an old friend, Hiter Lowry, who owned the largest grocery in the village, to offer the forlorn girl a job at five dollars a week to clerk in his store. The five dollars came regularly from the Judge's pocket, a fact which Madesin only discovered years later, but Mr. Lowry's offer was a bolt out of the blue.

"Nice girls did not work in public places unless extremely impoverished," Madesin writes. "And even the poorest did not clerk in a grocery store. The idea seemed to many of my friends just short of scandalous. Still, there was something to be said for it. Hiter Lowry was a kindly gentleman, a pillar of the Presbyterian Church, and the father of my closest friend, Hester. There could be no safer place to break a tradition than in his store, if broken it must be.

"The idea appealed to me. I was born with a love of business and I liked also to earn money. But the strongest lure was the utter disorder of the stock. Everything from the candy and tobacco shelves to the tables of china and glassware needed organizing. I took the job.

"Progress was slow because I used only my left hand. But by the time I reached the shelves in the rear of the store I had almost forgotten my useless arm. Not the shock and disappointment, however, for the inner scar remained. Then one day I found myself packing orders for the delivery boys to take out—with both hands!

"This therapeutic occupation was brought to a sudden end by a young man who, leaning across the cigar counter, convinced me that I could make more money by selling a *Child's History of the United States*. He guaranteed a minimum of two dollars a day but upon certain conditions. I must work every day, eight hours a day. Even more difficult, I must canvas the town street by street and every house on the street. I paid him five dollars for the privilege of doing what, in after years, I felt had been probably the hardest task of my life.

"It was a humiliating job for the daughter of the County Judge. Yet,

23

day after day I made myself go into the homes of rich and poor, friend and foe to sell the *Child's History*. While I earned more than my minimum commission, far more important, I learned something of the power of persuasion, and by facing and overcoming the disagreeable, I had put iron into my soul."

Gradually, her mother, her friends, and Madesin herself, grew accustomed to the idea that Judge Phillips' daughter, who had been to college and had almost become a famous pianist, could be a wage-earner. The experience changed Madesin herself from "lady" into "woman."

In the spring of 1904, Mrs. Joseph Burnside Skinner, the new principal of Jessamine Institute, asked her to head up the school's music department, at five hundred dollars a year, a good salary for the time. Madesin accepted.

"Teaching offered a release from just waiting—I knew not for what," she writes. "But I did not like trying to make musical velvet purses out of resistant little pigs' ears, just to please a mother's vanity. No job, however, could be merely a time-killer for me—it had to be a channel for the creative urge. I had no training in pedagogy, but my love for music was warm and vital. Often, when school hours were over, a group would join me around the piano for something beyond the prescribed lessons. We traced the variations of a theme, or tried reverently to comprehend the score of *Parsifal*. Then it was that music grew broad and deep, surging like life itself."

It may well be that those who gathered around the piano were drawn less by their interest in music than by the teacher's enthusiasm and by her personal magnetism—a quality which grew in her as the years went by. Although still physically frail, she radiated energy; although given to moods of high exuberance and black despair, she was as dependable as a rock.

During her first year at the Institute, Madesin was beset with anxiety about her mother. For years Miss Alice had been troubled by what she said was asthma. Now she was told that it was probably tuberculosis. The customary treatment brought little relief, and she was sent to spend the winter in the high, dry climate of the Southwest.

At the end of her second year of teaching, Madesin decided not to renew her contract. The teaching routine had grown wearisome, and her mother was home again. She settled down to her music and to a plethora of social and community activities, which she tried to enjoy.

"In the summer of 1906," Madesin records, "a New York writer of popular songs came to visit his aunts in Nicholasville. Doubtless, Paul Harris was one of many song writers in New York, but in our town he was a sensation. Young, handsome, successful, he played and sang his own hits, while we sat lost in admiration. In our eyes a professional writer of anything was a genius. Tin-Pan Alley was a glamorous term.

24

"Before long I showed him my songs. He liked them and said kindly things about them. Out came my five-lined music paper and off went the inner me listening for the melody which at some unexpected moment would begin to sing. Presently he suggested that I come to New York, stay for a while in Pelham with his wife and himself, and try my luck at finding a publisher for my songs." The idea was alluring but Madesin did not take it up and eventually Paul Harris returned to New York.

In November Miss Alice went South again to a warmer climate. The rains came to Nicholasville, bringing despondency to Madesin. "To eat, to sleep, to go to church and to the post office—was life to be like this?" Suddenly she answered 'no' to her own question and set out for New York with a round trip ticket in her pocket, a satchel full of unpublished songs, and sixty dollars in cash. Tin-Pan Alley had made its call heard.

The Phillips family off for a Sunday outing

25

4.   The Nation at War

The "Big Four" from Cincinnati was two hours late but it meant little to Madesin, who had wired Paul Harris that she would not go to Pelham until the following day. That night would be her own in New York. A man on the train had given her the name of a "safe" hotel but price, not safety, was her main consideration.

Entranced, she stood outside the railroad station, staring at the electric lights, the flow of carriages, the polyglot crowd, and was filled with hope. She took a hansom cab to the Martha Washington Hotel, sailed through the dreary lobby peppered with elderly ladies, engaged a room, and without stopping to unpack, set out for the Metropolitan Opera House. She bought the last of the Standing Room tickets. The occasion was memorable: the first American performance of *Madama Butterfly,* starring Enrico Caruso and Geraldine Farrar. Puccini, in the audience, received a wild ovation from the glittering throng. Spellbound, Madesin scarcely realized that she had stood through the entire opera, and found her way back to the hotel on foot, many blocks across town.

Fifty years later, when New York had long been woven into the fabric of her life, when she had held the spotlight in law courts, banquet halls or conference tables in many countries, she could still recapture the enchantment of that evening. Then, with a touch of whimsy, she wrote, "I too had made my New York debut that night—and returned to my old ladies' home, footsore but delirious with excitement."

The stupendous singing and the tumultuous applause still rang in her ears when she finally unpacked her bags and got ready for bed. Not one whit sleepy, she began to look over her songs, wondering how she would find her way into Tin-Pan Alley. Paul Harris had said that publishers were always looking for new talent, and she was confident that someone would like her work. The next step was to bring it to the attention of the right people and Harris had volunteered to help her.

"The next day," she wrote, "I went to the Harris home in Pelham. They were kindly folk. With breathless haste, I drank avidly of everything from musical talk with my hosts and their friends to visits to New York for sightseeing and window shopping." A week went by and she

26

had not yet offered her music to any publisher. She had had a wonderful time, but Pelham was twenty miles from Broadway, too far from the center of things. With her sixty dollars almost intact, she decided to take a room in town, and Harris gave her the names of the publishers to see.

Unprepared for Tin-Pan Alley's hard-boiled commercialism, for the dingy quarters, the battered pianos, the shirt-sleeved men in derby hats, the cigar smoke, the spittoons, Madesin never forgot that second week of February 1907.

If she was unprepared for Tin-Pan Alley, Tin-Pan Alley was even less prepared for her. The popular song business was a man's province. The old-timers were nonplussed by the appearance of a young woman in a countrymade suit and plain felt hat, holding sheets of music in kid gloved hands. "I began the long trail from one song publisher to another, wondering about the lack of musical culture I found in the men who sat banging on cheap pianos. They were kind, sometimes encouraging, but they usually suggested that I see someone else, a technique I came to appreciate later."

Inevitably measuring New York by the mid-Victorian standards of Nicholasville, she could not see that she was now confronted by the realities of the twentieth century. Judging her failure to penetrate the publishing jungle as her own inability to sell her wares, not understanding that the wares she had were totally outmoded, she did not succumb to discouragement.

"My intention to remain longer in New York was so settled that I wrote my friend Elizabeth Walker in Nicholasville to come and enjoy its wonders with me. Before she arrived I called at a teachers' agency to ask about a job for her, but just as I was leaving, it occurred to me that my sixty dollars was nearly gone and I, too, needed work. The woman in charge said she had something for me. The son of a wealthy manufacturer of tooth powder wanted someone to play his deceased wife's collection of sheet music so that he could select the pieces he wanted for his victrola and his player piano. The fee was a dollar an hour for a sight reader. Would the marvels of this city never end? A dollar an hour just to play the piano!

A few days later I was in the home of Edward H. Lyon, son of Dr. I. W. Lyon, creator and owner of one of the first popular tooth powders. Even Nicholasville was familiar with the trademark on the bright blue can—a cow-eyed girl with something resembling grapes dangling over her ears. 'Mr. Edward,' small, wiry, with a little goatee, sat beside me at the piano, handing me the music from a large stack. Sometimes I played only a few bars. Sometimes an entire selection. We had tea before a wood fire. At the end of two hours he gave me two dollars and asked me to come back.

"Before we met again, Mr. Lyon telephoned me to meet him at his office. When I reached the big building on West 23rd Street, he said his father had died suddenly, leaving his aged mother alone in her Englewood home in New Jersey. He and his brother wanted me to be her companion, but it would depend upon whether Mrs. Lyon would like to have me. She was not easy to get along with. The salary would be fifteen dollars a week.

"In a short time I was settled in the Lyon mansion, occupying the old doctor's bedroom, sitting in his high-backed chair at dinner, reading the daily Unitarian sermon to his widow, and listening to the chimes of a Tiffany clock tell the hours against the silence. Four servants cared for us. My job was to check and pay the monthly bills and to act as companion to the old lady. She rarely wished to see me before four o'clock, which gave me time to compose and also to go to New York. I went often, especially to the organ recitals at Wanamaker's, which seemed marvelous to me, and they were free.

"Having found a financial anchor, I sought out Harry Rowe Shelley, outstanding composer of church music and organist of the Riverside Church. With him I continued to study composition and wrote six songs. We had our lessons in the Sunday School room of the church; a blissful time, darkened only by an instinctive fear that God might strike Mr. Shelley dead—and incidentally me—because he irreverently smoked in the Sunday School room.

"With Mrs. Lyon we went to church, sometimes we shopped or called on a friend. At home I listened patiently while she talked about her fad, mastication. It was a tedious, often trying job, but it suited my purpose. We spent the summer months at The Mathewson, at Narragansett Pier, taking with us John, the coachman, and the horses, and I thoroughly enjoyed the gay life of this fashionable resort . . . But most of all the sea."

Madesin's frequent letters to her parents still expressed hope of finding a publisher, but the musical trend was running against her. Ragtime had been the rage in New York for several years, and public fancy might have swung back to *Hearts and Flowers* if William C. Handy, the son of a Negro minister, had not come up from Tennessee to peddle a new type of ragtime—the *Memphis Blues*. The contagious rhythms of his own people quickly became a craze barring a return to the sweet sentimentality of the Victorian era.

In the autumn Madesin went home for a short visit, her father having decided to sell Silver Hill and buy a smaller house now that his wife would be spending all her winters away from Nicholasville. When winter came, Mrs. Lyon had died and Miss Alice wanted Madesin in Florida. At DeLand, with her mother, Madesin kept a diary which only lasted a few weeks. The entries reflect a spell of purely social life with brief touches of romance that ended with the arrival of spring, when it was time to go back to Kentucky.

Miss Alice died just before the start of winter 1908 and Madesin, teaching again at Jessamine, was miserably unhappy. Not only did she feel lost at home and frustrated by the lack of a real career to pursue, but she was filled with remorse because she had failed to live up to the narrow ideals her mother had held up as a standard.

In 1910, dismayed by her own condition, she decided to go abroad with a party of young women escorted by a "Southern lady" she knew. Her first view of Europe, extensive though it was, left her with little more than fleeting impressions, a sharp contrast to the deep and thoughtful reactions that her frequent visits of later years were to evoke.

Nonetheless, she returned to Nicholasville refreshed and willing to embark on a new venture in partnership with her one-time pupil and childhood friend, Hester Lowry. They opened an Academy of Music in the building that had housed the now defunct Jessamine Institute. The venture was a major success, but one night, in the Academy's third year, the old wooden building burned to the ground. Three pianos, a large stock of music and all except eight of Madesin's compositions were destroyed. The shock did not lessen her love for music, but she ceased to look upon it as a means to economic independence.

Although the Academy was reopened in a new location and lasted successfully two more years, Madesin's chief interest was now in her father. "In his election years I campaigned with him" she writes, "stopping to talk to farmers in the field and shoppers in the country stores, attending political rallies in the hill country or down by the river. My father, first elected to office in 1874, was re-elected every four years until 1917—a record unmatched in the county!"

The German invasion of Belgium in summer of 1914 and the outbreak of war in Europe, barely stirred Nicholasville and there is no record to show that Madesin herself was particularly affected by it. A successful teacher, an increasingly respected leader in community and county affairs, still devoted to music and surrounded by friends, in addition to enjoying the companionship of her father, nothing appeared on the surface of the mental anguish by which she was inwardly beset. Three years earlier, headaches and what a doctor described as "neuralgic explosions" had made her seek medical advice during a visit to Knoxville, Tennessee. Found to be suffering from a low-grade renal infection and some measure of anaemia, she obediently took the prescribed remedies and appeared cured. This episode therefore would not seem to account for the nervous collapse which suddenly struck her in June of 1915. Her father took her to his doctor-son, George, Madesin's childhood idol, who placed her in a sanatorium where she remained six weeks.

Her recovery was complete and she returned home with a well balanced approach to life fully restored, her sense of frustration and de-

29

pression had gone. Her focus on music had been replaced by a new determination to carve out a career for herself in another field. She had decided to become a lawyer and her father gave her his full support.

Up to that time, only one woman had been graduated from the Law School of the University of Kentucky, but this did not discourage Madesin any more than did the prospect of daily twelve-mile trips on the trolley between Nicholasville and Lexington. The reaction of the male law students to the appearance in their midst of a female colleague, was published a year later in the *Lexington Herald* of December 21, 1916:

> Miss Phillips had not studied law previous to her entrance in the local college, but will receive her degree in June, 1917. . . . Some conservative students disapproved of Miss Phillips' entrance in their classes, believing their work would be retarded, but when the semester grades were posted on the bulletin board, their attitude changed. In the mid-semester report in November, Miss Phillips was accredited with eight A's. No better grade was offered. She carried twenty-one hours of classwork. The average schedule consists of twelve hours' work.

Behind this achievement lay the fact that Madesin was studying law because she wanted to. She was determined to succeed and unflinchingly self-disciplined, she was intensely interested in the field she had finally chosen to make her own. One of her papers, a critique of William Howard Taft's book, *Our Chief Executive,* was published in the *Kentucky Law Journal* and an accompanying editorial assessed it as a "highly scholarly review." In little over a year and a half, Madesin received her *Bachelor of Laws* degree, the only honor graduate in a class of fourteen men, and the first woman to be graduated from the Kentucky Law School with Honors.

At thirty-six, relaxed and easy in her mind, she hung out her shingle in Nicholasville. From the old brick building in the public square which she rented she could "look across the street at the Court House, the center of our town, where sat my father, the center of my life." Soon she had clients enough to feel assured that at last she had found her way when, quite unexpectedly, she faced another turning point.

1917 was the year in which the United States entered World War I, but Nicholasville was only a little less vaguely aware of this than it had been of events in Europe since 1914. Suddenly, one day, the voice of Miss Belle Bennet, the Southern Methodist leader who had visited the Phillips home when Madesin was in her teens, came into Madesin's office over the telephone from a nearby town. "How much do you know about the work of the Young Women's Christian Association?" asked the caller. "Not very much, I am afraid, Miss Belle," replied Madesin.

Miss Bennet, responsible for raising Kentucky's quota of funds for the National War Work Council of the YWCA, wanted Madesin's help in the campaign. This was a fulltime involvement requiring fulltime presence in Lexington. Madesin was hesitant, but "Miss Belle" was not one to take "no" for an answer. Presently Madesin found herself established as secretary-treasurer of the Kentucky Campaign Committee in Lexington. By dint of hard work and much imagination, the financial goal was reached and Madesin gladly went home.

She had only been back at her law practice a few weeks when a telegram from New York requested her to attend the first Conference of the War Work Council of the YWCA in Manhattan, all expenses paid. Surprised, she consulted her father and finally telegraphed back that she would come, but thought the expenditure would prove useless to them. New York's reply was immediate and brief: "Expecting you." She packed a small suitcase and went.

More than ten years had passed since her first visit to New York City. She was no longer thinking of Tin-Pan Alley. She was now a mature and settled woman, very satisfied with her growing law practice and content with her life in the small Kentucky town to which she planned to return as soon as possible. Nicholasville in her view was still a place "where all that a person had to do was to work hard, pay his debts and vote Republican or Democratic tickets, where people believed that they had always had the poor and slums and inequalities and graft, and therefore would always have them." While she did not share this·approach to life nor believe that Nicholasville was highly civilized or modern, she had learned to keep her doubts to herself and make the best of the good she saw. A decade of futile struggle to change the local attitudes had sobered her. Thus she took off for New York with a round-trip ticket in her pocket, but without impossible dreams or rosy illusions in her baggage.

Madesin's first impression of war-time Manhattan was electrifying. She writes: "They called it the 'Great War' in 1917. Crowded, hectic New York City was a continual pageant of flamboyant patriotism, flag-draped, parade-drunk, electric. Women were in the swirling center of the activity. From Times Square to the Washington Arch on lower Fifth Avenue, in every square, every theater, every crowded hotel lobby, women were singing, orating, selling War Bonds. They were driving cars, arranging block parties, serving coffee and doughnuts to 'our boys' in khaki, rolling bandages and knitting, knitting, knitting. Women in Red Cross uniforms, women in overseas caps, women in picture hats, swung their knitting bags as they walked briskly along the avenue. Women knitted as they rode the buses. They knitted as they jiggled baby carriages in the park. In office buildings, away from flags, parades and bands, women at machines were shouldering the work of men."

The headquarters of the National Board of the YWCA, at 600 Lexington Avenue, was the heart and center of the organized war work.

It had been designated by Newton D. Baker, Secretary of War, as the official channel for marshaling the energies of the distaff side of the population to "make the world safe for democracy."

A War Work Council, composed of one hundred of America's most prominent women had been provided with ample government funds. Women of leisure dedicated to good works sat on the Council together with social workers, lawyers, doctors, writers, with members of the National Suffrage Association and of the Trade Union League. The demands of war acted as a magnet, drawing together groups and individuals which had always gone their separate ways, or perhaps had never met before. The Council set up Hostess Houses at army camps, held dances and parties for the men in the services, staffed rest and recreation centers for industrial workers and, in general, tried to bridge the chasm between normal life and the life into which the nation had been catapulted by its participation in a major war. The Council, in effect, was trying to fit a chaotic mass of volunteers into a workable scheme of activities, while also endeavoring to deal with countless unprecedented problems brought on by the sudden entrance of millions of women into fields of employment previously covered by men.

It was into this sea of activity that Madesin was plunged by the invitation of the YWCA's National Board. At YWCA Headquarters, cordially welcomed by officials wearing blue-grey uniforms and tricorne hats, she found that a room had been reserved for her at the nearby Nurses' Club, but no one told her what she was expected to do. The Council Conference was already under way. Madesin sat through endless speechmaking and attended teas, luncheons and dinners with women in the public eye. Among these was Ida Tarbell, the writer known for her biographies of Lincoln and of other great figures, but even more renowned for her published investigations of American industry. Another was Mary Stewart, the educator who later played a major role in the Bureau of Indian Affairs and there were a number of public spirited wives of Wall Street millionaires, such as Mrs. John D. Rockefeller, Jr., Mrs. Herbert Pratt, and Mrs. John French to name but a few. At first Madesin enjoyed the sense of 'belonging' and being very much part of action which, to her, was new and exciting. However, after a few days of this routine, of long meetings in the hushed auditorium, of seemingly endless rounds of activities which she found somewhat repetitive, Madesin admittedly had begun to feel useless and fidgety. She wished she could go home where plenty of work awaited her return.

"Finally, I could wait no longer," she writes. "It all seemed too wasteful. I do not know with whom I talked, but I remember walking down Lexington Avenue with a National Board Secretary. 'Why did you wish me to attend this conference?' I asked. 'We wanted you to know something of our work,' she replied, 'hoping that you might become one of our field secretaries.' 'How many are there?' I asked. 'Eleven,' she answered. 'No,' I said, 'I would not leave my father, my home, my profession, for anything of which there are eleven. I am sure you can find one more without me.' I was not one to waste words or time. In Kentucky I had work to do. I said I thought I should get back home. 'Must you go at once?' she asked. 'No,' I said, 'I can stay longer, but since I cannot take this position, I should be wasting your money.' 'Isn't there some phase of our work in which you would be interested?' she asked. I hesitated a moment and then I said, 'Yes, I think I would be interested in doing something for business and professional women.'

"I remained in New York a few days longer. Several times I was asked to meet with small groups of Board Members to discuss ways and means of reaching the business and professional women who were unorganized. How would I go about it?, I was asked. This was unlike anything I had done before, but I made some suggestions which evidently were satisfactory, because I was told I could return home if I wished to and that a call to work with business and professional women would be sent me very soon."

Madesin returned to Nicholasville. If the call came, she knew she would have a difficult decision to make. Her law practice was growing. Working on her father's political campaigns, she had become well known in the Democratic party of Jessamine County. If women won the suffrage— the House of Representatives had already voted in favor of the constitutional amendment, the Senate, under pressure from President Wilson, seemed about to follow—she could hope for a political career in Kentucky. But most important to her was her father, now almost eighty and still her best friend and companion. They had kept house together for ten years since her mother's death.

On the other hand if the call came, it would be to wartime service, and she could not forget the exciting sense of 'belonging' she had experienced at first in the Council's Conference. Also, she knew that thousands of business women, lawyers, doctors, teachers, librarians, accountants were all moving in a fog of isolation which, somehow, had to be dispelled. The opportunity to organize them was not lightly to be put aside, and there was New York City itself, whose vitality pulled her like a magnet.

Judge Phillips understood his daughter even better than she realized. He helped make her decision even before she received the official call. He told her that he had sold the house and would be living with his older, widowed daughter. Madesin was thus suddenly relieved of any sense of obligation to remain in Nicholasville for his sake. When the letter came, inviting her to become a Staff Secretary specifically charged with working

33

with business and professional women all around the country, she accepted. The salary was $1800 a year—quite a bit less than she was earning in Nicholasville, but the challenge mattered far more.

Interestingly enough, she had a wholesome respect for the value of money earned and knew how to drive a hard bargain; yet she could always find reasons for putting service ahead of financial gain. There were several other such contradictions in Madesin's character. For instance, she always disclaimed any liking for things domestic and everything in her rebelled against the narrow house and family-centered life of Southern ladyhood. Yet, her affection for her home was deep-rooted and intense. Before leaving for New York, it fell to her to dismantle the house and oversee the sale of most of its contents. This, in her own words was "one of the most harrowing of all experiences.

"Our home must be broken up, its furnishings, familiar as a face of a loved one, scattered among those who will buy them. In a way, death itself is less poignant. For death has dignity, while in these small town sales of household belongings the very soul of family life seems laid bare, naked for whoever will see. We expose to cheap curiosity, relinquish to strangers, the familiar articles which have made a place home to us. To stand by, silent and helpless, as they are appraised at their market value, is a cruel ordeal. I suppose this is sentimentality. But old familiar friends seem somehow to deserve an end of greater dignity. Better by far to give them away or return to a pagan custom and consign them to the flames. The memory of a roaring bonfire, ending these symbols of a period of time well loved, would be better than the hideous nightmare which is sale day.

"At last, however, all was finished. My father was pleasantly established in my half-sister's home. My old-fashioned law office, opened a year and a half ago with such hope, was closed. I was ready to go, as were many others leaving their homes in those wartime days. After a while they would return from their strange experiences. I, too, had an assignment for patriotic service and once the war was ended and my work was done, I, also, would come home."

In April 1918 Madesin left Nicholasville telling herself that the persistent feeling within her that this departure was final was only the result of the emotional wrench. Once the war work was concluded she would return. Meanwhile she would give the best of herself to the opportunity which had so unexpectedly come her way. Often in her life she had felt, as she did then, that she was being directed by some impulse which she could not define or explain, but which she analyzed later in these words: "Forces which man does not yet understand, strange and often bewildering to him, lie behind the life-pattern of certain individuals. Of these individuals I was one. What is it that unexpectedly points a directing finger and says 'Turn here'? Or hovers over a wasteland, familiar, yet long

34

disregarded and commands 'Plant here'?

"Some will deny this exterior force entirely, claiming that the unexpected pattern, the new growth, is mere chance or, at most, the natural development from within the man himself, or the growth pressed up by long accumulated needs. But there is and has ever been, I suppose, in most persons a belief, if not fully resolved, that something beyond and far greater has upon occasion touched their life or determined their destiny. Call it as you will, the Good Spirit, Fate, Lady-Luck, or according to our Christian belief, God."

While Madesin could philosophize and usually did, she was also realistic in her appraisal of the more tangible aspects of life. Many years after this presumably temporary visit to New York, looking back on herself and her inexperience she wrote: "It did not occur to me that the material and moral equipment which had proven adequate in Nicholasville might not be sufficient in this more sophisticated field. I was to learn that some listen to what you say in speeches. Fewer understand what you mean. But everybody sees how you look. When I left home, the tailored shirt-waists and suits, a few 'Sunday dresses' and the can of talcum powder with whose contents I occasionally dabbed my usually shiny nose, would have seemed sufficient if I had given the matter any thought, which I did not."

If Nicholasville smiled at Lena Phillips' plain clothes, free-and-easy ways and beauless status, it knew also that she was honest, energetic and the daughter of the old Judge. "Such things gave me a sense of security," she notes, "and I knew exactly where I stood. This attitude I also took with me to New York. I looked, not down at the humiliation of failure or up at the satisfaction of success, but straight ahead, at just another, although bigger and probably harder, job to be done. Neither doubt nor fear tugged at my elbow. Mine was not the casual courage of the inexperienced, but the assurance of one whose family roots had not reached out to alien soil for well more than a hundred years. Looking back, my astonishment at my own serenity is surpassed only by amazement at the faith of the YWCA which engaged me to do a difficult job and something which had not been tried before. When I accepted I was totally unaware of what had to be done. I only knew that something had touched me on the shoulder, saying 'go'."

The Business Women's Conference, called by the War Work Council to consider forming a national organization of business women for war service was to be held on May 11th and 12th, of 1918. Invitations had gone out to key women in every state east of the Rocky Mountains. One of Madesin's immediate tasks was to call on women executives in the New York area, explain the purpose of the meeting, invite them, and secure their support. She was also sent to Washington to attend another Council

35

conference, of which her major recollection had personal significance. "We were received at the White House by the first Mrs. Woodrow Wilson. Her sister, the beautiful Margaret Axson, had been one of my closest friends at college and had visited me in Kentucky. I found myself remembering the day when the great man himself, then Governor of New Jersey, had addressed the Legislature in Frankfort, Kentucky. Of course I had been there to hear him and to meet Margaret's "Big Brother Woodrow.'"

Nearly a hundred women, most of them holding highly responsible positions, many already nationally known for their achievements, gathered for the opening session of the nation's first Busniess Women's Conference. "The discussions were lively and provocative," Madesin writes, "filled with the give and take of a group of enthusiastic individuals meeting for the first time in the hope of attaining a common goal. It is evidence of how far the vision of these women led them to look into the future, that many of the terms used in their resolutions in the interest of women and never before publicly used in such a context, gradually became the substance of organized demands and eventually of protest: 'protecting and promoting the woman worker,' 'equal pay for equal work,' 'promotion of business opportunities and business advancement,' 'development of training and efficiency.'"

Two of the several resolutions submitted failed to succeed, and while they "fared differently," writes Madesin, "they are amusing to recall. One, traceable to the then current popularity of peekaboo blouses and high French heels, required 'suitable dress for women in business.' It survived about six months! The other, asking for 'standardization of morals,' was not again mentioned from that day to this, so far as I can remember."

"Whatever we resolved, our purpose was a timeless one. We wanted more freedom and a greater degree of justice. Our banner was lifted under the guise of helping to win the war, but our inner urges went deeper than our words. Unconsciously perhaps, we were fighting for democracy. My own part in the conference was probably far more exciting to me than to the group. An inexperienced but self-reliant country frog had gaily jumped into an ocean of outer conflict and hidden rhythm." A YWCA report of the conference noted the following:

> "It is safe to predict that out of this conference will come a national movement for the promotion of the interests of women . . . that it is the first real attempt to organize all the business women of the United States is significant . . . that it should have come through the YWCA is also significant . . . As to the power which might be generated from such an organization . . . no one can estimate. It is safe to say, however, that it would be a force which could mold

36

public opinion, set standards and change economic and industrial conditions in such a way as has scarcely been dreamed of in days past. One may well expect to see great things done and done quickly."

Madesin appraised the conference in a single sentence, writing to her father: "We have started now an alliance of business women of the United States which will be a tremendous power for the betterment of the women."

The conference set up a committee of twenty-five key women from different parts of the country, called the National Business Women's Committee, which was charged with bringing to a head the quest for national unity. The National Board of the YWCA assigned Madesin, temporarily, to give her full time to this undertaking as its executive secretary.

Now it remained to develop the interest and support that would make the projected organization a reality. The executive secretary asked herself: How could the women be enlisted? What kind of organization would these unknown thousands want? "Out of my own experience came the answer," she writes. "I had learned what little I knew about organizing through the Methodist Church. I would go across the country, a missionary, to listen and to tell."

Her trip covered some nine thousand miles in four weeks. Detroit was her first stop; then Billings, Spokane, Yakima, Seabeck, Seattle, San Francisco, Los Angeles—a whirlwind of meetings, speeches, press interviews, luncheons, dinners. This preliminary tour was enormously successful. Madesin's charm and zest had endeared her to the women at the New York Conference, where she discovered the ability to hold an audience that she did not know she possessed. Now she found much larger and more diversified audiences across the nation equally responsive to her appeal and to her quiet arguments. She analyzed the trip in these words: "It was on this long journey that I first came to know some of the women who were to be leaders in the new organization. They, and others like them, had the knowledge and experience I did not have. But I had the fervor, the faith and, above all, the opportunity. The idea of a concerted movement among business and professional women was meeting with favor."

In Cincinnati, on her return trip, Madesin's barn-storming came abruptly to an end. A telegram from the National Board of YMCA informed her that she had been appointed director of the Women's Division of the Eastern Department of the United War Work Campaign, a fund-raising operation, already underway. She was to report at once to Chicago. "No one could have been more surprised than I at this new assignment. My work with business women was just beginning. It was far removed from a national campaign to raise funds."

37

The goal of the United War Work Campaign was $170,500,000. The money would be used in part for the recreation and comfort of the Armed Forces at home and abroad, and in part for the benefit of workers in war industries. The organizations co-operating in the campaign were the War Work Councils of the YMCA and the YWCA, the National Catholic War Council, Jewish Welfare Board, War Camp Community Service, American Library Association and the Salvation Army. Madesin was never able to determine why she, with comparatively little related experience, had been appointed director of the Woman's Division of the Eastern Department. Ten states were included in her department, which was expected to raise seventy-five million dollars of the total goal.

As soon as she arrived back in New York she established herself in an apartment on West 12th Street, campaign headquarters for the Woman's Division having been opened in that neighborhood at 200 Fifth Avenue. In addition to her administrative jobs at campaign headquarters, Madesin attended planning sessions with the five men who were the other Eastern Department directors, held innumerable conferences with women leaders, singly or in groups, and addressed campaign rallies in many states where she was usually the only woman speaker.

Glimpses of New York, then in the grip of war psychology, are scattered through Madesin's letters to her father—hastily written in snatched moments.

"Our Fifth Avenue is very exciting now, filled with the biggest and most beautiful flags you ever saw. At the Liberty Altar, almost opposite our campaign offices, there are constantly speeches, community sings, concerts and the sale of Liberty Bonds. . . The other night a lot of French soldiers were in a theater—I believe they call them Blue Devils—and a man said he would buy a thousand dollars worth of bonds if his wife could kiss two of those soldiers. Of course that was what she did, to everyone's delight. . . On Saturday there was a parade. The men from the trenches rode on top of the buses, and as they passed up Fifth Avenue people would begin to cheer. Everybody waved, handkerchiefs, hats, anything, and shouted, and the brave boys in their worn uniforms waved and smiled back. I heard they said they would be glad to get back to the trenches for a rest. While I was watching them there was a whirr overhead and right above us was a beautiful airship, just sailing by. It was the first I had ever seen and so lovely."

From a wealth of recollections of those days in 1918 Madesin writes: "America, we said, was fighting the war to end all wars. Therefore, one could be cheerful, at times as gay as the flags and music. The resultant rush and rhythm compelled participation.

"Against the backgrounds of parades, the United War Work Campaign moved feverishly to its culmination. The war momentum swept everything, even time, before it. Suddenly, or so it seemed, on November 11th, an armistice was signed in Marshall Foch's railway coach in the forest of Compiègne. Victory! The war was over. It was both too late and too early to abandon the fund-raising campaign. Too late because its powerful machinery had long been at full speed. Too early, because the same services would be needed during the period of demobilization. The campaign continued to a triumphal end. More than two hundred million dollars were raised."

There was victory in war, success in the national drive for funds. Madesin wound up the affairs of her campaign office and went home to Kentucky for an overdue vacation.

Madesin Phillips in her YWCA uniform, 1918

5. Organized Women: Asset or Onus?

In Madesin's own words, "Returning to New York after a month at home, was like going to a carnival ground the day after the show had closed. Flags were down and, although khaki-clad soldiers still thronged the city streets, roars of approval and encouragement were no longer necessary. America was quickly returning to business as usual. Of course, there was still peace to be made and pay-offs to be negotiated, but those who had sacrificed everything else 'to make the world safe for democracy' turned their backs on the unfinished job. They left it to the politicians who merely returned to their accustomed business of getting re-elected.

"The common purpose which had united us in fighting our enemies was already dissolved. The major political parties were once more fighting each other: since President Wilson and the Democratic Party approved a League of Nations, automatically the Republican Party must oppose it. This we were to see much more clearly later. At the time, pulses slowed down and the American people settled back to their old routines. The tide of events and human emotions which had once thundered in, was now sliding out, silently and irrevocably, dragging down the sands of public interest."

With the war over, the whole idea of organizing business and professional women to serve the ends of victory ceased to have meaning. Staring at the pin-scarred map on her wall where, according to her plan, local clubs were to be formed, Madesin was asking herself: 'What next?' Unknown to her, however, while she had been working for the War Fund Campaign key women from every part of the country had flooded the National Business Women's Committee with pleas that the efforts to organize a federation be carried on. Much to her surprise, Madesin was hastily requested to prepare a budget to cover the cost of getting a federation organized still as part of the War Work Council under the Secretary of War.

Given less than twenty-four hours in which to put her figures together, she met the deadline with some misgivings. "I felt that a budget was a Yankee device," she writes, "one never heard of, then, in Kentucky. A person just naturally knew about how much money would be coming in each year and geared his expenditures accordingly. In our family, that meant spending less than was earned and always laying something aside. The knockings of Fate were more familiar to me than budgets; nonetheless I made one which ran to about $65,000 and, with a wry smile at my own audacity, handed it in.

"I need not have worried. The War Work Council's budget exceeded one million dollars. No one disturbed my paltry $65,000, earmarked for the use of business and professional women. With the financial problem solved like magic, I turned my thoughts to how the American business and professional women could best be served. I had faith in the intelligence and ingenuity of the group. I believed that, if we could bring their representatives together in a convention, they would know how to define their purposes and program." Little did she know what an illusion that would turn out to be!

The YWCA re-appointed Madesin secretary of the Business Women's Committee. Her first step in trying to pick up the threads which had been dropped, if not altogether broken, when she had been so abruptly shifted into the War Fund Campaign, was to secure the support of the only major existing organization, the National Women's Association of Commerce, headquartered in Chicago. Returning from what appeared to be a very encouraging visit to the Association's President, she submitted her recommendation to the YWCA Board for a plan to unite all business and professional women into a single national federation, for which she had received support in Chicago.

Madesin made her point to the YWCA in these words: "Whereas the business and professional women of this country are without adequate national or state organizations, and because of this their great force and influence as a body is lost; if they were so united they could better serve their own conditions and those of working women in general, exert powerful influence in molding public opinion as to right standards of living and working . . . direct the vocational guidance of young women coming into the business world and promote fellowship among the women of the world."

It was agreed that a committee of six women—three from the National Business Women's Committee and three from the National Women's Association of Commerce, with Madesin as the executive secretary—would undertake to bring the two groups together. One major difficulty lay in the fact that while the Women of Commerce had been in existence for many years, the business women had not even been organized. Nevertheless, not to waste the interest and good will aroused by Madesin's visit to Chicago, the effort to achieve unification was initiated without delay.

Since the Chicago group was holding its national convention in St. Louis that summer, July 15 to 18, Madesin's committee decided that this would be the ideal time to hold a simultaneous meeting of delegates from as many business and professional women's clubs as already existed, and to hasten to create several more before that date. If this worked out, the two bodies would come together on the second day of their respective meetings, to decide for or against unification. Even if the outcome were negative the remaining sessions would be held as joint affairs, in order to keep a door open for a resumption of negotiations.

Above Madesin's desk, the map on the wall showed vast blank spaces where no business and professional women's clubs existed. Hence a great deal of promotion and publicity were needed in order to reach the thousands upon thousands of potential members and organize them in time for the July meeting. Where clubs were already active they would have to be brought together, state by state, into local federations, and an overall convention program had to be planned. There were only six months left in which to carry all this to completion.

With the confident outlook that was so typical of her, and with the organizing skill she had developed while working for the War Fund Campaign, Madesin immediatly set about outlining an ambitious plan of action. Having divided the United States into five regions, she placed each into the hands of an experienced organizer. The assignment involved making a survey of existing clubs, bringing them together into state-wide Federations and making sure that state delegates were selected to attend the meeting in St. Louis. At the same time they would have to try to form new clubs and, if possible, federate them as well.

The five organizers had been Madesin's choice. As they traveled around the country she sent them bulletins to keep them abreast of developments, help them to adhere to a basic organizational pattern, and to keep in mind the purpose of their undertaking. In a bulletin dated March 20th, 1919, she wrote: "Let there be no uncertain note concerning the following things: 1) Any federation or local club we attempt to create must be *non-sectarian*—at times it may be well for you to point out that our national executive committee includes a Unitarian, a Jewess, a Quaker and a Christian Scientist, and that we are trying to secure an equally prominent Catholic woman to join us. 2) Any federation or club must be *self-governing*—women must get together, decide what they believe should be done, and try to get things done by their own efforts. 3) Any federation or club must be *self-supporting*.

"Never forget that you are engaged in a very real and very constructive piece of work—something for which no money can pay—something which can only be bought with the best of your whole being—something that is part of God's great plan of making the world right and men and women free. Be practical in your work, but never lose the dream of our great vision of the future."

As Madesin, herself, saw it in later years, "It was a rush job and, I suppose, done in hit and miss fashion. Both hits and misses were perfect of their kind, however! The first appointment I made was a Director of Publicity—a person who knew not only newspapers but women, and who laid down a heavy barrage in the press on the importance of the cause and on the forthcoming convention. Her promotion covered the country, overshadowing the Women's Association of Commerce. In addition," Madesin reports regretfully, "she made of me a romantic and alluring crusader. Abstract causes must be personalized in order to be made palatable, but she could have 'hung' the stories about the coming federation on either the Chairman of the Business Women's Committee or on the Executive Secretary. For better or worse, she chose me and did much to give me a national reputation."

Inevitably, such publicity aroused jealousies; that June, the president of the National Women's Association of Commerce requested the YWCA to remove Miss Phillips, immediately and entirely, from federation plans. This the YWCA Board refused to do, but did make it clear that after the St. Louis convention, Madesin would not be officially connected with the newly organized group since her permanent position was with the YWCA. The Chicago group also demanded that when unification was discussed and voted upon at the St. Louis meeting, only the members of the Association of Commerce be allowed to vote. This request, running counter to what the Association had agreed to with Madesin several weeks earlier in Chicago, was also denied.

The short six months of preparatory work were coming to an end. Madesin had obtained a promise from the White House that President Wilson would send a message to the convention. The Call to Convention, stating Madesin's cherished objectives, had been widely circulated. In it were laid the foundations for *economic equality* of the sexes, showing the direction which the effort of American women must take now that their educational and political rights had been officially recognized. Calling for the establishment of a national organization of business and professional women "to bring about solidarity among women throughout the nation," it also contained the words "and eventually throughout the world," which clearly reflected Madesin's growing worldmindedness. In expressing this optimistic hope, she could hardly have imagined that, in little more than a decade, her international dream would become reality, since at the time even the prospect for a national organization seemed less than bright.

Indeed, the more was written and said about the unifying purpose of the convention, the wider grew the reaction that business women were much too individualistic to work together, that the differences with the Women of Commerce would be impossible to resolve and that a basic

43

cleavage within the business group, between those who wished to affiliate under the YWCA and those who did not, would be difficult to breach. "The impression that unification could not happen," writes Madesin, "was so general that the Women's Advertising Club of St. Louis, volunteering to produce the Convention Bulletin, decided to entitle it *'Can Happen.'* The title turned out to be symbolic of the outcome!

"On July 14th, the delegates streamed into the lobby of the Hotel Statler in St. Louis, obviously unaware of the storm in the offing. We were a group of gay, excited women from forty-five states, adventuring with a 'cause' and also come on a vacation. A huge streamer across the hotel lobby welcomed us. National magazines, such as *Good Housekeeping, Pictorial Review, Harper's Bazaar,* had sent representatives from New York to cover the meetings. A number of major newspapers had their reporters at the press table. Telegrams of good wishes from President Wilson, from William McAdoo, Secretary of the Treasury, and from Josephus Daniels, Secretary of the Navy, had been received among others and would be read from the platform. Commonplace as such things are today, in 1919 they were sensational.

"Colorful as we were and felt, surely nothing so picturesque and dramatic ever took place in a more drab and prosaic room. Perhaps it was because we were women's conventions—the Women of Commerce occupying a similar room on the floor above—that the Statler did not assign us the ballroom we had asked for, neither group having been willing for the other to have the best space! Each group had a salesman's room, long, narrow and unadorned, furnished with a few plain tables, a speaker's platform and the hard, narrow, straight chairs upon which so much of the world's best thinking seems destined to be done."

With more than two hundred delegates and almost as many visitors present, the Convention opened on the morning of July 15th. Before the Chairman of the National Business Women's Committee could express her words of welcome, a delegate from Detroit was on her feet with a motion: "Madam Chairman, I move that all newspaper reporters be excluded from the business of this Convention." Evidently sensing the crosscurrents already developing she probably wanted to save the meeting from predictably facetious headlines about women's squabbles, but Madesin was instantly out of her seat to reply:

"Madam Chairman . . . I am opposed to Miss Emery's motion. I am opposed to it for these reasons: First of all, we have nothing to conceal. (Applause) In the second place, if we had anything to conceal, we couldn't conceal it. (Laughter and applause) In the third place, the newspaper people of St. Louis and of this country have been the best friends that the budding federation has had. (Applause) We started a few months ago with nothing but an idea—an ideal—nothing else. We could say nothing that we had done, we couldn't even say what we were going to do. And yet the press of this country has given us thousands of free columns of real advertising matter. I, for my part, am profoundly grateful for it. Mistakes that would not look well in print will probably be made. But I, myself, would prefer to have these reported accurately, rather than from hearsay."

Madesin sat down, while laughter and applause greeted the comment from Miss Emery that "after such a burst of oratory" she would withdraw her motion. Madesin, too, had a comment to make in her later notes: "I had not then learned that, in women's organizations, the salaried persons who do nine-tenths of the work are expected to permit volunteers to do nine-tenths of the talking. When I made bullets, automatically I fired them myself."

Good spirits prevailed when the Convention settled down to business. Invited by the temporary Chairman to explain the purpose of the meeting, Madesin said: "We must pool our forces in a common effort for the things that advance our interest, advance the interest of other women and perhaps even of the men. Therefore, the purpose of this Convention is the formation of a national federation of business and professional women's clubs, which shall deal with these interests, attempt to place women where they should be, secure for them what they should have, and enable them to concentrate on making the world the kind of place it ought to be. Such an organization must be self-governing, non-sectarian and self-supporting." A delegate rose to propose that it be also non-partisan, and everyone agreed.

"The sessions," according to Madesin's report, "were long and hard, but in the end there was complete agreement as to the basic structure of the organization. The constitution and by-laws were hammered out line by line, the women arguing, changing and taking a vote over and over again, as women always will. It was because they really cared that every article, every word seemed so important. As usual, too, the fixing of dues brought forth a blaze of disagreement. Much was said about the poor working girl who might forever be denied the joys and benefits of federation if dues were fixed at twenty-five cents a member annually. But fixed they were. An airplane soaring into the sky would have brought no greater surprise then, than would the knowledge that within ten years those prohibitive twenty-five cent dues would have been raised to two dollars per member, annually."

Meanwhile, a special committee representing both groups was to work out the details of the proposed amalgamation, leaving nothing unsettled, after which the two major groups were to meet in joint convention to create the federation. That, at least was the theory. At all events, between their regular business sessions the two conventions had held joint extra-curricular programs to which a contingent of St. Louis men had been invited and had come.

"Men know so little about women," commented Madesin, "and even less about what to say to them as a group. One man said that the new organization would be 'the very quintessence of what the word peace would describe.' Another, in a flight of fancy, cried out 'Here is to the ladies, those white-winged doves of peace, whose presence amongst us is the surest harbinger of our eternal happiness in the life to come.' Comparing these masculine efforts with the thousands I have heard since, I remember what Dr. Anna Howard Shaw replied in the very early days of the Suffrage Movement, when someone asked her if she thought the general attitude of the men towards women's rights had changed. She said: 'Although eggs are still being thrown at women, I believe the quality of the eggs has improved.' Yet, even in 1919, women smiled and applauded many a fine-phrased insult to their intelligence, usually regarding them as compliments. Some women, at that Convention, who thought it was "wonderful that those busy important men should come to our meeting,' went back to their own business session to prove many admirable things no doubt, but never that they were 'white-winged doves of peace.'

"A storm was brewing. The hour for the joint meeting of the two groups approached but no word came from the Association of Commerce. We sent a message that we were ready. They asked for more time. Finally, we dispatched an ultimatum. Unless the Association responded by three o'clock, our group would organize without them.

"The waiting was anxious. Much was at stake, since the Commerce Women had strong State branches with powerful leadership, and to go our separate ways would add to our difficulties. At three o'clock a delegate rose to move that we proceed without the Commerce Association. It was a startled but determined group of business and professional women which then calmly organized the National Federation of Business and Professional Women's Clubs, adopted its constitution and by-laws and, by acclamation, elected its officers. We had not expected it to turn out quite like this." Among the resolutions presented was one which Madesin had not anticipated, nor was she prepared for the enthusiasm with which it was adopted. It recognized her part in the success of the Convention and her work in creating the Federation.

That same afternoon the first Board of Directors met. They elected as president Gail Laughlin, an attorney with a firm hand who knew how to face decisions as well as difficulties. "The choice of headquarters," reports Madesin, "was referred to a committee with power to act. Instructions were drawn up for an Executive Secretary who was to develop a program and make an organization where none yet existed. In spite of an empty treasury, the Board fixed the salary of the Executive Secretary at five thousand dollars a year. Such an amount in the year 1919 was munificent. The Federation, they said, must establish standards and set an example."

When nominations for an Executive Secretary were called for, three were made. One nominee received one vote, the other two votes, the re-

46

mainder were cast for Madesin, who had not even sought the job since she was due to return to the YWCA. During the Convention, she had been asked several times if she would accept the presidency. She declined "because I knew I should," she writes, but the offer of the key salaried position surprised her as much as it intrigued her. "The Board members were not my personal friends," she adds, "and most of them I had not even met until I reached St. Louis. Perhaps they could be so wholeheartedly for me because they knew me so little. For me, to become executive secretary of the new federation would mean to exchange security with the YWCA for insecurity, to leave a well-beaten road where many others were traveling, for trail-blazing through unexplored land. I asked for time to consider."

On the long train journey from St. Louis back to New York, she tried to keep her mind away from the tempting offer. She was too tired to think clearly. Besides, she planned to examine the whole situation thoroughly when she got to Wisconsin, with her father. His mere nearness was always reassuring and his influence steadying.

The following day, her briefcase bulging with papers, Madesin returned to her desk at the YWCA. Most of the executives were on vacation, but a cheerful "Welcome home!" greeted her from across the room. The voice belonged to the editor of the Council's department of Drama and Pageants, someone she knew very slightly. The young woman, instead, had observed her comings and goings for several months, had heard of the difficult convention to be held in St. Louis, and had looked upon it all as having the makings of a rather entertaining play. An actress and a stage director, Miss Marjory Lacey-Baker, was totally in the dark as to the inner workings of women's organizations.

Since it was approaching lunchtime, they went out together and Marjory was soon trying to keep up with the pace of Madesin's legs as well as with that of her unbroken narrative about the doings at St. Louis. Not daring to interrupt, the drama editor never found out what Miss Phillips meant by 'caucus,' 'laid on the table,' 'rescind,' 'the women on the floor above,' and other such mysterious terminology. Nor could she have guessed that that cross-town sprint with Madesin Phillips was the beginning of a friendship that was to continue for thirty-five years.

The last of July found Madesin at Lake Minocqua, Wisconsin, in the summer home of her beloved half-brother George and 'Sister' Hattie. She spent many hours drifting lazily in a boat with the Judge. Her father, perceptive as ever, knew she would have to make her own decision, and offered her little more than a review of all the possible angles she should consider. Grateful as she was for the friendship and support she had found among 'Y' leaders, interested as she still was in YWCA aims and activities, her pioneering spirit could not resist the challenge of developing something new and untried.

Her exhaustive letter to the YWCA says, in part: "It was one of the most perplexing days of my whole life. Every fibre of my loyalty and appreciation was strained in the thought of severing, even in name, my connection with the Young Women's Christian Association . . . and yet, I came to see that there would be no real change in the work itself, only in the name. Perhaps, this was the work I had been asked to do—to give a Christian leadership to those women in the business and professional world who had not hitherto been touched through our channels. . . I have given no answer yet, but I am becoming convinced of what I ought to do. . . When the presidency of the new federation was offered me, I declined it instantly and gladly, because I knew I ought to, but when this insistent demand came for my continuance as organizer of the new movement, I confess I heard it with some anguish of spirit. . . The task is so vital and so colossal that no sane person could approach it without great humility and a recognition of utter dependence on the forces of the spirit. . ."

Re-reading this letter some thirty years later, Madesin commented: "In 1919, some of the women who had insisted upon having me as executive secretary would have considered this letter too pious, written less by a feminist than by a preacher. But time has cured much of this seeming discrepancy, for, increasingly, a harassed mankind realizes that its welfare is inextricably bound to the social philosophy of Jesus Christ." This comment, like many others she wrote or spoke, has a prophetic quality, foreshadowing the demand for social and 'Christlike' reform which was to shake the church so profoundly in the 1960's and 1970's.

It was August 8, 1919, when Madesin Phillips notified the President of the National Federation of Business and Professional Women's Clubs that she was accepting the position of national Executive Secretary. Once again, she had had the feeling that the invisible finger, pointing the way, had indicated 'turn here.' Once again, the 'here' had been New York City.

In the early '20's Manhattan was a fascinating place in which to live. Or so it was for Madesin who remarked that "preoccupation with the war was gone. The theater was being reborn. There was music at Carnegie Hall and the Metropolitan and Manhattan opera houses were in full swing. Great organists and the finest of choirs could be heard free in the churches. One had only to choose."

She had found a small, two-room apartment in Greenwich Village into which she had managed to fit her new baby grand. The Mason & Hamlin, which thereafter followed her wherever she lighted, had been purchased on the installment plan—something the people of Nicholasville would have regarded as an unforgivable sin. Not Madesin, however, who, having recognized and accepted the merits of drawing up a budget, had also come to see the advantages of buying a piano 'on time.' The truth was that she could never have had it otherwise and making music was still an immensely significant thing for her spirit. She loved to improvise and, with her fingers on the keys, careless of time, she could let herself be carried into another, more distant and more comforting, world.

She enjoyed her new work, filled as it was with problems and hurdles to stimulate her resourcefulness, as much as she enjoyed 'having fun.' She used these words quite frequently in writing to her father, whose companionship she had never ceased to miss. Finally, she prevailed upon him to visit her in New York. Overjoyed at the prospect, she informed a few of her friends and made plans to give him an unforgettable time.

"On the whole," she writes, "my place was dingy and ill-equipped and the plumbing suffered from chronic disorders. 'If you had a pair of pliers,' my father said almost as soon as he arrived, 'I could stop the water running in the bathroom.' Of course, I had no pliers, but I did have some rich friends. One, whose husband was a Wall Street millionaire, had offered to send her limousine and chauffeur so that I could take my father for a drive around New York. I was all agog at such elegance, but the old judge took it as a matter of course. Presently he said, 'Don't you suppose that that fellow will have a pair of pliers?' 'What fellow?,' I asked. 'Why,' he explained, 'the man who will be running that car you said was coming for us. I thought I could borrow his pliers and fix that faucet.'

"I tried to explain to him that such a thing just was not done. Ordinary folks, like myself, I said, stood more in awe of the servants of the rich than of the rich themselves. But he did not and could not understand. To him a liveried chauffeur, or for that matter the chauffer's millionaire employer, was just another human being like himself, to be treated as any neighbor back home. He only valued the individual, not wealth or prestige. And until proven otherwise, he took it for granted that, like himself, any individual was glad to be helpful."

Anyone who ever came to know Madesin over the years would have to agree that, whatever else she may or may not have inherited from her father, this particular trait was certainly in her heritage. For her too, all through the years of her rise to prominence, her totally honest regard for the 'human person,' never changed. What counted, for her, was the intrinsic quality of the individual, and she believed, most deeply, that every individual was endowed with some measure of quality at its best. This golden nugget, buried in every person, was the treasure which she was so immensely adept at bringing to the surface in those with whom she shared an ideal, a cause, or even a bare hope.

Astride 1919 and 1920, the Federation was taking form on the foundations laid amid the aborted storm in St. Louis. Some of New York's most sophisticated women's magazines were interested enough in the venture to make an assessment of its programs and potential.

49

Harper's Bazaar wrote: "In detail the formation of this federation makes an interesting story, for the coordinating of several hundred women, each with different needs and aspirations, is no easy task. The federation is not political, but it has tremendous political possibilities. It is too soon to state in detail all that the federation may accomplish, but its usefulness, under proper guidance, is almost limitless. . . ."

Good Housekeeping indicated that "from the heart of this group, the future of America looks very fair indeed. The newly born Federation of Business and Professional Women has a glorious future. . . . The weight of its influence will be felt in the coming elections. . . . Politicians are watching it even at its birth. They see the handwriting on the wall and know that woman's day has dawned."

While Madesin herself never lost an opportunity to point out that the remarkable development of the organization, in its initial years, was due to the hundreds of capable women who had dedicated themselves to its advancement, the fact remains that what Susan B. Anthony was to woman suffrage, or Jane Addams to social work, Lena Madesin Phillips was to the business and professional women—at first in her own country, later around the world.

In little more than the batting of an eye, the federation's first year was gone. Summer of 1920 brought the second Annual Convention, this time in St. Paul, Minnesota. *Good Housekeeping* wrote up the event once more, pointing out that "a composite picture of the business woman as she appeared at St. Paul is eye-opening. The first impression is one of intense good health. Where is the fragile lady of yesteryear? In her place is a radiant creature with good physique, clear eyes, splendid vitality. . . She is intelligent and thinks clearly and forcefully. She speaks and acts with authority. . . In a word, she is a woman of affairs and there were five hundred of her at the St. Paul meeting. . . One hesitates to predict just what effect such groups of women will have on the world of tomorrow."

It was to these five hundred professionally trained women that Madesin presented her account of the federation's first year: New York had been designated for the national headquarters, but in the crowded post-war city office space was at a premium. A furnished sub-lease at a moderate rental had been found in the Flatiron Building on Fifth Avenue and 23rd Street, then New York's most publicized edifice. There, with a secretary and typist, the building of the organization had begun.

Some financial assistance having been indispensable until the federation could become self-supporting, Madesin had obtained a $15,000 grant from the War Work Council of the YWCA. With an office and a budget, an official publication had become feasible. An associate editor of one of the best known women's magazines, *Pictorial Review,* offered to edit it without pay. The first issue was ready for press with the title of *The Open Road* on the cover, when it was suddenly discovered that the title already belonged to another periodical. Quickly, the editor suggested *Independent Woman,* and forty years were to pass before that name was superseded by the one it currently bears: *National Business Woman.*

Madesin's report showed that the membership hovered around 26,000, scattered through clubs, varying in size from five members to sixteen hundred. A directory of the various businesses and organizations to which the members belonged, the first of its kind to be compiled and published, was proving extremely helpful to women in business or eager to get into the field. The records of women who had achieved distinction in their respective areas were being assembled. This, also, was a 'first.' The federation was beginning to receive national recognition and its existence was also becoming known abroad. In fact, that year, in New York, the National Federation had sponsored a meeting at which the principal speakers were professional women from foreign countries, in this case, France, Italy, Japan and China.

The report, naturally, revealed the formal and business-like side of Madesin's personality, but her sense of humor, tickled by the inevitable 'goofs' which occur at any major meeting, came forth in her private notes: "If this frisky, young organization came to the St. Paul Convention with 'a national reputation without a spot,' as some had declared, a few of its blemishes were soon fairly obvious. Some came to the surface in the contradictory provisions of the Constitution and the By-Laws, one of which seemed to permit voting by proxy, while the other appeared to prohibit. Delegates holding proxies—one member had as many as fourteen—favored it; those who had none opposed it violently. Feelings ran high, words were many, temperheat soared enough to all but blow the psychological mercury out of its column.

"Another point of tension was the treasurer's report. The president suddenly called a business meeting after the closing banquet. Dressed in party clothes, full of speeches as well as food, we filed droopily back into the Convention Hall. The treasurer, however, had gone to bed. In due course, room no. 344 reported that, given time, she would appear. When she finally did, it was complete with boudoir cap, her hair done up in curlers. Such frivolity as her appearance added to a group already weary with controversy and thirsting for a laugh, was hardly conducive to the dignity and pompous consideration which must always be accorded to finances in women's groups. It turned out that the president had not found the report made out in sufficient detail. All she did was ask for 'a more detailed report the next day' and adjourned the meeting!

"The Federation check book and some records having been located after midnight, a few generous souls volunteered to put their 'business heads' together at once, in order to get the report done."

At dawn, Madesin stepped into a cold tub, wondering why she was in St. Paul anyway! Later that morning, the Hotel Management informed her that the top of the table used by the presiding officer would have to be entirely scraped and refinished, because of the beatings it had taken from the gavel. "This," concluded Madesin in her notebook, "seemed a fitting postscript to a convention which had left the Federation still on its feet only by a miracle."

Madesin Phillips, Executive Secretary of the National Federation of Business and Professional Women's Clubs, in 1921

6.   The Bitter and the Sweet

The Federation had a new president—Mrs. Lena Lake Forrest. "She is a truly fine person and I like to be with her," Madesin informed her father. The feeling was reciprocal because the working relationship between the two women became a strong friendship, lasting a lifetime.

After a short rest, again at Lake Minocqua, Madesin entered the Mayo Clinic for an operation. This, of itself, was not a major matter, but her doctor brother was concerned by her general condition. The year had been hard on her. Not only had she traveled all over the continent to organize clubs, preside at meetings, patch up differences or participate in State conventions, but her sphere of interests had continued to grow. For instance, that year the League of Women Voters founded the Women's Joint Congressional Committee in Washington, D.C., before which Madesin was asked to speak and, while in the capital, she had been drawn into the activities and also the problems of the State Farm and Garden Association.

In Cleveland, at the end of a grueling week of sessions with business and professional women, she had been grounded by a spell of nausea which she could not quickly overcome. Her brother wrote her a long and affectionate letter, warning her of the dangers of over-fatigue, urging her to set time aside for rest and relaxation. The fact that her mother had died of tuberculosis was on his mind. That same spring a freak accident could have incapacitated her, even for life, when a huge pane of glass, falling from a window on a New York street, struck the upper part of her arm, flinging her to the pavement. The very deep cut was to leave a permanent scar. Her clothes, of course, were ruined. While the insurance covered all damages and costs, the loss of blood may well have accounted for her weakness at Cleveland later. However, she seems to have carried on her loaded schedule undaunted. In early May, telling her father that she had again traveled some 4,000 miles on a single trip, she expressed almost childish delight over the gifts she had received: wild flowers and a blanket from the Indians in whom she was deeply interested, a *Life of John Marshall*, by Devereux, costing, she noted, some $20.00, and wondering if she ought to accept it, toilet water, bathsoap, candy. . . But what

53

really pleased her "at heart," was that the clubs were increasing in number, size and activity.

Men listened to her with as much interest as women, never daring to offer her the idiotic compliments which had irritated her in St. Louis. That year, while ice and snow still covered the ground in Maine, more than 500 men and women turned out to hear her speak in Portland. If she was a feminist—and she certainly claimed and proved to be one—she was very different from many who appeared, even then, to be struggling, not for equality with men, but for supremacy over them. Madesin believed in true equality as she believed in God. In Portland, she made her views clear: "Of course, the ideal place for a woman is married and the head of a large family, but all of us can't do this and therefore we must not play seconds to men. We should be able to take our place at their side, as equals. As has been said, 'life is not a cup to be sipped, but a measure to be filled' and, please God, the business women of America will fill it, for they are the biggest unused power we have for good."

Her own family sense had deep roots. In Nicholasville, through her young womanhood, the family circle had been a wide one. As the youngest, she was central to it for many years. Once she had settled in New York by herself, she missed the family circle. Her father was the bridge to it and she crossed it as often as she could by corresponding with him. When she said, in Portland, 'the ideal place for a woman is the head of a large family,' she was saying what she meant. The appalling menace of over-population had not yet risen on the horizon of the world and she believed that equality had to put down roots within the family, if it was ever to flourish outside of it. Her conviction, that the economic factor was paramount in giving women the equality they had a right to demand, applied to the family as it did to the single working woman. She saw no conflict between family and career, only a question of mutable priorities. Most of the leading feminists in her time and earlier were married women.

The year 1921 brought Madesin little change of pace and no slackening of interests and challenges. But she had become more and more adept at keeping her evenings in New York free from business, in order to steep herself in music, the theater, the city's museums and galleries. One or more of her most congenial friends were usually with her. However, something different from all this was also in the cards for 1921 for which she was not prepared, if she had even suspected it might happen. This 'different element' in her professional life was a slow, steady growth of tensions and conflicts within the federation which had begun to poison the air, long before she was made aware of it.

When ideas, opinions or plans were at issue, Madesin could derive very real intellectual enjoyment from the clash of minds because, as she always said, 'the struggle is immensely broadening, regardless of the outcome.' Now, instead, she was up against a tangle of pettiness, which she was able to ignore until she became the target of all sorts of attacks, though none of them open, touching up her field work, her administration of the office, her handling of finances and compounded by a spreading misrepresentation of facts that in due course laid itself bare to everyone's view.

A letter—one among many in this vein found in her private files—written to a friend and colleague in Cleveland, who had warned her of the intrigues and dissension she seemed to be ignoring, illustrates a major trait of Madesin's character, which even her bitterest enemies were forced to recognize: she was eminently, one might say instinctively, fair.

"You are certainly a brick," she wrote, "and I truly appreciate your friendship. Forewarned is forearmed and I am glad to know the current gossip that may be important later on. Personally, I do not look for any real trouble. Practically all of the dissension is right here, in New York. There is a little group determined to 'knock' the national federation. Most of it one can explain: Mrs. C. lost her job and was previously disgruntled, I think, because she did not get to put out the Convention issue. N.P., I presume, still wants my job. J.N. expects the national office to do its own work as well as to organize New York State. . . So, you see, there is a reason in almost every place. We are going to have the best Convention ever. We have to. We cannot afford, for the third time, to use up in petty, gossiping quarrels all that it costs women to attend a national convention. . . If Miss L. comes, it will be, I imagine, to fight protective legislation and not me. . . ."

But Madesin was wrong. Miss L. continued her bitter personal attacks on the executive secretary. She also embarked on a campaign to form a National Federation of her own by trying to pull clubs and state groups out of the original federation, even though she had been among the latter's very first elected officers. Madesin, who liked to bring things out into the open, was baffled as much as she was hurt. Like all human beings she, too, had her faults and frailties, but hypocrisy or underhandedness were not among them. Her weapons were never concealed, the most effective of them being her tongue. Her remarkable gift of oratory was already beginning to be recognized, as was her quick repartee, and, in a debate, she knew how to use wit and humor with great skill. But always face to face. What made Miss L.'s attacks so difficult for Madesin to deal with was that, appearing out of the dark, they remained nebulous: substantial enough to generate confusion or doubts, yet not substantial enough to warrant serious rebuttal. As it was soon demonstrated, jealousy was the accuser's basic motivation. At the Cleveland convention, where sharp disagreements and all manner of trouble were expected, no such thing materialized. The meeting turned out to be a constructive one.

Mrs. Lena Lake Forrest was re-elected president and Madesin Phillips confirmed as executive secretary. Earlier in the year, speaking in Iowa, where she thought she sensed a slight unease among local leaders, a huge audience had been brought to its feet by the words in which she postscripted her account of how the Federation was born: "As women we now need a new kind of courage. We seem to live in an atmosphere of fear, we are afraid to express ourselves. . . Surely we cannot expect to achieve equality if we lack the courage to speak and stand for what we believe in our hearts."

Shortly before leaving for Cleveland, to set up the Convention, Madesin was stricken with a severe case of quinsy. Her throat had to be lanced, and Paula Laddey, an attorney active in federation affairs and one of her very good friends took her, almost by force, to her own home in Newark and placed her in the hands of a trained nurse. At the Convention, some who thought she looked 'tired and worn,' assumed it to be the effect of the gossip and the snide attacks, but she went about her business without showing the slightest concern either for her health or for what may have been said beyond her hearing. Her policy proved profitable all around. The mood of the Convention was good. By the end of September, having had her tonsils removed, she had fully recovered her bounce, but some of her enthusiasm for her job had disappeared.

She let another year go by, during which she still traveled a great deal, although increasingly pinned down by the quickly expanding bulk of office work. Markedly in that period, the basic theme around which she built her campaign for the establishment of more and more business and professional women's clubs all around the country, was contained in these words: "Make no small plans. They have no power to stir the blood."

Guided by her own motto, by the beginning of 1922 Madesin had decided to resign her job. If her blood could still be stirred, she would have to be working on a new and broader plan designed to lift the women's struggle for equality to a higher level. More and more encumbered by the ever growing administrative routine, she had neither the time nor the freedom of mind to make such a plan or even to dream about it. What fresh air is to human lungs, so was a fresh challenge to Madesin's spirit and she no longer saw a challenge in the office she held. There would be one in returning to the practice of law. After she had convinced Mrs. Forrest, the Federation President, that her decision was irrevocable, she communicated it only to two or three of her closest friends.

One of these friends was Paula Laddey, an active attorney then also Treasurer of the national federation. Miss Laddey offered Madesin a partnership in her New Jersey law firm which Madesin tentatively accepted. Quietly, she began to prepare to seek admission to the New Jersey bar. Forsaking all 'fun,' she gave up her evenings and weekends to serious

56

study. That she passed the test must have come as no surprise to anyone who saw the letter of reference given her by William A. Buckner, one of the most prominent members of the Kentucky Bar: "I knew of Miss Phillips long before I had the opportunity to know her personally. No woman there (Kentucky) is held in higher esteem. . . . At the University of Kentucky . . . she received the highest honors of her class and the highest honors ever received, up to that time, by a graduate of the Law School . . . she is a ready and fluent speaker, is possessed of a broad culture and of a personal charm which is rare. Her native endowment, her education, social position and character are such that the Bar of New Jersey will itself be honored, by honoring Miss Phillips with admission to its membership."

After the Convention, the announcement of her resignation brought letters of dismay flooding into the New York office. Typical of the hundreds of answers Madesin sent out, this one explains her reasons: "Essentially, I am a pioneer worker and the executive secretaryship is developing more and more into an office job. I have spent the keen edge of my initiative and resourcefulness, and I believe that a different type of person is now required. We should have someone with a full set of new ideas. I am planning to return to the practice of law. There seems to be sincere regret over my leaving, but I am convinced that this is the thing for me to do."

Full recognition of all that she had done to bring the federation into being, of her many personal sacrifices and of her unflinching determination to 'see things through' once they had been started—all this and more was expressed in a quite spectacular resolution voted at the close of the convention. Its concluding words said what thousands of business and professional women felt who had worked with her, or had been reached by her power to drive others forward: "Miss Phillips will always be the cornerstone of the National Federation and its abiding inspiration."

Willing to remain an active cog in the great national wheel, Madesin accepted appointment as National Membership Chairman. Reaching for membership meant reaching out to people. This was something which summoned the best out of her to the end of her life.

In practical terms, the federation had become an entity to conjure with on the American scene. It was financially self-supporting, its support was growing visibly and its formal alignment with the Suffrage Amendment, as with other legislation affecting the interest of women, had unquestionably carried political weight. As one observer put it, "The National Federation of Business and Professional Women's Clubs has come into a consciousness of its own, ready to pursue a self-determined course."

Lena Madesin was about to do the same thing, on a different path, and on her own. Seven years had already passed since she had first embarked on a legal career in Nicholasville, "only to be deflected from it by a surprising call to New York." America had been at war, then. Now it was, apparently at least, at peace and at ease. Without the excitement inevitably generated by the wartime mood, Madesin was now facing a totally unromantic struggle to achieve ease for herself. "Peace," she mused, "is something else. In people, it is a seed buried deep in the soul which must be nurtured without respite and made to grow from within." Spending time with Madesin Phillips, especially if a situation were difficult, often produced a strong feeling that peace was firmly established in her own inner being.

Once the certification of her admission to the New Jersey Bar was in her pocket, Madesin went to spend the rest of the summer at Lake Minocqua. With her father to hear her out, she reappraised her prospects and had his approval when she decided to establish her own law office in New York, rather than take the easier but less free-wheeling course of a partnership in Paula Laddey's established firm. Their friendship remained as strong as ever, and in the course of time they both agreed that Madesin's decision, though risky at the time, had been wise.

Now, however, she was entirely on her own, without a secure job or the prestige which she had built around the position of Executive Secretary of the Federation. Once, when she was at the half-century mark, looking back to that uncertain period she compared herself to a sailboat, tacking with the wind. The fact was, however, that she was a person of many talents, who needed to balance her interests by reaching constantly into new fields. Also, she was thrifty and had a few savings to fall back on while she sought the best means of making use of the law degree she had worked so hard to achieve. Above all, she was burning to measure herself against the standards and demands of the legal profession in a place as difficult and as unique as New York City. What challenged her most of all, she said, was "the prevailing tradition that men, and only men, were supposed to engage in the practice of law."

For the third time, she went back to school, knowing that the New York Bar examiners would give her a harder time than she had yet faced. At forty-one she entered the Law School of the University of New York. In 1923 she received a Master of Laws Degree, but the bar exam was yet to come. She took it, and failed. "No, I am not ashamed of you," Judge Phillips wrote to his crest-fallen daughter, "I don't know anyone who has done more than you and had so little help." Six months later, in June 1924, the letter he received from her had this to say: "Dearest Daddy: You are receiving a letter from a full-fledged lawyer in Kentucky, New Jersey and New York. . . . We were ushered into the luxurious Court Room of the Supreme Court, the Judges in their black gowns filed in, and we were sworn in. There were only about 115 of us because, as I know too well, it is very difficult to pass the examinations and then, for those who do pass, it is also difficult to be approved by the Committee on Character and Fitness. All of us stood and took the oath at one time, each giving his own name and all speaking at once. It was quite impressive. Afterwards the Presiding Justice gave us some good advice. . . I am glad it is over and while I may not have many clients right off, I will at least get started." Established in the law offices of John G. Turnbull, on Broadway near Wall Street, with access to his extensive library, Madesin mailed her engraved announcement around the country and hopefully waited for clients. They eventually came, but very slowly.

Actually, while preparing for the New York bar exams, Madesin's earlier contacts produced several requests for legal services on a fee basis, which proved to be a major financial blessing. Her first such client was the American Child Health Association, of which Herbert Hoover was president. Over a period of months Madesin surveyed the Association's activities, suggesting improvements in its management and ways to achieve broader public support. "We shall be building on your findings and recommendations for a long time to come," wrote the Association when the work was completed. Madesin had quite a talent for combining the intangible values of a cause with the mechanics required for its fulfillment. Probably this was one reason which made her a very tough lawyer, but also an inspiring leader of movements.

Next to seek her out was the Southern Women's Educational Alliance, regarded by many "as the bridge between the Southern girl and the right educational opportunity." The purpose appealed to Madesin who became the organization's consultant. It was from Dr. Orie Hatcher, its president, that Madesin borrowed a phrase she often used with great effect: "Human nature is very prevalent."

In the early part of 1924, she appears to have injected new life into the National Woman's Garden and Farm Association to which she was consultant at first and later the National Recording Secretary. Mrs. William C. Conant, of Weston, Massachusetts, who claimed to be "a New Englander, unable always to give expression to my thoughts and feeling as I should like" was nonetheless able to make very clear how her Association felt about Madesin's contribution: "Many of us went to the Annual meeting in Washington with the feeling that we were burying the remains of the National Farm and Garden Association. Not at all! A transfusion of life has been given it and we now feel that the Association is resuscitated and will leap forward with new life, usefulness and prosperity, thanks to your guidance. Hats off to Lena Madesin Phillips!"

The campaign of the American Woman's Association to build a combination clubhouse-hotel for single women in the center of Manhattan was already under way when Miss Anne Morgan and Mrs. William

K. Vanderbilt drew Madesin into their project. A veritable host of civic leaders and business women were selling stock to raise the three million dollars needed to finance it. Madesin's major contribution, here, was sheer oratory, even though she liked to say that the remarkable financial results of her speeches were due chiefly to the well known fact that Miss Anne Morgan was the daughter of the fabulous J. Pierpont! The club-house hotel endured successfully many years.

A change of occupation was not the only novelty to enter her life that year. She decided to try doing what so many single women did who had come to work in New York from elsewhere—share an apartment. It was once again in a casual way that she re-encountered Marjory-Lacey-Baker, now, like herself, pursuing a business career, far removed from her youthful and successful exploits in the world of theater. She was personnel manager for a major department store and looking for a place to live. Her father had died recently and her mother, being in very poor health and needing care, had gone to live with a married daughter. Their New York home had been dismantled and Marjory, for the first time in her life, was on her own. Pooling their resources, they moved into an apartment on East 30th street, much larger than either of them could have afforded alone. As it turned out, there was a sufficient difference of age and pursuits between them to make the combination interesting, yet enough similarities in their background, tastes and avocations to make it viable.

Eventually, as the years went by and the sharing of a home remained successful, they became working associates as well. Gradually, as their respective relatives of their generation disappeared, they became 'family' to one another. Photographs of Madesin in the twenties show a slender woman, with brown hair—cut short as was then beginning to be the style —grey eyes and good-looking clothes. The clothes were largely Marjory's doing. Madesin never had any more interest in her attire as a woman than she had had as a little girl and welcomed Marjory's willingness to keep her wardrobe up-dated and suited to the occasion. Marjory, on her part, became increasingly concerned with 'causes' she had scarcely known existed before she met Madesin. Indeed and much to her own amusement, she became a well-grounded parliamentarian, no longer baffled by Roberts' Rules of Order, as she had been the first time she heard the term 'tabling a motion' tumble from Madesin's lips. In later years, Marjory's work for the International Federation, when the organization could not afford good paid secretaries and such, was without price, efficient and devoted.

The year 1924 also marked the beginning of Madesin's entrance into the political arena. The presidential candidates were John W. Davis, Democrat, and Calvin Coolidge, Republican, to whom she had been introduced during one of her speaking tours in behalf of business women, when he was Governor of Vermont. A passing comment in a letter to her father, suggests that he impressed her "as being much too quiet a man to have presidential aspirations." Events, of course, proved her wrong.

Her interest in politics, first stimulated by her father's campaigns, had become increasingly lively. She was now convinced that women should not merely vote, but be active participants in all political battles as well. After attending her first national political convention as a Democrat, as soon as the campaign got under way she joined the speech-makers in greater New York. In the final days she shared a platform with Governor Alfred Smith, of New York, addressing an audience of more than three thousand men and women 'gone wild.' Regardless of her preference, she soon spotted the political handwriting on the wall and, when Calvin Coolidge became 20th President of the United States, she wired her father "disappointed but not surprised."

While the national campaign was hitting a peak, Madesin also worked for the re-election of Joseph V. McKee as Justice of the City Court of New York. In fact, he asked Madesin to be his campaign manager. "The first time in the history of New York politics," commented the press," a Justice has appointed a woman to fill this important post." Joe McKee won hands down and in the following year, 1926, when he ran for President of New York's Board of Aldermen, Madesin worked for him again, and again they scored a resounding victory.

As an active member of the Women's Democratic Union, Madesin helped to form the Women's Civic Organization which first met in January 1926 and had her for its secretary. People who asked why this organization had been created were given a leaflet which provided the answer in Madesin's words: 1) for a fuller participation in civic life by thinking women; 2) for the advancement of the State educational program; 3) for the promotion of better public health measures; 4) for the improvement of housing conditions; 5) for the sponsoring of progressive legislation in behalf of women and children. To be sure, she could well have been setting these five points on paper in the 1970's! Towards the end of that year, her friend Dr. Hatcher, of the *Southern Women's Educational Alliance,* hurriedly sought her advice on what to emphasize in a speech she was to make. Madesin sent her suggestions by telegram, dictated in the midst of a court case and when she was trying to get off to Kentucky for Christmas. But the pressure, evidently, in no way affected her clear thinking, her long vision or her wry, half-concealed humor. The text of the wire said: "Emphasize woman's limitations and weaknesses, such as unwillingness to assume responsibility, slavery to small things, lack of courage, initiative, as directly traceable to her history chattel, slave and entire background always meeting needs and demands of men. Today they live for first time in atmosphere of public opinion, recognizing them as more of equals, mentally physically. First real concept and treatment of woman as an individual human being with rights, capabilities approximating man's. Women have little idea today where they are going, they only know themselves released from confinement and are busy examining all things going in all directions. I think they should find balance through elimination of parasitic women, separating commercial and professional employment from their inherent self-sacrificing mothering treatment. On thë whole remove from business world sex as either help or hindrance. Advocate any piece of work being done by person best fitted, whether male or female. In some cases this might mean the husband minds the children while the wife runs the store, but no matter. Lena M. Phillips."

Although the Alliance was concerned far more with education than with economics as such, Madesin had not been able to refrain from touching upon this angle in her message. The concept of equality in pay scale, known as 'the rate for the job,' or, 'equal pay for equal work,' which the International Labor Office finally succeeded in placing on the international books, but not until the fifties, was already enunciated clearly by Madesin in the words: "Advocate any piece of work being done by person best fitted, whether male or female." Even this seemingly elementary aspect of economic equality between the sexes has not yet been fully achieved in the 1970's, in the U.S.

Despite all these activities, her ties with the federation never loosened, nor did her determination to see its members go forward ever lessen. As National Membership Chairman in 1924, she could report a membership just under 40,000. The Convention, held at West Baden Spring, Indiana, gave her a big hand for her efforts. At that gathering a number of women were wearing the new fangled bobbed hair for the first time. Those who did were the most 'progressive' and some admitted that they had had their hair fashionably cut more as a protest against the conservatives in their midst, than to be the first in style. At all events, at a meeting described by the press as "Bobbed Hair Breakfast," the conservative long haired women sat on one side of the room and the short haired ones—Madesin among them—on the other. That morning the iconoclasts reaped both cheers and boos, but the final triumph of the bob was not long in coming.

Being progressive, especially in regard to legislation, often required considerable courage in those days, because there were risks involved, not from a hairdresser's shears or from a booing congregation of breakfasters, but from powerful arch-conservatives around the country. From the floor of the Convention, Madesin led a hotly debated campaign to secure the federation's support for congressional ratification of the Child Labor Amendment and for participation of the United States on the World Court. Both of these recommendations were adopted, but not without evoking considerable public reaction.

Madesin described what happened: "Both the Federation and I, personally, together with other organizations and leaders of women, were attacked on the ground that we were reds and lending ourselves to the purposes of the Communists, by attacking the government. A contemporary clipping from the *Christian Science Monitor* quotes me as saying in reply: 'Our organization adopts its programs and policies not on the basis of the company they keep, but because our sound judgment and women's civic interest tell us that those programs and policies are for the betterment of conditions for men and women. Our choice is based on fundamental equities, not on color. (The Child Labor Amendment of natural course offered protection to black children as well as white.) We would rather be on the right side with radicals than on the wrong side with conservatives, or vice versa.' "

If this was the first attack of this nature, made upon her because of her readiness to go out on any limb that belonged to the tree of social justice at home or abroad, it was not destined to be the last. She never lacked the courage to stand by her most unpopular decisions, because she always made a decision with the fullest possible knowledge of the consequences that might be entailed. Had she not been a good lawyer this might have been otherwise. But a good lawyer she was and people respected her as such.

Evidence of this respect reached her one day in the form of an intriguing telegram from Portland, Maine, signed by Helen Havener, a brilliant young journalist on the staff of the *Portland Evening Express,* whom Madesin had met very briefly at a meeting, she did not remember where. The telegram said:

"Would you be interested in taking on rather unusual case as associate counsel with Senator Hinckley and Pinckney Glantzberg? Involves breaking the Hummel will. Small fee but nationwide publicity."

The story behind the telegram was even more intriguing than Helen Havener's message. Early in 1926, the daily press had carried front page accounts of the death in London of Abraham Hummel, a somewhat notorious New York lawyer. In the year 1907, when Madesin was staying with Mrs. Lyons in New Jersey, this shrewd defender of some of the city's worst criminals had been sent to prison on Blackwell's Island for subornation of jury in a divorce case. The prosecuting attorney, Jerome K. Jerome, had vowed to drive Hummel from the courts of New York and he did. After serving a year's term, Hummel left the country to live first in Paris, then in London, taking with him his two sisters and a nephew, but leaving behind his beautiful wife, Leila Farrel, of comic opera fame, and their small son. Leila Farrel died within a few years and the boy, Henry Abraham Hummel, went to live with his maternal grandmother in Portland—forgotten by the world and, seemingly, by his father as well.

Henry, now married, was driving a bakery wagon in South Portland

and playing nightly in a dance orchestra, when the news of Abe Hummel's death came over the wires, and Helen Havener was sent by the *Express* to interview his son. The Hummel estate, she informed him, reputed to amount to more than a million dollars, had been left not to him, but to his two aunts and a cousin. The young man told her that he did not want the money, and had not heard from his father in twenty years. Miss Havener's story for her own paper went around the world, headlined by the Associated Press, "Bake Cart Driver Spurns Millions."

In London the Hummel sisters denied that the bakery driver was their brother's son. Their refusal to acknowledge him hurt Henry's pride. He changed his mind and decided to prove his claim. Helen Havener, authorized by her editor to obtain counsel for the impecunious young man, asked Senator Frederick W. Hinckley, an outstanding attorney in Maine, to take the case. He agreed, on condition that he be given an associate lawyer in New York to handle matters at that end, a man, of course!—who thinks of women lawyers? Helen Havener did. An enthusiastic feminist, she suggested to the Senator that there might be advantages in engaging a woman, perhaps two. She proposed Madesin Phillips and Pinckney Estes Glantzgerg, another New York attorney, who had a summer home in Maine and was known to Senator Hinckley. Once accepted, both women plunged into a situation bristling with dramatic aspects, for, among other things, in his will Abraham Hummel had declared himself a bachelor. Unattended, his body arrived in New York in a casket of rosewood, trimmed with solid gold.

Between February and November, 1926, Madesin and Pinckney Glantzberg interviewed hundreds of people likely to throw light on Henry Hummel's birth and childhood, and on the home life of the flamboyant lawyer and his beautiful wife. They gathered scores of affidavits from such people as the nurse who had cared for Henry as a baby, from tradesmen who remembered the couple and the child, from old actresses who had played bit parts with Leila Farrel. They tracked down Mrs. Hummel's physician, her milliner, waiters who had regularly reserved a table for Mr. and Mrs. Hummel at Delmonico's. The photographs of Abe Hummel showed the striking resemblance between father and son, all of them corroborating the young man's parentage. Thirty-five witnesses had already been subpoenaed for the trial when the attorneys representing Hummel's sisters—the impressive firm of Davis, Polk, Wardwell, Gardiner and Reed—suddenly proposed a settlement out of court. The terms were not made public, but it was reported at the time that the estate had shrunk from the reputed $1,500,000 to a little over $50,000. But Henry Hummel had won his case, and women lawyers had scored a triumph.

Madesin had greatly enjoyed the case which, incidentally, found a place in New York's records as the most extraordinary of its kind ever tried up to that time. She also came to notice Helen Havener's remarkable sense of good journalism and of publicity. She drew her more and more into the work of the Federation to which Helen Havener contributed her remarkable competence in mass communication. Thanks to her skill, the press, radio and eventually television greatly enhanced the cause of women and the advancement of their rights. It was due to her that in a newsletter she published for the Federation's convention in Portland, Maine, that year, there appeared a news item destined to start off an interesting chain of events. It ran thus:

Vienna, July 20—Fraulein Marianne Beth, an enthusiastic advocate of women suffrage, claims the distinction of being the first woman to be admitted to practice law in Austria. Completing the University course, she studied law in her father's office and recently passed the examinations admitting her to practice.

Madesin quickly picked it out. It was one more prop to support her never-abated dream of reaching business and professional women in other lands to organize them as the American women had been organized. She remembered it vividly many years later, when Dr. Beth was among the first European women to answer her call.

The Hummel case was still pending when Madesin, again without the slightest anticipation of what lay around the corner, was pushed a step closer to her distant international goal. At the Federation's convention, in Iowa, which she attended as National Program Chairman, she was again asked if she would accept the presidency. This time she was willing to be nominated for it, "but," she writes, "I felt that there were loyalties due to another among us: Mary Stewart, a talented educator who had played a major part in the founding convention at St. Louis. There had long been a feeling that, at some point, both she and I should be honored with the office of president. The difficulty, keenly felt by many, lay in deciding who should serve first. . . . This is the sort of contention which tends to occupy much time and effort in young organizations. The less experienced members tend to find it easier and far more exciting to grapple with problems of personality than with matters of principle.

"Between sessions, as I strolled among the magnificent trees on the campus of Iowa College, where we were meeting, a member of the nominating committee joined me, saying: "Miss Phillips, some of the women in the convention think that Mary Stewart should also be nominated for the presidency. We did not know if you would be willing to run if there were another candidate." I looked at her, a little surprised by the question, but she was far more surprised when I said, quite simply, "Of course it is alright with me. You know, when I decided to run the field was wide open. As far as I am concerned, it still is.""

65

"Mary Stewart was nominated from the floor, but she withdrew her name. I was elected without opposition. As it happens, she never became president of the National Federation, but her memory lives very brightly, both at home and abroad, through the constant use of her beautiful and ageless *Collect for Clubwomen*."

Over the years, Mary Stewart's prayer has appeared in various formats, on cards, in anthologies, on decorated tiles, even in braille. Dropping its title, countless men's groups still like to use it at their meetings.

> Keep us, O God, from pettiness; let us be large in thought, in word, in deed.
> Let us be done with fault-finding and leave off self-seeking.
> May we put away all pretense and meet each other face to face— without self-pity and without prejudice.
> May we be never hasty in judgment and always generous.
> Let us take time for all things; make us to grow calm, serene, gentle.
> Teach us to put into action our better impulses, straightforward and unafraid.
> Grant that we may realize it is the little things that create differences, that in the big things of life we are at one.
> And may we strive to touch and to know the great, common, woman's heart of us all, and, O Lord God, let us forget not to be kind.

One may wonder what made Madesin take such a demanding office at that time. She was just beginning to build up a good law practice in New York; also the cause of women's rights was attracting an increasingly wide and varied following all over the country, many segments of which were turning to her for leadership. In trying to explain her decision one must recognize, first of all, that the more she established contacts with foreign women, the more she came to realize that an international movement, such as she hoped for, would have to be spearheaded by the business and professional women of the United States. They, in turn would need to have an increasingly strong, well-knit and forward-looking organization in order to offer the required leadership. She must have sensed that the time had come for her to place herself in a position within the national Federation from which she could work to bring all this to a head.

At about this time a theatrical producer and a supporter of the Federation, called Pearl l'Heureux, had made a study of Madesin's personality as keenly as if she had been about to cast her in a major role. It was for use in an article published when Madesin was elected Federation president. In it, she retraced the course of Madesin's career from her first visit to New York, noting that each time Madesin had changed course, it had occurred at the most propitious time. "She has the rare gift of knowing when the right moment has come to make a move. Few people have it. Lena Madesin Phillips never takes a step until the exact moment has arrived. But she seems guided by an instinct rather than by anything more tangible or specific, a gift which contributed greatly to her success as a pioneer. As a person," the writer added, "she is intensely human and extraordinarily witty. Not, however, the barbed wit that usually goes with the type of mind she possesses: her wit has the flash of a rapier, but without edge. No one ever cringes at the expense of her humor. This is a quality that enhances her native talent for leadership." As time would tell, it also drew in her wake some bitter enemies as well as many very loyal friends.

Representatives of the Federation at the tomb of Edith Cavell in Paris, 1928. Marjory Lacey-Baker is at far left, Madesin Phillips, the fifth from the left.

7. Broadening the Vista

Madesin was never one to waste time before letting other people know what was on her mind, especially if the carrying out of her plans rested on the willingness of others to assist. Thus, the first issue of *The Independent Woman* to appear before she took office presented her program for the ensuing year, highlighted by the question: "Will you follow?"

The Federation, born in 1919, could now be described as 'out of its infancy.' "The organization," she wrote, "has reached the mystic age of seven years, a number hallowed by tradition, signifying completion of a span and readiness for the beginning of new things. The time is ripe to bring our federation into new fields, to recognize wider opportunities and greater responsibilities and to claim both as our own. For some time, there has been an increasing desire among our members to come into closer contact with the business and professional women of other countries. Obviously this cannot be done both quickly and adequately at the same time. Therefore, it is fitting that at the start of a new cycle we extend both our vision and our reach. Perchance the reach may exceed the grasp —it should!"

Although her aim was the distant reach, this was not all she chose to project. She also showed what lay within immediate grasp, systematically, one step at a time, in a manner typical of the way her mind worked: "During the coming year, a commission on International Relations will undertake a survey of the need for an international federation, and of the ways and means of promoting it. . . . At our next Convention we may expect a comprehensive report. The following year should see a definite plan for establishing such an organization. At the end of the third year, our Convention should entertain leading representatives from foreign countries. With probabilities, by the close of a five year period, if not before, we can send a shipload of American business and professional women to a foreign country to establish, in cooperation with the women of other nations, an International Federation."

In her mind the dream had already taken shape, but she knew that before anything tangible could develop, a new and close interdependence

68

had to be established between the membership and herself. In order to explain this, she compared it to the relationship between a general and his troops: "Around the general are, or should be, gathered those of experience and vision against whom he may check his own ideas and plans, but his real strength is in the field. . . . With us, it is the rank and file of members all over the country who, with their officers, determine if a program, like a battle, shall succeed or fail. All that I can do must be done through you. If you fail, plans and programs are as nothing. As your president, I must lead, but will you follow?" Follow they did.

However, now that the Federation was raising its sights, abroad as well as at home, it needed the freedom to plan and to operate which come with financial stability. Thus, a long and hard fought campaign had been conducted to raise individual membership dues to $2.00. The majority, supporting the increase, were also aware that the struggle might weaken the federation by splitting the membership over the issue. The raise won by a good margin, even though some resentment remained among those who had opposed it. Writing about it later Madesin noted that "money was always a bone of contention among clubwomen in those days. Oddly enough, this was so even among working women who should have been able to regard money as the means to an end and not as an end unto itself. Actually in the course of the campaign some clubs withdrew their membership from the federation, others were hesitant and took no side, even though the vast majority voted for and paid the greatly increased dues."

The higher cost of belonging brought with it a number of compensations, one of which was that the Federation magazine would be distributed to the entire membership, thus eliminating individual subscriptions. This, in turn, meant increasing the circulation from 2,000 to more than 40,000 copies, a mechanical challenge of no mean proportions. Several significant new projects were also initiated and, probably more vitally important than any other single benefit, the Federation ended the year with a bank balance of some $17,000 after wiping out a $12,000 indebtedness. "With fitting ceremony," reports Madesin, "the Convention witnessed the burning of cancelled notes which the Federation had issued in 1921 to some of its own members."

Madesin rarely had any uncertainties in her mind as to the ends which should be sought by the means of available money. Now that the Federation was no longer strapped, a major concern was that the funds be wisely spent.

"Field organizers had to be engaged," Madesin noted later, "if the organization was to become something more than a group of women come together to serve their own interests or meet like-minded friends. A program would have to be developed which was far in advance of the general level of thinking in the country. The woman of today must realize that two things are of particular importance to her future: that she is a free, independent and capable individual; that opportunities are open to her, but that in order to enjoy them, she must have faith in herself, a full vision of her own potentialities and the courage to fulfill them. Woman now looks out upon a Promised Land, for the waters of the river have parted. But no person should be called upon to lift her bodily and place her in the Promised Land. The final step she must take herself."

The fact was that, in the 1920's, despite a growing number of highly qualified and prominent women who had joined the Federation and were influential within it, there were still too many members who had not even recognized the challenge thrown out by those who had broken ground in seeking economic equality for gainfully employed women. Arousing this awareness was among Madesin's major goals and all sorts of ways were devised to achieve it. The Federation published a guide to Schools and Business and Vocational Courses, facilitated the transfer of membership from one Club to another, distributed emblems and attention-getting automobile stickers. National Business Women's Week was inaugurated with considerable clamor around the country, and, as was its purpose, attracted the attention of business men to the broader activities and higher expectations of business women.

Madesin herself was considerably ahead of her time when she appeared before the Ways and Means Committee of the House of Representatives in Washington in 1926 to protest "against unjust discrimination against single men and women in the income tax exemption." At that time single persons had an exemption of $1,500, whereas married men had an exemption of $3,500 in addition to $400 for each dependent child. "The cost of living is much higher for single persons who must pay a maximum rate for all services," Madesin Phillips told the Committee, urging that the credit allowed single persons be raised to $3,500. "The government," she said, "could easily make this change, since the Treasury has each year unnecessarily collected about $600,000 over and above the government's needs." This remark, read in the 1970's, when the federal deficit is in the billions, must inevitably produce a smile, or evoke exclamations of disbelief.

But the ice had been broken. For the first time a woman's organization had testified on such a subject before a Congressional Committee and had entered a plea designed to benefit both men and women. A bill to this effect which came before the House and Senate, met with failure in the 1920's as it has ever since.

While holding the office of president of the Federation, Madesin was traveling constantly around the country and speaking without fees, a fact which seriously affected her personal situation. Later, in 1928, in order to keep some income flowing in from her law practice she took Barnet Muffs as a partner, renaming the firm Phillips and Muffs. Certain of the minor cases which she handled at about that time are worthy of note because they reveal the many economic difficulties women ran into merely because they were women. After nearly half a century this basic inequity still exists, even though less acute than in the 20's. One such case, involving a transfer of stock belonging to a married woman, caused Madesin to ask a member of the New York Stock Exchange to clarify the rulings affecting her client's position. He wrote: "As you probably know, owing to the fact that there are still some States which do not recognize the rights of married women to act as individuals, the New York Stock Exchange has ruled that securities assigned by a married woman are not a good delivery. In these cases a retransfer is necessary requiring an additional charge of 2¢ per share."

Interestingly enough, the unmarried woman who, not shy about admitting her status, called herself "Miss," came off much better in the stock investment field. He wrote: "Securities in the name of an unmarried woman with the prefix 'Miss' are a good delivery and need not be retransferred. If the prefix 'Miss' is not added, or if the shares are in the name of a widow, the assignment must be acknowledged before a Notary Public, otherwise the shares are not a good delivery and must be retransferred."

In the matter of salaries all women, married, single, admittedly 'Miss' or otherwise, came off poorly as compared to men of equal skills. This, too, has not yet ceased to be true today. In 1927 the monthly review of the National Employment Exchange, showed that a bookkeeper received $45 a week and up if a man, but only $30 if a woman; a woman cost-clerk could earn only up to $25 a week, a man up to $45; a male secretary could earn as much as $75, but a woman could not seem to get beyond $40, for the same skill and experience. Madesin and other women had been fighting these inequities a long time, but even more difficult to overcome was the intangible factor of 'attitude' then prevalent in the working world, whereby woman was considered to have inferior potential capacity merely because she was not a man. This 'attitude' was commonly accepted in lieu of facts demonstrating the contrary.

To change this prejudice—for such it was—public attention had to be drawn to the achievements of women as well as to their unused and underestimated potential. Everything revealing woman's contribution to the economic picture became grist to Madesin's mill. Although not by nature a 'joiner,' she began to respond favorably to requests from women's organizations seeking her endorsement, her support or her legal counsel. In each case she undertook a commitment because it offered a hitherto untried approach to her main goal, the achievement of woman's economic

71

equality. Thus, she became Vice-President of the *National Council of Women of the United States,* was closely identified with *New York's Exposition of Women's Arts and Industries,* already in its fifth successful year. In a legal capacity she was still actively associated with the *Southern Women's Educational Alliance* and the *National Woman's Farm and Garden Association,* to mention only two of her steady clients.

At about this time, having done well with her installment purchase of the baby grand, she invested in a Ford car on the same easy payment system. Her letters to her father, which continued to be frequent, warm and usually gay, reveal no mention of this renewed trespass on the traditional financial mores of Nicholasville. She enjoyed the car and stole out of the city whenever she could to rediscover "real country scenery." Occasionally, her "theft of time for my other self" as she put it, covered a weekend during which she went by train to see her father. At 88, he was reasonably well and contented, but in the previous year his condition had caused her grave anxiety. Suddenly this tall, sturdy man, who had always been so splendidly well and strong was beset with ills, for the most part imaginary. He lived to be 95, but that year he was greatly troubled and unhappy about a burning sensation in his hands and feet and by the fear of death. His son George finally decided to put him for a month in Dr. Sprague's Sanitarium for mental and nervous diseases in Lexington, where Madesin herself had been so thoroughly healed of her nervous breakdown years before. The Judge, too, made a complete recovery. In August, during one of the many visits she made to him that year, she found him "much better than I had expected." Christmas in Nicholasville was, once more, a gay family affair.

Returning to New York in the fall from a dash to Kentucky, Madesin discovered that her new car, parked before her apartment on 30th Street, had been stolen. Although she was able to get another to replace it, the shock of it lingered with her for a long time. A car stolen and not recovered was an exceptional event in those days, even in crowded Manhattan!

The following year Madesin instituted a policy for the Federation well supported by her close associates—namely that public interest in the activities of business and professional women must never be allowed to lag. It was a spectacular innovation which other organizations watched with some amusement, some critical comments and, lastly, with admitted if somewhat envious admiration. Oakland, California, had been selected for the Federation's National convention. Two bright young members, whose business was travel, decided to organize a Convention train, known as the 'President's Special' to run three thousand miles from New York City to Oakland. As a piece of promotion for the Business and Professional Women's Clubs it was a roaring success. In Madesin's words, "It was the biggest all-woman train that ever crossed the country. Starting from New York, it picked up delegations as it traveled, finally running in three sections and carrying one thousand members. It also carried not only an abundance of pullman porters, but maids as well, and even more unique, it published a daily newspaper on board."

Helen Havener of Maine, to whom Madesin owed her involvement in the famous Abe Hummel case, published a daily bulletin on board entitled *Once in Awhile*. Besides news, gathered at each train stop as well as on board, and some rather eclectic features, it also carried a 'lost and found' column which, on one occasion, announced the loss of one porter, inadvertently left behind in Albuquerque. When the three sections pulled into a station, they were met by large crowds of friends, relatives and local members, headed by the Mayor and other local dignitaries. Speeches, lavish hospitality, entertainment typical of the area, sightseeing and the like provided material for the publication. Madesin herself described some of this extraordinary journey as follows:

"At St. Louis, the first stop, the reception was designed to celebrate the birth of the federation in that city in 1919. At Kansas City, Missouri, a very moving service was arranged for us at the World War I Memorial. At Colorado Springs, a trip to the summit of Pikes Peak—16,000 feet. Our exit from Colorado Springs evoked the early days of the Far West. An ancient stagecoach, garlanded with columbine, the state flower, flanked by the prettiest of our young members as outriders and preceded by a brass band, carried us to the station, followed by a long procession of motor cars and busses.

"Our day in New Mexico began at Santa Fé, a city old when the Pilgrims landed, where we again disrupted traffic and amazed the passersby as we paraded through the streets in cars and busses, led by another old-fashioned stagecoach. This time, by request, I sat on top, accompanied by a venerable Indian, Old Sage San Tiego, of San Domingo Pueblo. The Governor welcomed us at Old Palace.

"At Grand Canyon we were greeted by Arizona's Governor Young, and at sunset witnessed the ceremonial dances of the Hopi Indians. Here an aged chief placed an Indian rug about my shoulders, making me a member of the Hopi tribe, with the name of Chickawana which, so far as I could make out, meant Chief Lady of the Snake Dance.

"In Los Angeles we had the thrill—and it was a thrill in those days —of a reception given for us by Mary Pickford, then Queen of the Motion Picture World, and of being guests 'on the Lot' at Hollywood. Rarely have I had so gay, uproarious and yet rewarding audience as when I addressed a large gathering of men, at the well known Los Angeles Breakfast Club.

"After ten days of this rollicking adventure across the vast expanse of America, from the Atlantic to the Pacific, we finally arrived at Oakland. Carefree we seemed and mostly were, but we had also seen our country and ourselves in a new light, had reviewed our objectives as an organized body of self-supporting women and caught a glimpse of the mission that might be ours overseas."

The mood of the Convention was remarkably internationalist despite the growing isolationism of the country as a whole. Indeed, it was a sign of Madesin's influence that the Convention, with its 2000 delegates, threw its support behind any policy or effort designed to bring the United States into the World Court! A few years earlier, Madesin's advocacy of such a position had brought on the charge that she, and others holding her views, were 'reds.' Now, a majority of the nearly 50,000 members of the federation had voted to stand at her side on that same issue. Madesin regarded this far less as a personal victory than as evidence of the advancing world-mindedness of the clubs. "It was education and planning that did it," commented Madesin, who was an ardent believer in the merits of both.

The only negative note struck at the Convention came from the report of the chairman of the Commission on International Relations. Miss Harriet Taylor, traveling through Europe for her own affairs, had interviewed many women engaged in business or a profession in their respective countries and, on the whole, had found them reluctant to take the first step towards an international association. Their argument, in general, was that they should secure recognition at home and build a national organization before attempting to form an international body. Actually, however, the political climate had also played a role in their reaction: many Europeans had become somewhat suspicious of the motives of American policy after Washington's refusal to join the League of Nations, while the fluctuations of U.S. foreign policy, the flaunting of the wealth of 26,000 post-war American millionaires and the nations' youthful and aggressive vigor coupled with its inexperience in world affairs, had given rise to considerable resentment. Against this background, Miss Taylor's failure to arouse enthusiasm for an international federation was hardly surprising.

Nevertheless, the Convention urged that contacts with European women be carried on and other avenues of cooperation be sought. Madesin, elected president for a second term, continued to advocate international cooperation, undeterred by the lack of immediate response from abroad. In the autumn, that year, a mail vote by the federation's board of directors gave full approval to a plan worked out by Miss Taylor, whereby Madesin would lead a party of U.S. members on a tour of Europe, not merely to sightsee, but also to meet with their counterparts in various countries. The time was to be July 1928.

One day in early March, 1928, Judge Phillips received one of his daughter's fairly frequent letters. Like many others, it was written at night time, on a train. As usual, she was off on a speaking tour, covering several Mid-Western states. In the middle of the second page, he stopped and muttered. "What? What? She's a fool!" Then he read the passage from his daugther, to be sure he had understood. Madesin said: "This afternoon a dozen of us took a ride in one of the new big monoplanes— a party arranged in my honor. They are wonderful planes, each having three powerful motors, comfortable wicker chairs, a toilet, an aisle to walk on, windows, electric lights, heat. We went up 4300 feet and traveled 100 miles an hour. It is very comfortable if you weren't so far from land. A wonderful sight all around, of course. But I won't make a practice of going up. I don't really enjoy it much, although I doubt if it is any more dangerous than riding in an automobile. . . ."

A few days later he wrote back, still the father having to admonish the child: "I was very much surprised to get your letter telling me that you had been up in an airplane. I was sure that you had better judgment than to do such a foolish thing and want you to promise me that you not do so again and I am sure you will make this promise." The letter ends with the admonition ". . . and stay close to the ground." There seems to be no record that Madesin ever made him such a promise, although to the end of her life, traveling as much as she did, she flew as infrequently as she possibly could.

Transatlantic passenger flights, of course, still lay far in the future and the Goodwill Tour booked passage for its fifty-two travelers on the S.S. Carmania. The New York press, which covered the midnight sailing on July 20th, 1928, called this "the largest group from any organization to go in a body to Europe." Madesin, who knew that the trip was costing each woman $795 of her hard earned money, plus all the rest that vacationers can never refrain from spending, especially if it is their first trip abroad, wondered what had really motivated them. "Probably the answers would be as varied as the women themselves," she writes, "but, running like a common thread through all of them, would be a belief in the influence and prestige of the Federation, a desire to see Europe and the eagerness to make some contribution to international understanding in the interest of real peace."

A couple of weeks before the tour started, the National Federation, holding its Tenth Annual Convention, prevailed upon Madesin to remain as President for a third term. Her strong reluctance to accept was dictated mainly by the ever increasing activity developing with the office and by the professional and financial sacrifices entailed in her case. She finally yielded to the argument that she ought to lead the Goodwill Tour as Federation President, since this would prove to the Europeans that she had a mandate from 50,000 American women.

The itinerary included England, the first stop, where a second contingent of American business women joined the group making the number sixty-five, then France, Belgium, Holland, Germany, Switzerland and Italy. In addition to sightseeing, the program took in the Olympic Games in the Netherlands, a boat trip down the Rhine and a visit to the League of Nations in Geneva. However, the events which Madesin was anticipating most eagerly were the meetings already organized with the foremost professional women in each country, where ideas would be freely exchanged and much reciprocal knowledge acquired.

In New York the group received an official sendoff by Madesin's old friend, Acting Mayor Joseph V. McKee. On board, Madesin occasionally brought the group together to preview what lay ahead and to plan how to achieve the tour's ultimate goal—ensure the support of European women. Her enthusiasm for what they could accomplish was contagious. Presently, these gatherings, held in the public dining room, attracted a sizable audience of regular passengers, who came again and again, apparently fascinated by the proceedings.

"The tour director, Mary Kennedy," writes Madesin, "became a past master at meeting every sort of situation with imagination and equanimity. Problems ranged from retrieving a member lost in a shopping crowd, to allocating with reasonable fairness among sixty-four train-weary women the very few bathrooms available in hotels. In England, we landed at Plymouth, reversing, so to speak, the trail of our Pilgrim forefathers. The group that welcomed us there included Caroline Haslett, a woman of charm and distinction, an electrical engineer who was the director of the National Electrical Association for Women, and well known on the continent as well." Later Miss Haslett played a leading role in the growth of the International Federation.

Before leaving the United States Madesin had secured the personal interest of Herbert Hoover in the purpose of the tour. As Secretary of Commerce he had alerted U.S. Commercial attachés in the European capitals who, in the course of the formal dinner at the end of each visit, informed the travelers and their local guests of economic and other significant matters prevailing in their area. On each such occasion Madesin gave a brief concluding address which highlighted the advantages inherent in an international organization of business and professional women. She always drew enthusiastic applause, because she could lace hard facts and sound reasoning with sparkling wit and in England, as everywhere else, Madesin became at once very popular, while true friendships developed between tour members and their European hostesses. Nonetheless, the idea of an international association was not being accepted, as Caroline Haslett explained in an article published in a London magazine:

"An organization of business and professional women," said the article, "would undoubtedly help considerably towards the closer understanding of those working for economic freedom. . . . The difficulty in this country appears to be that women are far too busy with their own jobs to spare the necessary time. . . . This, I think is entirely wrong. It should be possible for the women doing highly responsible administrative and executive work to find time to take part in world wide movements, such as those in which her male colleagues are engaged. . . . But, I think that at the moment, the main thing is for women to make good each in her own trade or profession."

In Paris the group found that practically no professional or business women's clubs existed in France. There were, of course, hostess-conducted visits to institutions and business houses, many interesting conferences, some social events, much sightseeing, and a memorable excursion to the Aisne-Marne American War Cemetery. "As Americans, we placed a wreath at the base of the flagpole from which fluttered the Stars and Stripes, our eyes filling with tears. In London, as women, we had placed a wreath at the foot of the Edith Cavell Memorial."

The impact of the visitors on the sophisticated city of Paris was the subject of an illuminating article cabled from Paris by Dora Miller, an American correspondent:

"The arrival of a group of American business women has taken Paris by storm. . . . American business women are no longer unfamiliar figures in Paris. They come and go, stylists, buyers . . . they come individually. But sixty-four all at once! This was a revelation to Parisians. They simply couldn't comprehend so many women, representing so many vocations, coming to Paris on such a serious mission. . . . It was supposed they would want to attend teas and be entertained in a very feminine way. . . . They found that these women were really in search of facts, and that they were interested rather than bored by long dissertations on economic conditions and the status of self-supporting women in France. The earnestness of their manner, the intelligence of the questions they asked, won the respect of those who came in contact with them. The American business woman has won her spurs as far as Paris is concerned. . . .

It was an enormous asset to the basic purpose of the tour that, from London to Rome, there was always substantial publicity. The reaction of the foreign press everywhere was markedly favorable to the "sixty-four women we met all at once." Reporters, cameramen and American correspondents greeted the travelers at every arrival point. Members with unusual vocations provided a harvest of feature stories while Madesin held press conferences everywhere, her numerous speeches, brief or formal, being invariably reported in the local press.

77

In Belgium, a conference with a dozen of the country's outstanding professional women revealed them very progressive in their thinking about the place of women in the world of affairs, whereas their compatriots on the whole were as conservative as the French. A distinguished attorney, Marguerite de Munter Latinis, viewed the situation much as had Caroline Haslett, but like her, later became a backbone of the International Federation.

"In the Netherlands," writes Madesin, Rosa Manus, a veteran suffragist and a friend of America's Carrie Chapman Catt, had arranged a luncheon where the Dutch women we met included a Member of Parliament, the Curator of the State Museum, a Town Councillor, and a score of others who had won distinction in various professions. They told us that there were a few clubs in Holland, and that women had advanced more in the professions than in business. Among the latter was Clara Mijers, executive assistant in the Amsterdam branch of the well known Bank of Rotterdam."

The encounter between the American and the Dutch women brought surprising results. In December of that year, the *New York Herald Tribune* published an article headlined '*Women Conduct Bank for Sex in Amsterdam*' and subtitled: '*Branch is Launched on Idea Patrons Will Cease Hoarding Their Savings at Home.*' The gist of it was that, as a result of her meeting with American women on the Goodwill Tour, from whom she learnt about women's departments in U.S. banks, Miss Mijers immediately proposed to the directors of the Rotterdam Bank, the erection of a Woman's branch in Amsterdam. Although it was then summer and vacation time, details were worked out and the bank opened on December 15th, the first of its kind in Europe, of course. The rush of business the first day was ten times what had been anticipated, most of it devoted to the opening of new accounts by women, renting of safe deposit boxes, inquiries in regard to insurance which the Bank was also prepared to handle. Clerks had to be borrowed from other branches to take care of the crowd. A leaflet printed by the Bank explained one angle of the venture as follows: "Mesdames, considering that more and more women are becoming independent and that, nowadays, they make more tours abroad alone, we think they will appreciate being enlightened by a woman on financial and travel questions." Handling travel was also a novelty, as was the fact that the woman's bank remained open one hour longer than the regular banks, to encourage young working women to use it instead of a Postal Savings Account. Best proof of success was found in the compliment paid Miss Mijers by the president of another bank, saying: "We admire your pluck, and our competition will now have to be all the keener!"

"In Germany," Madesin recalls, "some of us had meetings with the leading women in Berlin. Although the Weimar Constitution, enacted eight years before, had given women equal rights with men, the *de facto* status of the German women was still limited by the *kinder, kirche, küche* tradition. Even so, many were convinced that if an international organization was formed, Germany would join. So it did, until the tragic events of history intervened."

In the twenties, and despite the crushing defeat suffered by Germany less than a decade earlier, women were already extremely active and well organized. They played a role in the Republic's various political parties; at least one of them, Frau Mendl, had been a member of the Reichstag for that whole decade and another, Frau von Tilling, was president of a Federation of twenty women's organizations. "But," Madesin noted, "we probably found our closest counterpart in the League of Women's Commercial and Clerical Workers, with 60,000 members. Although they spoke little English, we understood each other and sensed the darkness of the days through which they had passed, never suspecting those yet to come, for them and us all."

"In Switzerland we found a national organization of business women that seemed a small counterpart of our own, with 2,500 members and business clubs in seven or eight cities. In the Swiss capital we saw the first Women's National Exposition, called *Saffa,* far in advance of anything to be seen in the United States. It covered five and a half acres and had been conceived, organized and executed by women, its exhibits representing every phase of their interests—professional, commercial, educational and domestic.

"At Geneva, we had several very profitable meetings with prominent members of the Secretariat of the League of Nations and of the International Labor Office. The dinner, that night, was presided over by Dame Rachel Crowdy, widely known for her work as Chief of the Social Questions and Opium Section of the League.

"The new Italy through which we journeyed was a startling revelation. Most of us having known it was a country with a great past, we now found it a modern nation intent on building a fitting future. Premier Mussolini was at the height of his power. Italian women were engaged in commercial and professional work in growing numbers and many held high administrative positions. Although, in general they lacked equality of opportunity with men, especially in regard to advancement, it was clear that they were making a major contribution to national life."

Less than a decade later, the turn of events was to cause Madesin to look back and exclaim, not without dismay: "In those days Mussolini had not revealed the poison which Fascism carried in its fangs." Indeed, in 1928 practically all the prominent women Madesin contacted in Italy felt certain that the following year they would be sufficiently organized to join an international federation of business and professional women, they would be doing so freely, not subjected to the control of their own government. In the long run, such was not to be the case.

As to what the Goodwill Tour accomplished, Madesin herself was not certain, but the numerous American requests for an encore persuaded her to plan a second trip for 1929. Letters from participants had been gratifying. Typical of many, were such remarks as: "I now find myself reading every bit of foreign news I can get hold of. . . ." "I have given informal talks on Europe to other clubs, to church groups and, recently, to over 100 high school teachers." "The tour has given me a broader view of what our Federation can do if it really tries."

For Madesin the tour had been a heavy drain on her physical resources. Several of her friends, noting how thin and wan she looked, had urged her to take a real rest, but this was precisely what Madesin could not afford to do. The year 1928 could hardly have been leaner; her earnings had amounted to less than $900. She had given up her apartment to become a paying guest in the suburban home of Mrs. Lacey-Baker, Marjory Lacey-Baker's mother, nearly one hour's train ride from the city into which she traveled every day.

When the autumn arrived she was sufficiently recovered to become deeply involved in at least two major aspects of the agitated political situation then prevailing in the nation. One concerned the Kellogg-Briand Pact, signed in September by the representatives of fifteen nations, but now facing the hurdle of ratification by the United States Senate. Although President Coolidge strongly favored the treaty, the isolationist trend all over the country was strong enough to make congressional approval seem very uncertain. With other leaders of national organizations, Madesin embarked on a widespread campaign to arouse public demand for speedy as well as favorable action on Capitol Hill.

The other cause which commanded her attention and activity was the presidential campaign. Herbert Hoover, Republican, and Alfred E. Smith, Democrat, were running in a race that was gaining momentum at a precipitous rate. Disturbed by the small number of women who had gone to the polls in the previous election, the Democratic Party called on Madesin to help organize an energetic 'get-out-the-women's-vote' drive, national in scope. The enduring friendship which she developed then with Mrs. Franklin D. Roosevelt later drew fire from Roosevelt's opponents in the National Federation, starting up one of several major storms which broke upon Madesin's head when she was president. Although these outbursts of antagonism from within her own organization sometimes filled her with dismay, they always left her undaunted and her position unchanged.

8.   A Goal is Reached

Carrie Chapman Catt who, in 1920, had been so largely responsible for achieving women's suffrage, in 1928 created the National Committee on the Cause and Cure of War. Its first objective was United States ratification of the Kellogg-Briand Pact. The Committee, consisting of the presidents of the most influential women's organizations in the country, prominently included Madesin, not merely because she represented the already prestigious National Federation of Business and Professional Women's Clubs, but perhaps even more so because of her firm belief in the Committee's ultimate purpose which was to promote a top-level study of the causes of war and to attract the world's best minds to a serious search for the means of eliminating them.

As was to be expected, powerful groups and individuals involved in the highly profitable armaments industry did not allow the creation of Mrs. Catt's Committee to pass unnoticed. Having failed, at first, to prevent its establishment by opposing it in the open, they soon resorted to undercover calumny and red-baiting. Carrie Chapman Catt, Jane Addams, Madesin Phillips and scores of other distinguished Americans were accused of favoring the reds or of being Communists themselves. The slanderous campaign raged on for at least two years, while Madesin and other women smeared in this fashion, struggled against many odds to stem the tide of false charges and prevent it from destroying their respective organizations.

Despite these miserable currents, on January 15, 1929, when the Senate of the United States ratified the Kellogg-Briand Pact, one thousand women, disregarding threats and smears, assembled in Washington from every part of the country, to attend the fourth annual conference of the Committee on the Cause and Cure of War. Madesin headed a delegation of business and professional women representing twenty-one states. She was also chosen to preside over the one-day Open Forum held to analyze and discuss the inconsistency inherent in the fact that none of the signatory governments had made the slightest move to consider the reduction of armaments or of armed forces. The principal speakers were James T. Shotwell, of the Carnegie Endowment for Peace, Arthur Bullard,

81

formerly of the League of Nations, Reinhold Niebuhr, the theologian, James G. McDonald, of the Foreign Policy Association, Sidney L. Gulick of the National Council of Churches, and Bruce Bliven, of *The New Republic*. The conclusion was reached that the effectiveness of the treaty was vitiated in large measure by its failure to provide measures of enforcement and that public opinion, in America and elsewhere, had to be aroused to demand such measures. The Committee was instructed to plan an educational campaign along these lines, directed to the membership of the organizations affiliated with it and to the general public as well.

Viewing this campaign in long retrospect, it is evident that the effort did not bring about the needed strengthening of the treaty any more than the Pact itself served to prevent World War II. Yet, the work which was put into it could not be counted less remarkable because it fell short of its goal. It may also be said that, if the campaign achieved nothing more, it served to stem the tide of isolationism in many sections of the United States.

At about that time, for instance, the National Federation, supporting Madesin's world-mindedness, decided to replace its first temporary commission on International Relations with a permanent Committee to deal with this area of activity in even greater depth. The first chairman was an internationally known newspaperwoman, Majorie Shuler, of the *Christian Science Monitor*. "Eventually," foresaw Madesin, "this Committee will have its counterpart in every single Club and in every State Federation. Its purpose is to lead the membership into a clearer understanding of international issues and problems, while also enabling women to place their personal or collective influence behind wise and just international solutions."

Throughout 1928 Federation demands on Madesin's time had greatly increased, to the further detriment of her law practice. As in the previous year, three fellow attorneys, Pinckney Estes Glatzberg, John C. Turnbull and Charles Abrams had handled some of her legal work. Finally, in the fall of 1928 she took Barnet Muffs, who had also worked in her behalf, as her partner. Interestingly enough, when he occupied space in her office paying $90 a month to cover stenographic services and other facilities, he was providing Madesin with practically all of her income! Little wonder then that, as July 1929 drew near, which would conclude her third and final term as Federation President, she was thinking seriously of how to expand her law practice as soon as she could devote full time to her true profession.

However, when July came around and with it the Federation's Tenth Convention to be held at Mackinac, most of her thinking was centered on devising a strategy to bring the International Federation into being. Her attitude towards it was almost fatalistic, in the sense that she knew that whatever else she might have to sacrifice to this dream, she would inevitably allow the dream's demands to be paramount. In fact, her financial situation was such that she was having to dig into capital to keep afloat. A letter to her father shows that she asked him to buy some of her Kentucky Bank stock. Although the Judge's health had not been good and Madesin had been seriously concerned about it, despite his 91 years his mind was perfectly clear and able to help Madesin out of her difficulties. He now had a male nurse with him and was no longer able to write letters, but during her frequent little visits to Nicholasville Madesin heard him admonish her against her improvidence with his usual good sense, tinged at once by his traditional conservativism and his deep and loving regard for his daughter's aspirations.

At the Convention in Mackinac, looking back on her three years in office, Madesin saw the gains that had been made, but was still far from satisfied and said so in her final report: "At St. Louis in 1919 an inexperienced group of some two hundred women came together to form an organization. They were without plan, program, money or knowledge of the field, yet their voice has now been heard across the seas. In the past ten years we have developed an excellent instrument with which to work, but let us be quite clear that an organization, as an individual, must justify its existence by what it accomplishes. The greatest assurance of permanence lies in usefulness.

"At this time, however, it is generally admitted that the entire woman's movement has struck an impasse: for the rank and file of working women there is yet neither equal opportunity nor equal pay, while as to detail, to drudgery, to whatever is unremunerative, they are always welcome. . . . Wiser heads than mine have been unable to find a panacea for this predicament. Nonetheless, it is certain that once we women, as a group, can rise above envy, jealousy or fear of feminine competition, and are ready to promote rather than to block the advance of any qualified woman, we shall have torn down a major obstacle to our equality with men. Therefore, I strongly advocate promotion of women by women. To those who would be critical of this idea, saying that we must not indulge in sex discrimination, I answer: 'True, but such discrimination already exists. . . .' "

The Convention applauded long and loud, but the advice was scarcely heeded. Some three decades later, Mrs. Franklin Delano Roosevelt, ever active in the politics of her party and eager to promote women, was still justified in voicing the same complaint. To be sure, she did so not about business and professional women in particular, but about women in general who appeared incapable of giving their full support to other women.

From Madesin's standpoint, the lack of solidarity among women was all the more regrettable in that business and professional women, as an organized body, had actually performed many services whose value to the country as a whole had been fully recognized. For instance, an occupational survey of the women engaged in business and the professions had been published in cooperation with the University of Michigan; another study likewise published, covered all the commercial schools in the country; a study had been made of certain aspects of federal taxation and a proposal designed to correct inequities had been taken to Capitol Hill, attracting national attention and support. In her report Madesin strongly recommended that such projects be constantly expanded in scope and multiplied in number.

Finally, she highlighted one more plan whose fulfillment ranked in her mind second only to the creation of an international organization—the establishment of a permanent home for the national Federation. She said: "Because Washington attracts the greatest number of our countrymen and is the headquarters of many important organizations, because of our own legislative, educational and international programs, I think that our home should eventually be located in our national capital. . . . We should begin now to make plans for the purchase of property there. . . ."

Relinquishing the Chair, Madesin herself moved, "that the incoming president appoint a building committee to present to the 1931 convention a definite financial plan, by which we might purchase and establish national headquarters in Washington." The motion had been swiftly carried when, suddenly, Lena Lake Forrest, a past president, asked for the floor. Holding in her hand a check for five hundred dollars, she announced: "Here is a gift from one of our pioneers, to buy the first foundation stone of the National Federation's home in Washington." Then she quickly called the donor, Dr. Ann R. Ranes of Chicago, to the platform.

"In less than a minute," as Madesin clearly recalled, "the vast auditorium became a pandemonium of cries from other contributors, the improvised recorders frantically trying to keep up with the givers. The convention went wild with excitement when a second pioneer, Georgia Emery said, 'Put me down for one thousand dollars in the name of Lena Lake Forrest!' There were gifts and pledges for the living and for the dead, in the name of the pioneers, in the name of mothers, mothers-in-law, grandchildren, in the name of the Goodwill Tours, of 'my good husband,' of 'the husband I didn't get,' of nieces and of teachers, in the name of the retiring president and in the name of the international federation yet to be."

The conclusion of this extraordinary outburst is reported in the *Independent Woman* as follows: "When the giving finally appeared to wane, Miss Phillips rose to resume the business of the convention, but each time she did so, the enthusiasm would wake afresh. At one point a delegate from San Francisco leaped to her feet. 'I can't give a large sum,' she said, 'and I am wondering how many others there are who want to subscribe something in honor of Lena Madesin Phillips. How many will join me in giving ten dollars in cash at once?' Hands went up all over the hall. Tellers hurried from aisle to aisle collecting the bills in hats and rushing them to the platform. Finally, when the collection was finished, came the motion of a North Carolina delegate that the spontaneously created fund be known as the Lena Madesin Phillips Building Fund. Approved by a voice vote, the new fund could boast of nearly twenty-five thousand dollars!"

From this unexpected beginning, a fund-raising campaign was launched. Gift committees were appointed, quotas established and for several years contributions came in from members all over the country. But the passing of time and the course of events entailing another World War, caused the project gradually to slip into limbo. It emerged again in 1954 when the sixth of the special committees appointed over the years to present a comprehensive project for the building, proposed a three-year plan to raise $325,000 needed in addition to contributions already received. Enthusiasm was rekindled and the goal was reached. The national headquarters of the U.S. Federation of Business and Professional Women's Clubs, at 2012 Massachusetts Avenue, N.W., in Washington, D.C., was dedicated on September 22, 1957, but Lena Madesin Phillips had not lived to see it.

It was from that same 1929 Convention in Mackinac that Madesin's international project received its first major impetus. A young Italian mathematician, Dr. Maria Castellani, who had been lecturing in the United States, addressed the convention as the Federation's first foreign guest. With wit and humor, she interspersed her impressions of America with a report on the notable advances made by business and professional women in Europe since the end of World War I. Her talk was climaxed by the announcement that Italy had already taken the first steps toward forming its own federation of business and professional women's clubs, this being entirely the fruit of the Goodwill Tour. An attorney from Montreal, Miss Dorothy Heneker, added to the enthusiasm aroused by Dr. Castellani by informing the Convention, in behalf of the Canadian delegation which she headed, that a federation was about to be founded in her country as well.

The mood had thus been set for the motion presented by the International Relations Committee which recommended "that at an early date, and as soon as they deem it advisable, the Executive Board, upon the advice and consent of the Board of Directors, be empowered to take steps towards the calling of an international conference, to be held at such time and place as seems consistent with our growth and progress." The motion drew loud applause. Madesin, still the Convention's presiding officer, beamed as she acknowledged its passage.

Once the new President had been elected, she immediately asked Madesin to accept the Chairmanship of the International Relations Committee, "in order," as she put it, "to give you opportunities to progress with plans for an international organization." When Madesin rose to accept the appointment, a voice was heard from the floor moving that Lena Madesin Phillips be given the title of Honorary President of the National Federation. The voices of the seconders were drowned in the standing ovation that ensued.

In a matter of days Madesin was on board the *S.S. Bergensfjord,* taking some thirty Federation members on the second Goodwill Tour. This time, however, the tour was divided into two sections of approximately equal size, one going north, the other covering the countries visited the previous year. Madesin, always an avid reader of Sweden's Selma Lagerlöf, Norway's Sigrid Undset, and Denmark's Isak Dinesen, had chosen to lead a group to these three northern countries, plus Germany, Czechoslovakia, Hungary and Austria, joining the others in Paris, prior to the return trip on the *S.S. Aquitania* in early September. Once the New York skyline was out of sight on the outward journey, Madesin began to relax. The office of Federation president, despite the heartaches it had involved, had been very rewarding. Inclined by nature to look to the positive side of any situation, even when the negative appeared overwhelming, she knew that just the motion unanimously approved at Mackinac empowering her to set up an international conference was, in itself, worth the whole of her three year effort. That such a conference would take place, she had no doubt. What did concern her, it seems, was how much more aware the European women might be than the Americans of the price that would be exacted of them in hard work and self-abnegation by the equality they sought to achieve.

In her satchel were notes she had made when reading Gertrude Atherton's 1927 book, *The Immortal Marriage,* a novel based on the life of Pericles and Aspasia, who lived at the height of Athens' greatness. Aspasia has been called "the first modern woman" because she knew what she wanted and dared go after it in the face of custom, law and prejudice. Though some 2500 years had passed since then, customs, laws and prejudices of an almost identical nature still had to be faced in 1929, as Madesin observed, and today's feminists are still confronted with similar obstacles. Aspasia's victories were remarkable: she won the right to be loved by her husband in a society where a law required men to be married by the time they were 30, but where right-thinkers ignored women except for childbearing and housekeeping purposes, where it was regarded as unsophisticated for a man to love a woman. The love between Pericles and Aspasia lasted through all the misfortunes and contumely that arose from it. The second victory was that Aspasia sat at the banquet table of

86

Pericles around which gathered such men as Socrates, Phidias, Aristophanes, Sophocles and others like them, and that these great luminaries were glad to have her there. Her third victory was that she brought other women to the table with her and had them not merely accepted, but enjoyed as table companions of the great. The fourth was probably the most significant: the wives of several prominent men dared come to her home to learn to read and learn to think. When Aspasia was brought to trial for these sins, her life in jeopardy, it was her husband who defended her. When he showed the Athenians that he was ready to stake his own life for hers, coolly and deliberately in a court of law, Aspasia had indeed achieved the fullest equality. A pencilled annotation in Madesin's hand on the page where the drama unfolded reads: "How many women, today, could make the same claim?"

Madesin's appreciation of the intangible values involved in Aspasia's striving for equality, provide an interesting contrast to her constant insistence that equality must rise from economic roots. This ambivalence was one of her assets and must have stemmed from the fact that she was unquestionably an artist, with innate musical talent, whereas the vicissitudes of life had transformed her into a practitioner of the law. Artistic temperament and a legally trained mind had merged within her personality without destroying each other. Once she had decided to make the equality of women her major cause, single-mindedness in driving toward her goal was something she had in common with Carrie Chapman Catt, who had agreed to lead the fight for woman suffrage on condition that this become the single purpose of all the militants until it was attained. Madesin was convinced that woman's journey to equality would have to follow the economic route, and promoted this objective persistently.

In the late forties, when World War II was over and America was becoming increasingly prosperous, she kept on her desk a clipping with these facts: American women are already in control of more than 41 percent of the nation's individual wealth; they pay taxes on more than three and a quarter billions of individual income each year; they are the majority of stockholders in the country's largest corporations; they constitute 40 percent of investment bond-house customers; they receive 70 percent of estates left by men and 64 percent of estates left by other women; there are more than eight and a half million gainfully employed women; if they maintain their financial ascendancy, all the wealth of the country will be in women's hands by 2025. The prophecy may well come true, since a comparison between the figures given for the late 40's and those applying to the early 70's show a marked increase in woman's favor.

Probably Madesin had come to realize the importance and power of money as a means of attaining the higher levels of equality, because she, herself, had often had occasion to wonder just where her next month's rent would come from. Capable of driving a hard bargain in behalf of someone or something she believed in, her professional record demonstrates that she never hesitated to pass up an opportunity to earn what her work or counsel were worth in order to serve a good but penniless cause. Forcefully insisting that all people, men as well as women, should be fairly and equally compensated for their work, she could easily persuade others to adopt this concept; yet she made no effort to see that it was applied to her. If a friend criticized her for this contradiction she did not take to it kindly. In fact, whenever she invited criticism she listened carefully and learned from it, but when criticism was unsolicited, her smiling grey eyes turned to cold steel and her self-discipline was heavily taxed to restrain an outburst of displeasure. Her self-discipline, it must be said, was remarkably enduring.

Docking at Oslo, the *Bergensfjord* was met by the president of the Norwegian Council of Women, Fru Kjelsberg, a government industrial inspector and a very influential citizen, heading a party of other distinguished women. One of them was Nanna With, a journalist and lecturer who later became the first president of Norway's federation of business and professional women. In Stockholm the first woman elected to the Upper Riksdag or Swedish Senate, Kerstin Hesselgren, welcomed the American party and she too, like her Norwegian counterpart, was accompanied by the nation's most prominent women. Stricken with a severe case of influenza in Stockholm, Madesin rejoined the tour in Copenhagen, where, once again, imaginative hospitality was provided by the country's leading women. The next stop was Germany, a rather bewildering Germany in that summer of 1929.

"Emerging from the spell of Hans Christian Anderson's home land," writes Madesin, "we came face to face with reality in Germany, a country in political transfusion. It was ten years since the Weimar constitution had changed an ancient monarchy into a modern republic. In Berlin on Constitution Day we saw the young new Germany march through the streets to commemorate its independence. Little did we know that independence would end under the baleful influence of Adolph Hitler, and that in less than twenty years much that we saw would be rubble.

"With some of the women who met with us around the conference table, we had talked during our previous visit; others were newcomers. Nearly all held administrative positions, and one was a member of the Reichstag. Their reaction was heartening, as was that of others we met in Munich, who spoke with pride of their women leaders: 'Even today we cannot ask for anything that they have not already sought and worked for.' Someone remarked: 'Life here has a special kind of faith since women have helped to draw its lines.'

"After Germany came Czechoslovakia, and the highlight of our visit to Prague: meeting Senator Frantiska Plaminkova. A powerful personality, a leader of many national and international organizations, she was to become a most valuable officer of our International Federation. Through an interpreter she addressed us at dinner on the woman movement in her country, adding that she did not believe in organizations that included representative women only. She seemed deeply interested in our American Federation and our plans for a world organization. Her remark, that she and her country-women always preferred 'to get under the pioneer's burden rather than be in the group that just walks behind,' was revealing of her spirit.

"With us that evening also were the only woman holding an official position in the Ministry of Foreign Affairs and another, who became Mayor of the City of Prague. We learned that the Czech women not only had the vote, but, like the men, were also required to use it."

Two days in Budapest allowed only for a glimpse of the old and the new cities—Buda and Pest, but this was sufficient time for the Hungarian women to evaluate Madesin's brief speech. The second day of the visit, there, their spokesman announced that they would begin at once to organize professional and business women's clubs. A Hungarian federation was created within the next three years and in 1938 Budapest was the scene of one of the International Federation's most brilliant congresses.

"In Vienna," wrote Madesin, "our coming aroused much interest, and on the day after our dinner meeting, the leading professional women told us they were ready to take the first step, organizing a club, without delay. Dr. Marianne Beth, the first woman in Austria to become an attorney, later became a vice-president of the International Federation, and Alice Schalek, the first woman reporter allowed at the front in World War I, came to the United States to lecture to our clubs. In Austria, as in Hungary, we found that the economic situation was extremely grave."

In Paris, while most of the group was being entertained and shown the fashions as well as the sights, Madesin and a few of the women who had been with her on the earlier tour continued to explore the prospects for a French organization. Although French individualism was still far removed from the American concept of a federation, the idea was beginning to take root. Its most enthusiastic advocate, Madame Mary Laudner, an educator, became founder and first president of the French federation. Meanwhile, the Paris edition of the *Chicago Tribune* said of *les femmes d'affaires américaines:* "The city of light, love and laughter, where a woman is still only a woman and not a lawyer or a banker, has prepared to give its official welcome to the sixty American delegates, representing the emancipated woman in her every phase, scheduled to arrive here tonight." Across the ocean *The New York Times* in an editorial headed "Our Astonishing Women," noted that "the Frenchmen who gave the official welcome expressed their amazement at the importance of the positions held by these Americans."

A rather interesting sidelight on the second Goodwill Tour was that all the conferences and meetings had been arranged by the European women themselves, whereas in the previous year the entire project had depended on the assistance of the U.S. Department of Commerce. The spontaneous eagerness of the Europeans to cooperate was a clear sign that not only had ice been broken, but that the goal—an International Federation—was coming into view.

In October 1929 the stock market crashed, wiping out thousands upon thousands of bank accounts, including Madesin's. The belief of Americans in their perpetual prosperity was shaken. Mills and factories were closing, pushing up the level of unemployment. Suicides, too, were increasing, especially in the large cities, but the individuals who had not been drastically hit, or not touched at all, kept life moving on as usual. There were many who, like Madesin, though dealt a serious blow by the crash, paused long enough to take stock of their losses and then resumed their activities with dogged determination not to yield to discouragement, let alone despair.

When November came around the National Council of Women asked Madesin to become its president. Although she did not accept, she became interested in a plan to give women a prominent role in the Century of Progress Exposition to be held in Chicago in 1933. The mere fact that the many distinguished women active in the Council were looking ahead and making very ambitious plans, impressed Madesin as a healthy indication that the womanhood of America was very resilient and, in a crisis, not inclined to self pity or apathy. For the time being, however, she must keep her own mind focussed on plans that would again take her to Europe the following year, not merely on a third Goodwill Tour but, far more important to her, to the first International Conference of Business and Professional Women.

In November Madesin called together her International Relations Committee and in January 1930 sent a personal letter to most of the women she had met in Europe during the previous tours. Written in behalf of the U.S. Federation of Business and Professional Women's Clubs, it was a remarkable specimen of diplomatic tact, yet forceful enough to command a clear-cut reply:

"It is our purpose to call this year an international meeting to be held at Geneva, the latter part of August, for the consideration of the special problems which concern women actively in business or the professions, and for the further consideration of the advisability of forming an international organization. . . . Will you be so kind as to advise me whether, in your opinion, it is probable that your government would send one or two women as official representatives. . . . It is in no sense the desire or intent of our organization to superimpose anything upon the women of other countries. We have assumed leadership because our organization has so largely met the needs of the business and professional women of our own country."

The answers were encouraging and in April the former invitations went out to Canada and to the thirteen countries included in the Tours. The wording was in French and German as well as English: "*The International Relations Committee—of the—National Federation of Business and Professional Women's Clubs—of the United States—invites you to attend a meeting of—professional and business women—of all countries for the discussions—of their mutual interest, to—be held at Geneva, Switzerland—August 24, 25 and 26, 1930—For further information write to—Miss Lena Madesin Phillips, Chairman—35, Boulevard des Capucines —Paris, France.*" Harriet Taylor, then in Paris, was to receive the replies.

"Within the membership of the National Federation," Madesin writes, "some skepticism as to the success of the meeting was to be expected, and a certain degree of hostility to any 'foreign entanglements.' Isolationism was an old story in the United States. Memories of World War I, little more than a decade away, were still painful. But many women shared my conviction that the diverse fragments of a common desire were coming together to build a structure useful enough to serve, and strong enough to bear, the wear and tear of human relationships. A sense of identity with world affairs was clearly on the increase throughout our organization, with its leaders in the vanguard."

This was further borne out by the fact that close to a hundred members from twenty-eight states had registered to participate in the Third Goodwill Tour which would find its major highlight at Geneva's international conference. The tour was having three sections, and the leaders of each were appointed delegates to the Geneva Conference with power to act in behalf of the U.S. Federation.

Madesin's group went north once again, and, after re-visiting Norway and Sweden, crossed the Baltic Sea into Finland. "As our ship docked," she writes, "we could see a group of men and women who had come to receive us. Among them was Anni Voipio, writer and civic leader, who later founded the Finnish federation, and Fanny Bonn, sales manager of one of the world's largest timber companies, a most unusual position for a woman. Finland already had several associations of women, each covering a different occupation, but we noticed that our idea of uniting them all into a single organization, which was new to them, had aroused their interest.

"We left by night train for Russia, not without fears and some

91

misgivings, of course. We had no thought of organizing a federation in that country, but since we were to be so close to its border, we had set aside eight days for Leningrad, Moscow and Kiev. No member of our party regretted it for it was an exceedingly enlightening experience.

"We visited museums, modern welfare institutions, cathedrals, factories, the palaces of the czars, always aware of the skill with which our charming young women guides avoided answering any of our more probing questions about what we did not see of life in the USSR.

"Our only contact with Russian women other than the guides came toward the end of our stay in Moscow. Having expressed the desire to talk with women who were members of the Communist Party, a tea was arranged by VOKS, the Society for Cultural Relations with Russia, to which a dozen such women came. Most of them held high-ranking office, all were persons of great drive, very intelligent and extremely courteous. There was no problem of status in their country, they said. They worked shoulder to shoulder with the men and received equal pay for equal work.

"One of them, a government inspector, referred to her days in prison and her exile under the Czarist regime. I told our interpreter that we would be interested in hearing about her imprisonment because none of us had ever met a woman who has been in prison for her political beliefs. My request evoked great hilarity and much conversation among the Soviet women, which we did not understand until the interpreter explained that not only the one who had spoken, but all of them had suffered imprisonment, some many times, before the revolution.

"The next five days were spent in Poland. Arriving at eight in the morning, we were received at the railway station by a delegation headed by the Mayor of Warsaw. I was impressed by his welcoming speech, which gave us statistics about women in business, vocational information and many other interesting facts. The next morning a conference with our Polish hostesses gave us hope that a federation would be formed at a not too distant date.

"At the closing dinner given by the Polish-American Chamber of Commerce, a string quartet played our National Anthem. It sounded beautiful but somewhat strange to our ears. I later learned that one of the musicians, knowing only the melody, had devised the accompanying harmonies. A heart-warming tribute, I thought, to us and to our country.

"At the Hotel de Ville in Cracow we were greeted by city officials and by members of the Chamber of Commerce with their president. In that lovely tenth century city we met with one of the most spirited groups of women we had encountered anywhere in Europe, who represented a wide range of professions. At our first conference they decided to organize at once. In Poland, as in Finland, women were associated as occupational groups, and the idea of uniting business and professional was new to them and also very attractive. We felt certain that some day there would be a Polish federation of business and professional women—and there was."

As the result of the previous visit, Austria's first Club had been established in Vienna and was already growing. This fact amazed many Austrian women who, like other Europeans, had found the whole idea of uniting without men, quite inconceivable. A Viennese lady said so to Madesin. "I do not understand how you Americans can seem so content to have meetings without men, to be happy although unmarried. It is very different in our country. Your associates have told us that they can have a splendid banquet where women have a fine meal, some speeches and no men. This, with us, would simply be unheard of."

After Vienna and Oberammergau, while the group went to Lucerne, Madesin, on her way to Geneva, responded to a last minute request to speak to a meeting of the *Dolgozo Nok Klub* (Working Women's Club) in Budapest. To the reporters who met her at the train, she said: "I shall speak of the conditions which affect the American business and professional woman, and of our United States Federation which has more than fifty thousand members. Representing them, we are going to Geneva in the hope of likewise uniting our colleagues on other continents. In Europe this movement has already begun in earnest."

Ten years had elapsed since July 1921 when, as executive secretary of the two-year old National Federation, Madesin had captioned a section of her report to the Convention with the query: "International Federation?" The query was about to be replaced by an affirmation.

The choice of Geneva for the international conference was a logical one. The League of Nations, now entering upon its second decade, was headquartered there, as were many major international organizations. Several very distinguished women were representing their governments either as full-fledged delegates to the League and members of commissions, or serving in the International Labor Organization. Their cooperation was indispensable in launching the organization Madesin had been striving to achieve. In fact, for several months she had been corresponding very actively with two prominent and capable women stationed in Geneva: Dr. Maria Castellani, ILO actuary, and Marie Ginsberg, librarian for the League's economic division. Although both succeeded in enlisting the support of many of their most outstanding colleagues, as Dr. Castellani later remarked, "Their scepticism was not dispelled until they met Dr. Phillips. Quickly sensing her wisdom and experience and noting that she rarely if ever failed to say or do whatever was right in the circumstances, they recognized her as a leader and were willing to co-operate with her in every way."

Arriving in Geneva with only two days in which to prepare for the conference, but greatly aided by Helen Havener who had come from America to handle press and publicity, Madesin immediately engaged the handsome old wood paneled Salle Centrale on Geneva's Place de la Madeleine for the business meetings. "Its lights were not bright and its equipment far from modern," Madesin noted, "but it had enormous dignity. A little balcony housed a pipe organ and for one Swiss franc per day a musician was hired to provide music before and after the sessions. With plants and flowers we set the stage for the founding of a world organization of business and professional women, the first of its kind in the already long record of the woman movement."

On the eve of the conference, Madesin invited the leaders of all national delegations to a preliminary discussion of procedures and activities. The group was outstanding: the Italian government had sent its own representative in the person of Angela Maria Guidi, later an Undersecretary of State in her country; Austria was represented by Marianne Beth, lawyer and philosopher, the first woman to receive the coveted Kant Prize; Finland by Armi Hallsten-Kallia, of the League's Institute of Intellectual Cooperation, precursor of UNESCO; the presidents of the two newly formed national Federations, Dorothy Heneker of Canada, and Maria Castellani of Italy, and others such as Marie Laudner of France, Geline MacDonald Bowman and Charl Williams of the United States, soon to achieve that office in their respective countries.

Great Britain was represented by Helen Fraser, director of a large manufacturing company; Hungary, by Dr. Brode-Erone, journalist; Germany, by Dr. Hildegarde Boehm, an executive of the Social Welfare Association; China, by Mrs. T. V. Lee, then a resident of London; Switzerland, by Dr. Gourfein-Welt, chairman of the reception committee for her country; Belgium, by Dr. Marguerite de Munter-Latinis; Sweden, by Edith Lindbloom; Holland by Mrs. F. T. Hartog-Plaut; India, by Srimati Gayatree Devi. Madesin's fears that only very few of the countries invited would send a delegate had been dispelled. Sixteen were represented by well over two hundred women.

Chairing the pre-conference meeting, Madesin made it clear that any decision regarding the formation or rejection of an International Federation would rest entirely with the delegates. She pointed out that the success of the United States Federation had convinced its own members of the value that women in other countries would derive from a similar organization, and were ready to share their experience and offer guidance if requested. Ultimately, however, the last word belonged to those who spoke for the fifteen other nations. After each delegate had given a brief account of the status of women in her own country, the group engaged in a thorough discussion of what form the prospective organization should take, its constitution, and its program of activity. They planned the agenda for the conference and agreed to prepare the draft of a constitution to be submitted to the conference, if such were to be called for. It was at the conclusion of this meeting that Dorothy Heneker of Canada moved that a recommendation be presented at the conference that "an International Federation of Business and Professional Women be established at this time." Seconded at once by Dr. Marianne Beth of Austria, the motion was approved.

The next day the Salle Centrale was filled to capacity. The first announcements of the unusual meeting, carried by the press, had aroused enormous interest and there had been a surprising demand for invitations. The Secretary-General of the League of Nations had appointed Princess Gabrielle Radziwill to represent the League and to deliver a message in his behalf. "The League looks forward to cooperating with you," she said. "The major link which unites men and women is the link of mutual work and when they talk together of things which concern them both. It is only through organization and federation that we can hope to know each other's needs and to attain what we want. . . . The work you are going to do, I hope will bear fruit in every country."

Madesin, as temporary chairman, sat on the dais between women who officially represented governments and major international bodies, but her eyes were on the delegates, whose presence really represented the fulfillment of her dream. "I doubt that I shall ever forget," she wrote later, "the thrill of the meeting in Geneva, for there were delegates from countries that only twelve years before had been at war with each other. Side by side they listened to the proceedings and joined in the animated discussions. Each had her own point of view and never hesitated to express it, but their expressions were always without a trace of rancor."

The brief addresses by eleven delegates contained ideas that were subsequently built into the structure of the organization. The long-range effects of cooperation between members of each country, as between countries, were emphasized, and proposals were made dealing specifically with the advancement of women in the professions, the liberal arts and in business.

On the second morning the conference voted unanimously to establish an international organization to be named International Federation of Business and Professional Women. Its objectives were to promote friendly relations between the business and professional women of all countries, to co-operate in the interests they held in common and to work for high standards of service to communities and nations. The federation was to be strictly non-partisan and non-sectarian. It would have two types of membership—active and associate. The first would be national federations of business and professional women's clubs or associations of business and professional women; the second would be clubs of business and/or professional women in countries where no federation existed. Individual associate membership would be taken out by women in sympathy with the purposes of the organization. The annual dues for national federations were fixed at ten dollars, or their equivalent, and for associate members, either clubs or individuals, at five dollars. The Board of Directors would be composed of eight officers—a president, four vice-presidents, corresponding and recording secretaries, and a treasurer—and one representative from each of the member countries. The framework was simple but strong enough to endure with practically no major change for many years.

The third session was devoted to "The Handicaps of Women in Business and the Professions," a subject discussed mainly in relation to married women and to legal disabilities by which women were affected in different countries. These appeared to be of similar nature everywhere, varying only in degree, and all agreed that a woman's professional qualifications and not her status should be the decisive factor in employing her or otherwise.

The ornate banquet hall of the Carlton-Parc Hotel was the setting for the official dinner. After all the dignitaries had offered the good wishes of their respective governments or organizations for the success of the new Federation, a spokesman arose for each of the sixteen national delegations to pledge support to the new international body. Madesin's own words were direct and incisive: "Let us build together and see what we can make. Here is an opportunity for hard, even controversial work, and the likelihood of being undervalued and misunderstood. But here is also the opportunity for new service."

Then, much to the Chairman's surprise, an Italian delegate asked to speak. "Your project of creating an International Federation of Business and Professional Women has been carried through and crowned with splendid success. The representatives of sixteen nations assembled here wish to thank you once more for your great gift to them. We feel that this event is a major step towards establishing new fundamental ideas on the real value of women in today's world. We ask you to accept this small token of our gratitude. . . ." Across the base of a small silver clock which she handed to Madesin was this inscription: "Presented to —Miss Lena Madesin Phillips—founder of the—International Federation of Business and Professional Women—by the representatives of sixteen nations—assembled at the First International Meeting—held in Geneva, August 24, 25, 26, 1930."

For a full quarter of a century the clock remained on Madesin's desk, testifying to a pursuit undertaken with faith and to a cornerstone laid with determination and hope.

At the final business session, on the following day, the report of the nominating committee, with Mme. Mary Laudner of France as chairman, resulted in the election by acclamation of the following officers: *President,* Lena Madesin Phillips, of the United States; *Vice Presidents,* Ester Danesi Traversari, of Italy, Yvonne Netter of France, Marianne Beth, of Austria, Helen Fraser, of Great Britain; *Corresponding Secretary,* Miss Dorothy Heneker, of Canada; *Treasurer,* Miss Henrietta Corson Harris, of the United States.

Responding for them all, the International President said: "We, your newly elected officers, accept our responsibility and the opportunity to serve you. You have trusted us, and we are trusting you for the future development of our organization. I hope that together we shall build something of great value and beauty. On behalf of all of us I thank you."

Princess Radziwill, rising quickly to her feet, had a final word for the delegates:

"I have seen and observed many organizations, and the life of each has depended on the executives. In this instance you seem to have found the person who has knowledge, determination, insight and capacity for work. The choice of Lena Madesin Phillips is not only excellent, but it is a guarantee of future developments."

That afternoon the Board of Directors held their first meetings to set in motion the organizational machinery and to implement the decisions made by the delegates. Four resolutions, dealing with major concerns expressed during the business sessions, called for: (a) the drawing up of lists of professional bodies which did, and those which did not, admit women; (b) setting up national bureaus to seek and collect all information and publications relating to the work and status of professional business women; (c) establishing hospitality committees to provide contacts and courtesies for visiting members from other countries; (d) requesting the United States Federation to permit the use of the *Independent Woman* as the official organ of the International, by allocating a certain portion of space to the reports and other writings of the latter.

Not all the resolutions submitted to the business sessions had had plain sailing or had passed. "Opinions clashed over two resolutions," writes Madesin. "One, proposing that world peace be made one of the International Federation's objectives, required that 'the Federation pledge its individual and organized influence to the eradication of the psychological causes of war: fear, ignorance and greed.' One after the other, several delegates rose to state that although the desire of all women was for peace, the Federation, at this time, must limit itself to the specific purposes for which it was organized. This resolution, finally referred to the incoming board of directors, was later adopted, but not as one of the basic objectives of the organization."

That differences could be aired so frankly at the initial sessions of an organization not yet fully in being, was something which, in Madesin's view, offered proof of two highly important facts: one, that from the start the delegates were concerned with issues ranging beyond their personal interests and two, that they knew they were free to speak their minds and take whatever stand their conscience dictated. In effect, broad concern and freedom of expression were very much a part of her own personality, and when they surfaced in the group she had gathered together Madesin felt encouraged and gratified. The date of August 26, 1930, when the International Federation of Business and Professional Women became an accomplished fact, was made all the more memorable by the honesty with which divergent views were set forth.

The founding of the International Federation of Business and Professional Women, the Salle Centrale in Geneva, 1930

9. First Taste of Politics

The European delegates left Geneva eager to establish or strengthen their own national federations; the Americans, eager to inform their Clubs and also the men and women of their communities of the event they had witnessed.

Madesin's attention, instead, was claimed by the practical aspects of the new situation. "I had brought home an international baby," she wrote, "difficult to rear, without home, staff or money." However, she herself provided an immediate home, free of cost, in her law office on the seventeenth floor of the Woolworth Building in New York.

Barely had she picked up the threads of her law practice when she was approached by a committee representing several women's organizations concerned with corruption in the administration of New York City. They urged her to seek appointment to the office of city magistrate, recently vacated by Judge George H. Ewald, assuring her that they could marshall wide support for her candidacy.

Two major considerations caused her to accept the invitation. First, since embarking on a legal career she had hoped some day to follow her father's footsteps to a judgeship. A city magistracy could be a step in that direction. Second, she recognized that by campaigning for this office, whatever the outcome, she could register her protest against the very small number of women in top positions in the city's administration. Actually, the situation of women was no better at the national level. In ten years since the granting of suffrage, only eight women had been elected to Congress, not one to the Senate, and the judges were very few, Florence E. Allen sitting on the Supreme Court of Ohio, being a notable exception. Women, on the whole, still "sat below the salt," although many, in both political parties, had grown increasingly rebellious.

Mrs. Oliver Harriman, a socially prominent New Yorker and Madesin's friend, accepted the chairmanship of her campaign committee, and an army of enthusiastic campaigners left no stone unturned in their efforts to obtain endorsements for their candidate. The Mayor of New York, James J. Walker, was deluged with letters and telegrams from political committees, women's organizations and a host of individuals, urging her appointment. Marguerite Moores Marshall, in her column in the *New York Evening World,* October 6th, 1930, perceptively analyzed Madesin's qualifications: "We have found the following to be characteristic of Lena Madesin Phillips during an acquaintance of ten years—a sense of justice, a sense of balance, a sense of humor, a distinguished gift for human contacts. And it seems to us that these are qualities of value to a city magistrate and to the city he or she serves."

Madesin herself stated in a leaflet prepared for campaign distribution, "The magistrate's court is the people's court. To it come not only hardened criminals but occasional offenders. It needs broad human understanding as well as the administration of justice. One must have, of course, legal knowledge and experience. It is not enough to punish. One should be able to safeguard against repetition, and even in the punishment to direct constructively. Because I believe that herein is an opportunity for public service, I would count it a privilege to become a city magistrate."

As a member of the American Bar Association, of the County Lawyers Association, of the Order of the Coif and of Phi Delta Delta sorority, Madesin had a wide acquaintance among her legal colleagues, and many rallied to her support. The League for More Women in Public Office was organized to make her appointment their first project. Its provocative name aroused a lively exchange between columnist Franklin P. Adams (F.P.A.) in his much quoted *Conning Tower* and the League's chairman, Mrs. John Kendrick Bangs. Among the women, well known in that day, who sponsored her candidacy, were ex-governor Nellie Tayloe Ross, Lillian Wald, Mrs. Charles Dana Gibson, Ruth Hale, Mrs. Daniel O'Day, Estelle M. Sternberger, Aida de Acosta Breckenridge, Anne Morgan, Dr. Valeria E. Parker, Anna Steese Richardson, Mrs. Stanley P. Woodward, Mrs. Job Hedges.

Whenever the matter came to her attention, Madesin consistently refused to allow her standing in the National Federation to be exploited for her political advantage. Nonetheless, her friends in several states, on their own initiative and without consulting her, successfully sought endorsements from their governors, senators, congressmen, mayors and other public officials. Cordell Hull, who shortly thereafter became Secretary of State, wrote about her to Mayor Walker of New York: "I know of no other American woman who, in my judgment, possesses superior qualifications and claims for appointment to high judicial position." Messages of this tenor came from Governor Horton of Tennessee and Governor Dillon of New Mexico; the mayors of Indianapolis and Boise, Idaho; Jouett Shouse, executive officer of the Democratic National Committee and William Harman Black, a Justice of the New York Supreme Court, to mention but a few.

In the thirties, however, as indeed in the seventies, no amount of enthusiasm, hundreds of letters of endorsement from prominent figures, public meetings, appeals to entrenched city officials, or popular support from countless organized groups all around the country, could prevail against the political machine which was unable to bring itself to appoint · a woman. Tammany Hall sent a man to the office of City Magistrate.

The brief digression into politics did not mean that Madesin's "international baby" was being neglected. On the contrary, in October, while she was deep in the campaign, Madesin had called the first meeting of the International's Executive Committee. Geographic accessibility had determined its composition, and the Geneva Conference had empowered the elected secretary, Dorothy Heneker, who resided in Montreal, the treasurer, Henrietta Corson Harris of Springfield, Massachusetts, and the President in New York City, to act for the board of directors.

Financing was the committee's most crucial concern. Little aid, beyond their annual five or ten dollar dues, could be expected for the present from the groups in Europe. Mary Kennedy generously contributed $500, the total amount of her commissions from the travel agency for enrolling members for the three tours, but a year's income must be obtained in order to meet current expenses. It could be anticipated only from the associate members of the International: every one hundred associate members would mean five hundred dollars. Madesin now sent her first appeal letter to clubs and individuals all across the United States and the response was rewarding. The number of associate members grew from year to year, becoming an informed and sympathetic body of supporters.

An appeal outside the membership, made to internationally-minded women, brought, as a first such gift, $1,000 from Mrs. John D. Rockefeller, Jr. However, the income was never adequate despite the giving.

A monthly bulletin called *Widening Horizons* soon made its appearance, with Helen Havener as volunteer editor, while the *Independent Woman,* thanks to the National Federation, allocated two pages quarterly for material submitted by the International.

The committee accepted the invitation from Austria to hold the first congress in Vienna the forthcoming summer, in 1931. The general interest aroused by the Geneva conference, and the encouraging accounts of progress in the formation of clubs overseas, suggested the advisability of doing some field work to consolidate the development. Dorothy Heneker volunteered to take a leave of absence from her law practice to assume the task. In a period of three months, visiting thirteen countries, she brought new clubs to life in many cities.

101

While Dorothy Heneker went abroad, Madesin embarked on a closely packed lecture tour west of the Mississippi, but before leaving a difficult decision suddenly had to be made. She had been nominated for the presidency of the National Council of Women of the United States, having been a vice-president for several years. She must either withdraw her name at once or be prepared to take the office. Founded in 1888, the Council consisted of thirty-one national associations with an approximate membership of five million, and had the makings of a very influential body.

For more than a year the Council had been considering an impressive three-fold project to be realized in connection with the Chicago Century of Progress International Exposition in 1933. The brain child of Dr. Alma Garlin Spencer and Estelle Sternberger, the plan included an international congress of women to explore new paths in the conduct of world affairs; the writing and publication of a history of woman's work in America in the last hundred years, and an exhibition of the work of organized women. The financing of all this was still to be thought out.

Forty years earlier, Dr. Anna Garlin Spencer had attended the historic conference on women's rights held at the Columbia Exposition in Chicago, when, for the first time, women who had fought independently for equal citizenship and for women's right to full education, had finally joined to promote a concerted plan for the future. Dr. Spencer, now almost ninety, regarded all this as only a first step and felt that another one should now be taken.

Although the scope of the Spencer-Sternberger plan, and its relevance to the troubled times rising in the 30's, appealed to Madesin, she believed it would be wise for her to decline the nomination. However, after several personal appeals from the Council's Executive Committee, she agreed to accept and, in due course, was enthusiastically elected. Two factors, among others, may have influenced her change of mind. Estelle Sternberger had been active in the Council of Jewish Women and Madesin had already perceived the black cloud of anti-semitism projecting itself on the European horizon. She felt strongly the need to cooperate with any group or individual fighting discrimination. In her European contacts she had also seen the quality of women active in the International Council of Women, of which the U.S. National Council was a branch. Indeed, several of them had been active in forming several of the federations of business and professional women.

She had barely been elected when something which she liked to describe as "Phillips' luck" threw open an unsuspected door. Samuel J. Kimball, Chairman of the Board of the Exposition of Women's Arts and Industries of which she had long been a vice-president, asked her if the Council might be interested in establishing educational scholarships for young women. He could obtain funds for this purpose, he thought. Madesin made a counter proposal, which was to provide funds for the Spencer-Sternberger three-pronged project. Kimball's imagination was quickly captivated and the result was a plan so unprecedented as to appear almost unbelievable.

The Postal Telegraph-Cable Company, then under fierce competition from a rival firm, was looking for ways to increase its patronage and, as a means to that end, to acquaint the nation's women with its services. The company was prepared to invest one hundred thousand dollars in a campaign that would forward the Council's project while increasing the company's clientele.

The first step was for the Council to obtain the signatures of one million women to a petition addressed to "all the governments of the world," inviting each government to send their most representative women to the Chicago congress. Petitions were to be distributed to all of the Postal Company offices across the United States, where they could be signed or taken to meetings for signature, after which Postal would deliver them anywhere. It was a gigantic enterprise, but since the membership of the organizations affiliated with the Council totalled several million women, the Council agreed to undertake this campaign and to accept Postal's gift of one hundred thousand dollars in return. Suddenly a tempest began to develop in the National Federation of Business and Professional Women's Clubs which, as a member of the Council, was a participant in this plan. Attacking the project as rank commercialism to which business women should not stoop, certain members attempted to force the Federation to withdraw from the Council. The Postal Company plan went through nonetheless, and so did the project which it was designed to benefit. This was not the first, or indeed the last, of such tempests which Madesin was able to weather while holding one or another of the many offices she filled.

The need for office space in which to carry out this monster-sized operation was met by Madesin with characteristic acumen. She convinced the management of the conservative Vanderbilt Hotel, at Park Avenue and 34th Street in New York that if they donated the use of a three-room suite for the duration of the project, they would find an increase in the hotel's business due to the patronage of Council guests and dinner meetings. Next, in order to have both her major activities under one roof, she moved the headquarters of the International Federation of Business and Professional Women from her law office to the Vanderbilt.

The arrival of autumn 1930 saw the beginning of a two-year outpouring from the National Council's offices of form letters, leaflets explaining the petitions and how to handle them, publicity releases and other promotion, reaching out to a vast multitude of women being urged

103

to invade the Postal's offices from coast to coast. The staggering goal of one million signatures was reached early in 1933. The signed petitions were forwarded in great stacks to the U.S. Department of State to be presented to foreign governments through official channels.

Meanwhile, thanks to Postal's gift, the program for the Chicago Congress, the writing of the women's history and plans for the exhibition began to move steadily forward, even while the actual opening date remained, as far as Madesin was concerned, quite comfortably distant. Except for long and stimulating conversations about all this with Dr. Spencer and with Charles and Mary Beard, two remarkable friends Madesin cared about very much and who were also involved in the Chicago plan, she did not have to give much time to the Council's major project at this point.

Her other "causes" were also well in hand: preparations for the Fourth Goodwill Tour were almost completed and the National Federation's 1931 Convention—the first biennial one—to be held in Richmond in July was still well in the offing. Feeling freer than she ever had to take her mind off her "causes," she plunged avidly into her law cases, keeping all other commitments to the barest minimum.

As soon as the worst of the New York winter was over, she yielded to an urge which had come upon her every spring since she had left Kentucky—the urge to be in the open air and to have a piece of land to call her own. Now that the International Federation had become a reality, it was as though Madesin were suddenly allowing herself to place her determination and perseverance at the service of a personal cause, rather than, as had been usual with her, a public one. Almost every weekend, with Marjory Lacey-Baker and some other friends in her car, she explored the countryside in the vicinity of New York, looking for a spot near enough for commuting, but far enough to be a refuge from the mounting pressures of the city. Although nothing was for sale that spring which suited her purpose and her purse, and although at a certain moment she had to suspend her pleasant quest, she never stopped planning the little house she intended to build, or marking on the map the areas she would investigate as soon as the business of summer had been attended to.

At the Richmond Convention, where she was scheduled to be the principal speaker, she first reported as Chairman of the International Relations Committee. With justifiable pride, she was able to announce: "The International Relations Chairmen and Committees have grown from 69 to nearly 700 in two years, although an even more effective development of our international programs would occur if the remaining 500 clubs followed suit!" Then, having recommended that the Goodwill Tours be continued, she turned to the financial position of the International Federation, appealing to the U.S. Federation "for the tangible support of at least one five-dollar associate membership in the International from every U.S. Club."

Next she raised the convention's sights to the broader aspects of foreign affairs, focussing on two issues which were then highly controversial all over the country: one, was participation of the United States in the World Court, the other, a petition urging limitation of armaments, drawn up by the National Committee on the Cause and Cure of War, to be sent to the Geneva Disarmament Conference. The sponsors of this petition were seeking the signatures of one million American women. Madesin quietly and firmly asked the Federation to accept a goal of 50,000 signatures from its membership. On this matter as on U.S. participation in the World Court she received support. Looking back on it later, she marveled at the scarcely hoped for success of her dual plea at a time when the mood everywhere in the country was becoming conspicuously nationalistic.

Indeed, the Richmond Convention was outstandingly international in character, highlighted by a message from Virginia-born Lady Nancy Astor and by the addresses of four guests from overseas: Emma Chiera, from Italy; Indegarde Bergstrum, from Sweden; Dorothy Heneker, from Canada; and Mary Laudner, from France. The latter's exclamation, "This is a marvelous gathering such as I have never seen before!" epitomized the reaction of her fellow Europeans to their first American convention.

Madesin's main speech was sadly prophetic, coming as it did, only eighteen months before Adolph Hitler became Chancellor of Germany. "Cooperation among all peoples cannot remain a dream," she said, "but something that must become actuality if our civilization is to survive. We cannot afford to wait long in this changing and changed world. It is now—not in the next century or even in the next generation, but now—that we, and the men and women of all nations, must recognize that as no man lives unto himself no country can live unto itself.

"I believe the world is fast approaching a climax, and too many of us are bound by inherited states of mind. The present is darkened by economic depression, preparation for war, unemployment, poverty. Yet we still meet these new problems and crises by standards set by our diplomats a century ago. They are not going to work any more.

"We follow the traditions of a political party, without caring enough to want to understand them. We permit a League of Nations to become a political football. We sneer at the idealism of Virginia's great lover of peace, Woodrow Wilson. We shrug our shoulders, saying 'My country first and our flag. We must not have entangling alliances.' We insist that our tariff walls be raised in order to protect our industry. We are not willing that other people should share equally with us.

"I am concerned not only about world affairs, but also about our own new organization, for such attitudes are antagonistic to all that is fundamental in the philosophy of the International Federation. Thus I challenge you tonight, as I challenge myself, to forget the nationalism we have been taught to revere almost too much, to open our consciousness to a new feeling for people, our own and those of other countries. It is my prayer for all of us—that we may be consumed with a desire for world understanding and world peace, for world fellowship and world prosperity."

The warm and apparently very sympathetic reaction to her warnings was still echoing in her mind when she packed her bags and collected her papers to hurry off to Europe. The First Congress of the International Federation was taking place in Vienna at the end of July, and as soon as it was over she would be leading one of three sections of the Goodwill Tour. This time her group was to cover completely new ground for Americans—the "turbulent Balkans," as that picturesque region was often referred to in the thirties.

Not many days later, sitting under a big red umbrella on the terrace of the Schloss Kobenzl in Austria, Madesin was writing to her father. "We had a fine crossing. We enjoyed our days at sea and had some excellent conferences in preparation for our International Congress of 1931. I came directly to Vienna with Helen Havener, our publicity chairman, to go over arrangements with Dr. Beth, chairman of the Congress Committee. Now that all seems in readiness, I have escaped to this hotel for two days of quiet to prepare myself for the not so easy task of presiding over the congress.

"This is an ancient castle, surrounded by great forests. There is a marvelous view and the gardens are full of lovely flowers, many varieties well known to you. The meals are served out on the terrace and I have just had my breakfast. . . ."

The delegates to the International Congress seemed to have no inkling of the economic distress that was engulfing Austria in 1931, where there were close to six million unemployed. "The Austrian Congress Committee," Madesin records, "had neglected nothing that could add to the comfort and enjoyment of their guests and to the smooth functioning of the meetings. They were held in a stately old palace now the headquarters of the Vienna club which has nearly five hundred members. The opening reception was held in the Grand Salon on Sunday evening, July 26th, attended by ambassadors, ministers and other officials from the fourteen countries represented by delegations.

"For the first time there were women from Norway and also from Czechoslovakia, the nation that gave us a great leader, Senator Frantiska Plaminkova. We had talked with her two years earlier in Prague, and having come to Vienna, she seldom failed to attend congresses and board meetings, earning everyone's admiration and affection for her un-shakable devotion to her people, her country, and to the cause of freedom. For this, she was fated to pay the ultimate price at the hands of the Nazis: persecution, torture, then death before a firing squad."

When the treasurer, Henrietta Harris, presented her report for the fiscal year ending May 31st, it showed a balance of eight dollars and thirty-four cents. The income had been $3,979.30, the expenditures, $3,970.96. Undismayed by the financial situation, firmly convinced that funds would somehow be forthcoming, the delegates voted unanimously to set up an office in Geneva. Miss Heneker had agreed to serve as executive director for a year.

In the Federation's first twelve months, the Canadian federation had established thirteen clubs, the Italian, approximately forty. In addition, there were clubs in Vienna, Amsterdam, Brussels, Helsinki, Lausanne, Oslo, Paris and Stockholm, two in Great Britain, five affiliated groups in Hungary, and organizing committees at work in Czechoslovakia and Poland.

Exhibitions for the sale of member's handwork and handicrafts were being organized in several countries. An art show had been held in Rome and another was planned in Budapest. Dr. Marianne Beth was making good progress in her survey of discrimination against women by professional and commercial organizations.

One full day was devoted to the problems of growing unemployment. The main address on this subject was given by Ober-Regierungsrat Dr. Hilde Oppenheimer, of Berlin, a distinguished economist, whose remarks are still surprisingly pertinent. Twenty million people in Europe and America were out of work at that time, and she pointed to over-production and poor purchasing power, replacement of workers by machines, and, in some countries, lack of credit, maintaining that while there would always be some unemployment, it could be reduced by extensive public works and shorter working hours combined with un-employment insurance. She pointed out that "a little work is better than no work at all, especially for its moral effect."

To Madesin it had soon become very clear that shortly, if not at once, the International Federation would have to make a choice as to which direction it would take. Would its programs be aimed at ameliorat-ing the plight of individuals, as might be achieved with a multiplicity of limited projects in mutual help? Would it instead try to meet the need for research into the more fundamental questions involving the general improvement of the condition of women? In other words, would they choose to give immediate though limited assistance to a few indi-viduals, or pledge support for an extensive, long-range program to bring about fundamental social changes?

At the next Board Meeting in Paris, in 1932, the pull toward devoting the energies of the member clubs to mutual help in the professional and business field was still strong, but the Board itself chose to grapple with the fundamental, world-wide, problems. Two decades later, Madesin was still trying to decide in her own mind which course was the best. "As the years have passed," she writes," one sees by reviewing old records of ideals, ideas and achievements, that one of the primary purposes desired and followed by a large number of European members, which was to offer commercial assistance through advice, trade and other methods, has almost been entirely lost. Perhaps such practical matters do not combine well with the larger issues involved in international problems or programs." Almost inevitably, by 1933, the Board had voted that "owing to economic conditions and high tariff barriers, international exhibitions through our Commercial Exchange Committee are not feasible at the present time."

"Today" Madesin continued, "we have a more powerful, influential organization than then, despite the loss of this special material branch, but somehow I wish we might have kept both, those who wished to encourage trade among women or create business for women, and those who saw larger concepts involving such ideals as freedom, peace and justice. Both the practical and the ideal are needed. If one must choose, I think one would choose the latter. But I still feel the loss of that other pull, by which we drew a certain following of women who needed Federation help and who, in turn, could have been a great asset to it."

At the farewell banquet in Vienna, addresses were heard from five prominent delegates: Deputy Eugenja Wasniewska, Poland, on politics; Dr. Maria Munk, Germany's first woman judge, on law; Hofrat Ehrenhaft, Austria, on education; Dr. Anna Maria Speckel, of Italy, on journalism; and Mrs. Flora Drummond, of Great Britain, spoke of "the immense power inherent in collective endeavor." A masculine note was introduced by Vernon Bartlett, speaking for the League of Nations.

The final business session adopted resolutions endorsing the principle of equal pay for equal work and urging the appointment of women judges. It is interesting to note at this point that the Women's Liberation Movement of the seventies is still struggling, without too much success, to force acceptance by the United States of these very same demands which have now been implemented in many other countries of the world.

International officers were continued for another year. Additional vice-presidents were Dr. Marguerite de Munter-Latinis, of Belgium, Senator Frantiska Plaminkova, of Czechoslovakia, Baroness Marta Armfelt, of Sweden, Dr. Maria Castellani, of Italy.

Immediately after the Congress, Madesin and nineteen companions went to Budapest for one day and, from there, started their tour through the Balkan countries.

"In Hungary the banks were closed, but there was no indication of anxiety on the part of the Budapest friends who met us at the station. With them was Count Apponyi, nephew of Hungary's 'grand old man,' carrying a small American flag," Madesin writes. "In the Balkans we carried our message to entirely new groups. They were more Eastern than European countries, rarely visited by American tourists. We met there perhaps fewer, but hardly less competent or distinguished, business and professional women. Sometimes their first query about our organization was, 'What is your peace program?' And while at that time we had no clearly defined 'peace program,' expressing our first efforts largely through increased international understanding and good will, we could tell them how women's organizations in many countries, and we among them, were collecting millions of names to be sent to the International Disarmament Conference at Geneva in 1932, to prove that the women of the world were in earnest in their desire for peace. These were, on the whole, countries of danger, deprivations, economic crises, great sorrow in the past and equally great uncertainty as to the future."

The tour included Yugoslavia, Bulgaria, Rumania, Turkey and Greece. After World War II, when the first three of these five countries became Communist ruled, Madesin, always trying to replace prejudice with knowledge and antagonism with understanding among her more vehemently anti-communist friends, would bring out her notes and pictures dating back to the 1931 tour, in the hope of placing some of the pre-war facts in their proper perspective. The gaps she had seen between the minority of 'haves' and the majority of 'have-nots' in these societies were always deeply etched in her mind. "The deprived majority could not be expected to bemoan freedoms erased by Communist rule, because they had never had them in the first place," she would say.

"In Belgrade," Madesin's record continues, "we saw a city totally rebuilt after its destruction in World War I. It was a place of enormous contrasts, where peasants in homespun mingled on the streets with smartly dressed men and women, and lumbering oxdrawn carts were given right-of-way by motor cars. Several hundred women's organizations throughout the country were affiliated with the National Council of Women of Yugoslavia. A strong feminist movement for greater recognition of women's role was underway.

"Next we spent two and a half days in the Bulgarian capital of Sofia, an ancient settlement grown to a city of 250,000 inhabitants. The women at a conference represented a variety of professions, from ethnography to home economics, and many were engaged in literary careers, in the arts and in teaching. We were hopeful that this was fertile soil for our work. We saw Bulgaria as a kaleidoscope of neat red-tiled villages, purple laden vineyards, black and white sheep grazing, oxen pulling plows, dark forests.

"Our three days in Bucharest, Rumania, were not only the high point of our tour, but also the most rewarding for our purposes.

"Traveling overnight from Sofia, we arose at dawn in the small port of Ruiscuik, to take the little steamer across the Danube to Giurgiu. As the steamer docked, we saw a solemn procession of men and women marching slowly toward the pier. Weary and rumpled as we were, we were ill-prepared for this official delegation headed by the Mayor of Giurgiu. When greetings and short speeches had been exchanged, to my utter surprise I was led to an open carriage, the horses with bells a-jingle, and we drove in state, followed by a line of slow moving cars to a lovely old inn for an outdoor luncheon. A special train took us to Bucharest. Another group of dignitaries was on hand to escort us to our hotel, where in every room we found a note of welcome from the Prime Minister, and flowers from our hostess, Princess Alexandrine Cantacuzène, President of the National Council of Women of Rumania.

"A round of functions included a visit to the Dowager Queen Marie at her summer palace in Sinaia, a half-day journey on the train. She received us very simply, with her daughter Queen Marie of Yugoslavia, who was visiting her. We talked chiefly of world affairs, and at the end she said: 'Tell the American women that I think it is good for us to come to you, and for you to come to us. If we can teach that the Atlantic Ocean does not separate us, we shall have accomplished much.'

"King Carol, her son, also received the group after we had strolled through the luxuriant gardens to the Royal Palace.

"At Zamora, Princess Cantecuzéne's castle in the heart of the mountains, was where we were able to discuss with Rumania's most influential woman, the reason for our visit. Her interest was obvious, her questions keen, and within two years a Rumanian federation was organized under her presidency, which lasted seven years.

"Turkey had recently come through a social revolution. In Istanbul, veiled and unveiled women moved through the narrow streets, the wide boulevards, and the teeming bazaars. The women of the new Turkey were aggressive, alert, modern. Selma Ekrem, the young author of *Unveiled,* who had lectured in this country, Nebahat Hanim, our dark-eyed vivacious hostess (Hanim is a suffix indicating "woman") and Saffet Hanim, who gave us an unusual amount of publicity, were typical of the new Turkey.

"But the most remarkable woman we met, 'a perfect example of Turkey's two-job wife,' was assistant manager of the Pera branch of one of the largest banks in Istanbul. Although the mother of six children, she was incredibly young in appearance, and with her husband had worked out the management of the household on a completely co-operative basis. We were told that the husband supervised the buying and gave directions regarding the meals, while she did the sewing and arranged for the care

110

of the house. Other Turkish women told us stories illustrative of their emancipation and we found them working at a variety of pursuits. There were two women judges in Istanbul.

"The Turkish Women's Union, which entertained us at tea, was one of the largest and most influential organizations in the country, and we were told that it was highly probable that a professional section of it could be formed, to affiliate with the International. Probably for lack of money at this time, we let slip here an opportunity for a strong, useful branch."

An all day sail through the Sea of Marmara and the Aegean Sea brought the party to Greece.

"No city in the world is quite like Athens," Madesin commented, "with its magnificent marble stadium, its wide, well-paved streets, its pepper trees and, towering sentinel-like above, the Acropolis, crowned by that matchless and mournful ruin, the Parthenon. But with all its antiquity, grace and beauty, we found here also modern and interesting women, working zealously in many new fields. One was the Attorney for the Bank of Greece. She had a large private law practice in addition to her banking interests and had, that very morning, conducted five divorce cases. Another was an official of the telephone company. These women were enthusiastic about forming a branch of the International and gave us a list of eighteen cities where they had appropriate contacts for our work. They hoped to form groups which might affiliate with the International. Alas for their dreams and ours! We lacked the funds with which to send qualified field workers."

Shortly after returning from Europe, Madesin resigned as national chairman of the International Relations Committee. She had served in some official capacity through eleven of the first twelve years of the Federation's existence. For three, she had been executive secretary, for five, chairman of three different national committees, and for three more, the national president. She felt the Federation could profitably use new blood while she might be seeking a new vantage point from which to survey the vast international fields in which women would increasingly have to conduct their battles for recognition and equality.

Meanwhile, that September she was receiving recognition from her own University of Kentucky Law School, which had just been granted a chapter of the Order of the Coif. The letter which Madesin received from Professor Forrest Black said, in part: "The Order of the Coif is the outstanding honor society for law school graduates. According to the preamble of its constitution its purpose is 'to foster a spirit of careful study and to mark in a fitting manner those who have attained a high grade of scholarship.' It is the *Phi Beta Kappa* of the law school world and an invitation to membership is a signal honor. The faculty of the University of Kentucky

Law School has voted that you be invited to membership.' The formal installation was held on Saturday October 17, 1931, which Madesin probably attended, although her records seem to indicate no mention of this fact. At all events, she took pride in her membership and made no secret of it.

The Board of Directors of the International Federation, Geneva, 1934. Madesin Phillips is in the center of the front line, flanked by Senator F. F. Plaminkova of Czechoslovakia (left) and Dr. Maria Castellani of Italy (right).

Philsfolly

10. A Prophetic Challenge and a Bit O' Land

The blossoming of spring came earlier than usual to New York in 1932 and Madesin, pulling out her well marked maps, headed for New Jersey to resume the search for her bit of secluded land. Lady Luck was on her side or, as she preferred to say, the invisible finger was pointing to a certain turn in the road. A twelve acre lot of land was there for the bidding, five miles from Boonton, the nearest village, and within easy commuting distance from Manhattan: rocky woodland, enlivened by a captivating brook which meandered through the thick underbrush as if unable to decide which way to go. Madesin and Marjory, instead, were in no way undecided. They knew this was the place they wanted and, in short delay, became co-owners of that "rugged piece of earth."

Every spare moment thereafter was devoted to planning the house, but not until late summer could work be started, and not until the glorious reds and golds of the autumn foliage had emblazoned the landscape was it ready for occupancy.

The summer, as usual, was heavy with commitments which Madesin undertook with renewed vigor, thanks to the prospect of the retreat that would soon give her all the refreshment she could possibly want. The Board of Directors of the International Federation was meeting in Paris in mid-July. Owing to Madesin's unrelenting winter efforts, the organization had received sufficient contributions, both from public spirited friends and from five dollar associate memberships, to engage Dorothy Heneker as international executive director. In a small apartment, at 2, rue de Malagnou, in Geneva, vacated by Dr. Maria Castellani then retiring from ILO, the International Federation established European headquarters almost side by side with the League of Nations.

Twenty-four members of the International Board from sixteen countries, met in Paris at the old-fashioned and cozy Hotel Mirabeau where, after a formal opening, the Duchesse de la Rochefoucauld, president of France's National Association for Woman's Suffrage, gave them an interesting view of the background and current situation of the movement in her country. The business sessions began with an animated discussion designed to answer the question 'When is a federation a Federation?' The definition arrived at in Paris in 1933 is still valid: "For the purpose of membership in the International Federation of Business and Professional Women it is considered that a National Federation must be a recognized union of at least three organized groups of business and professional women." An accompanying memorandum added that "a group or club must be an organization composed of at least 75% of business and professional women engaged in earning their living, with a definite constitution and by-laws and properly appointed officers."

Budgetary plans and various recommendations brought in by specific committees were all accepted save two, dealing with the League of Nations. Here, a conflict of national viewpoints developed over a proposed endorsement of the League's Equal Rights Treaty and over the work of the League's Committee on Economic Sanctions. "We were not yet sufficiently united for positive action," writes Madesin, nor strong enough to risk violent disagreement among ourselves. Instead, we requested Miss Heneker to report on the course followed by the Treaty in the League itself, while the Economic Sanctions proposal was referred to the Federations for more careful study. Most importantly, however, the International agreed to continue to collaborate with the Disarmament Committee of Women's International Organizations and with the International Institute for Intellectual Co-operation, later transformed into UNESCO." The president of the U.S. Federation invited the directors to hold their next annual meeting in America, an invitation accepted with appreciation.

By the time Madesin returned to the United States, political excitement was rising to a high pitch all over the country. "The campaign to elect Franklin Delano Roosevelt," she writes, "was just beginning and the interest was spreading from one end of the country to the other. Mrs. Roosevelt asked me to be National Democratic Chairman for business and professional women. I would have liked nothing better, but it was a salaried position and I knew that, because of my official connection with the International Federation and the National Council of Women, I could certainly not take on a political job on that basis.

"Nonetheless, I also felt that, as an individual—not in any official capacity—it was my right, or even my duty, to express my personal opinion in this extremely important political campaign. Thus, I offered, as a volunteer, to write to women I knew throughout the country, asking them to support the candidate in whom I so strongly believed. My form letter, written of course on my personal stationery, brought a flood of replies. Those of my political persuasion thought it was wonderful that I was helping. Those of the opposing party expressed criticism and even reproach."

This appears to have been somewhat of an understatement on Madesin's part, for she actually became the target of sharp attacks rather

114

than mere criticism. Such phrases as 'You have used the position to which you have been elevated to further partisan politics' were among the mildest. Despite the much larger number who approved of her action in supporting Franklin Roosevelt, the condemnations affected her deeply. Many years passed before she could re-read the antagonistic letters with equanimity. Her candidate won, but Madesin herself could neither vote for him nor participate in the excitement of waiting for the returns. On the eve of the election she was suddenly taken to the hospital for major surgery.

Fortunately for her, the house in the woods, which had been only in the planning stage when she left for Europe, had been completed in October. The hands which could draw exquisite sound from a keyboard were also skilled with hammer and saw and Madesin had not only directed the workmen, but had also been their most diligent helper. Christened *Philsfolly,* it now provided her with the perfect setting in which to recuperate from her bout with death, surrounded by the softened tones of the late autumn scenery.

Built of fieldstone found on the property, the simple lodge had a high peaked roof and a great stone-floored living room, with some twenty windows reaching to the rafters, ample room for the piano, bookshelves built into every available wall space and a huge woodburning fireplace. An overhanging balcony which, as Madesin wrote, "seemed able to absorb an inordinate number of cots for overnight visitors, made it the perfect place for informal entertaining. It was unique in that we would not permit any so-called modern improvements. Electric light, telephone, running water, radio, all were taboo. Kerosene lamps and candles were our choice. It became also a perfect place for rest and recreation not only for us, but for many of our friends. As for exercise, there was always wood to chop, water to carry, flowers to plant, birds to feed, meals to cook for an indefinite number of people. . . To it came some of our most influential leaders, men as well as women, for discussion and planmaking. Here we could dream as well as work for what was perhaps one of the most difficult organization-building jobs. . . ."

The year 1933 found much of the Western world in the depth of a major economic depression and the United States among the hardest hit. For any American who, like Madesin, had close ties on both sides of the Atlantic, the situation was made all the more trying by Adolph Hitler's January election as Chancellor of the German Republic. Anti-Semitism was building rapidly throughout his Nazi-governed country. The strong German Federation of Business and Professional Women disbanded rather than sacrifice integrity, or renounce humanity toward its Jewish members. Streams of Jews and of anti-Nazis were pleading for admission to the United States. Although the mood of the country and the economic situation were far from good, every effort was made to give them safe haven. Madesin was among those actively involved in trying to make arrangements for their entry.

Meanwhile, the National Council of Women had been moving steadily ahead on its major project connected with the Century of Progress Exposition in Chicago, due to open in May. A large group of prominent American women were on its advisory committee. They included, among others, Jane Addams, Carrie Chapman Catt, Florence E. Allen, Harriet Stanton Blatch, Lilian M. Gilbreth, Ruth Bryan Owen, Frances Perkins, Eleanor Roosevelt and Mary E. Woolley. Hildreth Meière, the painter, was completing a sixty-foot mural illustrating the epic moments in the onward march of the American woman from 1833 to 1933. Inez Hayes Irwin was writing the history of organized women in America for the last hundred years, entitling it *Angels and Amazons*.

Mary Beard, the historian, was organizing the Congress of Women, a six-day meeting, with roundtable discussions, seminars and other features, for which more than one hundred leading men and women from the United States and other countries had agreed to speak or lead discussions centering on the theme: "Our Common Cause—Civilization." A number of overseas members of the Federation had been chosen as program speakers who, later, would attend the Board Meeting in New York. In some cases their expenses would be paid from the fund available to the National Council of Women; in others by their own governments, thus assuring their presence at both events.

The Century of Progress Exposition in Chicago opened duly in May and within it a notable section organized by the National Council of Women, in full accordance with the Spencer-Sternberger plan, highlighting the contributions of women to the advances of the previous century. The week of debates which Madesin was to chair as Council President was scheduled for July.

Like a bolt out of the blue the news reached her of her father's death. "Just as the year drew toward what was, for me, a milestone in my life," she writes, "the very roots of my being were torn away from a security I had always known. My beloved father died quietly at the age of ninety-five. I knew that his going was better for him, but life for me lost some of its meaning and was never quite the same again. It was a moment of great grief."

Nevertheless, when the women's Congress opened on July 16th, 1930, Madesin was in Chicago, calling to order a most extraordinary gathering of intellects. Shortly before she rose to speak, someone handed her a gavel and a message. When she stepped forward, instead of rapping the lectern she held up the gavel for all to see, exclaiming: "I know of no more auspicious thing that could have happened to us today than, unexpectedly, to have received for the opening of this Congress, the gavel in my hand. It was used in 1888 by Elizabeth Cady Stanton to open the first International Congress of Women in Washington; it was used by May Wright Sewall in 1893 at the next, equally memorable, Congress of Women in Chicago during the Columbian Exposition and by Susan B. Anthony at every one of the suffrage conventions over which she presided until the end of her life." A great burst of applause drowned the staccato sounds of wood rapping on wood to call the Congress to order.

In the vast audience of men and women were economists, scientists, statesmen, educators, writers, musicians, welfare workers, and other professional people who had come from every part of the United States and from as far away as India and Japan. The listing here of only a few of them shows how widespread and serious was the interest aroused by the Women's Congress: the Hon. Margaret Bondfield, the first woman member of the British Cabinet; Henry T. Rainey, Speaker of the U.S. House of Representatives; Mme. Marcelle Kraemer-Bach, founder of the International Association of Women Lawyers; Lilian Gilbreth, celebrated consulting engineer; Dame Rachel Crowdy, former Chief of Social Questions and Opium Traffic Section of the League of Nations; Jane Addams, founder of Hull House, the first social settlement in the United States; Muthulakshmi Reddi, Deputy-president of the Madras Presidency, sometimes called the Jane Addams of India; Baroness Shidzue Ishimoto, Japan's leading feminist; Christine Galitzine, National Director of Public Assistance of the Rumanian Ministry of Labor, Health, and Welfare; Ernest Gruening, then Editor of *The Nation;* Paul H. Douglas, Professor of Economics, University of Chicago; Mary Anderson, Director of the Women's Bureau, U.S. Department of Labor; Yi-Fang Wu, President of Ginling College, Nanking; Carrie Chapman Catt, America's great leader for suffrage and peace; Charles and Mary Beard, eminent historians; Rosa Manus, veteran suffrage leader of The Netherlands.

For her address Madesin had chosen to ask a question: Shall It Be Progress? With her usual sensitivity to the interaction of present and future, she foreshadowed the whole social direction which the women of another generation, some forty years later, would give to their own, more agitated struggle for liberation from inequities and injustice.

Madesin said: "I have put this question because I believe that organized womanhood and our own civilization are at the turn. I am convinced that, today, organized womanhood falls far short of what it could and should do. It offers a half loaf to a world starving for the fullness of spiritual food. It is content with half-gods, therefore the whole gods cannot appear.

"Today's idea of progress is comparatively new. It implies that a condition of general growth and happiness will ultimately be enjoyed which will justify the whole process of civilization, and that this condition will result largely from the efforts of men and women, uninfluenced by any other force.

"If you believe that all a person has to do is work hard, pay his debts, and vote for the political candidates of his choice, you will miss the true meaning of this conference. If you believe that we have always had the poor and the slums, inequalities and graft and will always have them, you start with a handicap in this Congress. If you believe that the Golden Age ended with the Greeks, you cannot catch that glimpse of a new world of peace and plenty, of security and opportunity for all, that has actuated the movers of this program.

"But if you can see civilization as a living, growing, changing thing; if you can discard old beliefs and theories, your fathers' as well as your own, and know that new conditions demand new treatment; if you can be willing to let your works justify your words when you speak of the brotherhood of man; if you can refrain from covering greed and selfishness with the benign cloak of Providence, then you are ready to begin to answer our question.

"Shall it be progress for organized womanhood? If so, we must take definite steps beyond the path which our pioneers have worn smooth. Women already have broad human sympathy. . . But it is not enough. . . It is easy to 'resolve'; it is difficult to act. Words, by and large, have become an outlet for the speaker rather than a contribution to the listener. Until women and men are willing to support their words by militant action, we are justified in hoping for but little.

"I believe we need a restatement of our inherited social code. Charity does not express love as much as does the willingness to accept a redistribution of wealth, employment and opportunity, that will eliminate the need for charity. World friendship is not expressed so well by sending shiploads of food and clothing to less fortunate people as it would be by a world-wide plan to obviate the need for these spasmodic generosities.

"A passionate desire for peace proves itself more clearly by curtailing the manufacture and traffic in arms than by exchanging polite words. We cannot truly desire the welfare of all, in our own country and elsewhere, unless we are willing to participate in the changes necessary to secure such welfare. The day of magic and superstition is past. If we want the things of which we talk, we can have them only at their price.

"The price lies in three things: first, an understanding of causes and effects and of the relationship between the many factors which, united, produce certain results that work either for the betterment of a few or for the good of all; second, a spiritual growth which will enable us to realize that material things at the cost of social justice bring neither happiness nor success; and third, the awareness that civilization is served not by the theory of social justice, but by its practice, and that the practice may

118

require drastic changes perhaps in our concepts and certainly in our social standards.

"We cannot have changes by mere wishful thinking. Change is the result of forces which we must deliberately control. Change may come through revolution, but it can also come through orderly planning, consciously and determinedly carried out. . . .

"If we accept these three requirements in principle, the obvious question is: What can women do? They can go home from this Congress and continue to study, of course; they can try their best to grow in that spiritual grace which we, as a nation, have always been so sure is ours; or they can set to work in an orderly way in their own communities. . . The test is here and now. . . Shall it be progress?"

Challenged by the question, the Congress steadily gained momentum over six full days and evenings of extraordinary give and take. The range of countries represented was impressive: Argentina, Armenia, Austria, Bulgaria, Canada, Chile, China, Cuba, Denmark, Finland, France, Germany, Great Britain, India, Ireland, Italy, Japan, Latvia, Mexico, Norway, Panama, Poland, Puerto Rico, Rumania, South Africa, Sweden, Switzerland, Syria, The Netherlands, Turkey, and Uruguay.

The problems facing civilization, in a year destined to become crucial, were dealt with from a variety of angles expressed by titles, such as these: "The World As It Is"; "The World As It Could Be"; "Economic Security Through Government Under Communism, Fascism, Democracy"; "Women in a Changing World." Problems facing the younger generation came to light in the words of college students at a forum on "Youth Plans for a Civilized World." Roundtables discussed security through employment, buying power and government; security against destructive forces—disease, crime, prejudice, war; opportunity through education and leisure.

There was an international women writers' conclave; seminars on problems of rural young people and on social hygiene, a pageant, musicales and an international music conference. Finally, a day devoted to a discussion of the findings from the six roundtables and how to fit them into a plan of action.

The banquet was highlighted by a unique feature. The Postal Telegraph-Cable Company had arranged a demonstration of coordinated communications whereby some fifteen telegrams, cablegrams or radiograms were sent from the dinner to leaders throughout the world, inviting them to respond to the question, "What is the best road to a social order assuring security and opportunity to all?" Flashing electric lights on a large map of the world indicated the approximate course of each message as it was sent and received. The replies were fascinating. One, from Amelia Earhart, said: "To me there seems no more direct road to what world

119

civilization truly means than that lighted by education and social tolerance." Another, from George Bernard Shaw: "The first step is to prevent men from discussing civilization in the absence of women, and women from discussing it in the absence of men."

This one must have especially delighted Madesin, who that year had been incensed by derogatory remarks which Mussolini had directed at women in an interview appearing very widely in print. She had answered him, likewise in print. The dictator had said about American women "The conquest of public life by women has assumed vaster proportions in the United States than anywhere else. . . . Hitherto we have never heard of any woman who succeeded in giving new and original imprint to any branch of political activity. We have not noticed any difference in the policy of the governments of Great Britain or the United States since women got their electoral rights. On the contrary, we have seen that this influence has been inferior to what has been prophesied, in fact in some cases absolutely negative; so much so that the United States backed out of their desperately defended position (*on prohibition*) and are about to resume a 'wet' regime."

Madesin replied, "Premier Mussolini's statement that 'woman is not adapted for participation in political life' does not prove much. Perhaps there is something wrong with political life . . . and there *is* a vast difference in the policy of the government of the United States 'since women got their electoral rights.' The whole trend toward disarmament and peace marks that difference and it is a trend largely attributable to women. As far as prohibition goes, if the women brought it in, certainly they took the leadership in pulling it out. Mr. Mussolini despises our popular form of government. He refuses it to Italian men as well as women. Why expect him, then, to be enthusiastic about woman suffrage? As for the Italian women's attitude toward it—it is easier to live in peace than to engage in strife in order to get the vote."

In Chicago, certainly, woman's contribution had not failed to make an impact. During the five months of the Century of Progress Exposition, thousands of copies of Inez Haynes Irwin's *Angels and Amazons* were sold; thousands of visitors viewed the historical exhibition in the Hall of Social Science; echoes of the Women's Congress were heard in many lands; the depth and sweep of the program opened up new perspectives on the modern meaning of civilization itself.

Mary Beard, writing to Madesin after it was over, made her evaluation saying: ". . . . the whole make-up of the Congress with few exceptions, was indicative of a revolution in women's minds . . . such publicity as I have chanced to see has reflected my own impression: that it marked a true advance for women."

The first meeting in the United States of the Board of Directors of the International Federation was held at Chautauqua, a beautiful spot in New York state. The European women, most of them seeing America for the first time, were fascinated by this unique combination of a summer resort and a center of organized intellectual activity. In the mid-1930's Chautauqua was famed for the eminence of the speakers heard on its platform during the summer season. Among the notables who extended an unplanned and much appreciated welcome to the foreign visitors, were Mrs. Thomas A. Edison and Mrs. Franklin Delano Roosevelt. The First Lady, there to address an audience that overflowed the huge amphitheater, unexpectedly invited the BPW members from overseas to share the platform with her and to speak briefly of their respective countries—an experience which none of the visitors ever forgot.

When the International settled down to business, it had reason to be proud of what it had accomplished in three years of existence. A British Federation had been formed, with Caroline Haslett as Chairman of the Administrative Council; a Rumanian Federation, under Princess Alexandrina Catacuzène; a first Club in Warsaw, founded by Anna Paradowska-Szelagowska; in Spain, a first Club was established in Madrid by the illustrious Isabel de Palencia, unhappily as short-lived as the Spanish Republic, and a Club in Seoul, Korea, the first in the Orient, presided over by Mrs. Induk Pahk, the distinguished writer. Thus there were nine National Federations and eleven other countries had individual Clubs. All of this had been built on sound foundations, reflecting Madesin's oft-repeated principle that "one must create as quickly as may be, but as slowly as must be."

Unexpected problems arose as each country tried to establish clubs or create a Federation. In Norway, for instance, housewives regarded it as an insult that they could not join, arguing that they too had a profession quite as important as that of self-supporting women. The Norwegian Press, seizing on the complaint, had publicized it widely and the government had levied a heavy tax on the National Federation. The pros and cons of the housewives' case were debated at the Board Meeting, but no conclusion was arrived at, nor indeed has the problem been resolved to this day. Madesin suggested that a questionnaire on the subject be sent to all Federations and individual Clubs to get at least a general idea of where the membership stood.

But if Madesin was always cautious at International meetings lest she appear to press her own convictions on women of other countries, she left no doubt of the side she was on when she was speaking for herself. The changes in the social and economic structure of the United States under Roosevelt's New Deal were highly controversial. Yet, from one end of the country to the other, she spoke out in favor of welfare measures and of 'planning' and against every form of discrimination.

After long hesitation—for there was much to be said on both sides—she had concluded that protective legislation for women, for which Mrs. Roosevelt, Mrs. Catt, Francis Perkins and other of her friends had fought so long, was discriminatory in practice. Madesin felt that working conditions must be improved for men and women alike by legislation applying to both as well as by collective bargaining between management and unions, rather than by the enactment of laws protecting 'the weaker sex.' Consequently, from 1933 to the end of her life, she supported the Equal-Rights-for-Women Amendment which had still not been passed by Congress in 1971.

In the 30's a night-work Convention, applying internationally, prohibited women from doing night work of any kind. The International Federation scored a victory when a motion, presented in its behalf to the ILO by Caroline Haslett, finally produced a revision of its text. An added paragraph stated that "this Convention does not apply to persons holding responsible positions of management and who are not ordinarily engaged in manual work." The change exempting business and professional women from restrictions on manual workers, evoked Madesin's gratification. "One must feel pride," she said, "in noting the positive position taken by the International in the often complicated situations confronting gain–fully employed women. In only four years our organization has advanced from its beginnings, when aims and ideas had been so diverse, to a sound basis of concerted legislative action."

"In art-loving Europe," Madesin also reported, "the Committee on Music and Fine Arts was most successful at the hands of Antonietta Paoli-Pogliani of Italy, herself a distinguished painter and sculptor. She was able to organize art exhibitions in Oslo, Vienna, Paris, Budapest and in several Italian cities. High tariffs and stringent government regulations had barred all exchange exhibitions of handmade goods between countries as planned by the Commercial Exchange Committee. However, local shows in eighteen European cities had resulted in publicity and sales. Dr. Marianne Beth's study of discrimination against women in the professions was proceeding effectively, while Helen Havener had developed a major publicity angle for the International Federation as a whole, through a series of radio broadcasts over major American networks featuring eminent women from Finland, Hungary, Japan and South Africa. Dr. Maria Munk of Germany, concerned with the position of married women which she had studied extensively, proposed a resolution stating that the International Federation "stands for the principle of equal rights as to nationality between men and women." Strongly supported and much publicized, the resolution highlighted a problem which was officially recognized and finally resolved only several years later.

As soon as the Board Meeting came to an end, Madesin fled to

Philsfolly where, axe in hand, she was out in the woods, replenishing her supply of logs for the winter weekends that lay invitingly ahead. It was always open house at *Philsfolly*. Colleagues and friends would come, sometimes for the day, sometimes for a weekend or longer.

Selma Ekrem of Turkey, a apeaker at the Chicago Congress, startled and delighted to see the International President in denim slacks, exclaimed: "You have made me very envious! Now, I shall not be satisfied until I have a stone house, overlooking the Bosphorus. Then I hope you will visit me and be sung to sleep by the nightingales!" *Philsfolly* had whippoorwills, but no nightingales!

Among frequent guests were a group of Federation friends calling themselves the Co-Ops—the Cooperating Committee—who, during the week, helped as volunteers to meet the mounting volume of work at the International office in New York. Madesin's correspondence alone was monumental, one of its major purposes being to increase and maintain the five-dollar associate memberships, now growing into the hundreds.

The Co-Ops, twelve or fourteen of them—if one dropped out a new-comer took her place—met once a week for early dinner and worked at the office for three or four hours, each on her own assignment. Most of them had important executive positions, but when they came to the International's little office they typed and filed and kept the accounting, taking anything and everything in their stride. Another reason for the huge bulk of Madesin's correspondence was that she used it to impress herself on the minds of people who might some day give her a helping hand. For instance, after addressing the Electrical Association of New York, in December that year, its president wrote her the following note: "Your address at our luncheon, while entertaining, could not be passed up as momentary, for the cheering message had a lasting effect on those who, like myself, had been quite despondent. Your optimism and vision for a greater future was a grain of inspiration that will grow in many hearts and was just the encouragement needed by so many." Madesin saw fit to thank him even briefly, saying: "Thank you for your kind letter. Perhaps you will be glad to know that it was a cheering message to me on a blue Monday. Of the services performed by each of us to the other, who knows but that yours was the greater?" The Co-Ops enjoyed writing these lively notes and often were treated to a clear view of how well they paid off!

The autumn fires blazing through the New Jersey countryside became the fires of another political campaign for Madesin. Although she could ill afford the time, she spoke and wrote in support of the Independent candidate for mayor, Judge Joseph V. McKee, whose campaign for Justice of the City Court she had managed so successfully ten years earliers. This time, however, he was opposing Fiorello H. LaGuardia, Fusion candidate, who was elected by a vast majority and proved to be one of New York's finest mayors. Her personal disappointment was soon displaced by her growing admiration for the winner.

Another matter in which she was engaged that autumn had a less fortunate outcome. The National Council of Women, not content to rest on the laurels of the Chicago Congress, became involved with the unemployment of women. A Council committee worked out a National Leisure Time program to be presented to President Roosevelt—designed to organize and maintain cultural and recreational activities for men, women and children. It was to be administered by the Council through its constituent bodies and other organizations across the country, educational, cultural, labor and religious groups having given assurance of their participation.

"As I re-examined it twenty years later," Madesin writes, "I was still convinced that it was a good plan, and still surprised that the President did not accept it. Naturally, we were very disappointed."

Concerned as she was by America's serious problems, Madesin could never confine her efforts within national boundaries. Her world was "one world" long before Wendell Willkie made it a household word. Early in 1934 she had urgent words to say on the subject: ". . . eventually we must have security and opportunity for all races, classes and creeds of men, with peace and goodwill among them. One might be expected to limit this challenge in a time of growing nationalism but I prefer not to. I could never be content with prosperity in America and starvation in India. . . Knowing as I do, the leading women of some twenty-six countries, I cannot draw a line around the United States and say 'Let us be prosperous and happy here—no matter about the others.' This may be a psychological reaction, but there is also the hard fact that today no country can live alone. . . Just how to find security and opportunity for all, we do not yet know, but certainly it is a challenge to the women of the world to participate in the pathfinding. . . ." She repeated this over and over during winter and spring, speaking around the country.

11.   As the Storm Gathered

As so often happens when one major enterprise is successful and others follow in its wake, the Chicago Congress of Women sparked a number of initiatives designed to advance the cause of woman's equality it had so eminently served. Outstanding among them was a project of considerable magnitude, spearheaded by Mary Beard, called the *World Center of Women's Archives*. Madesin, whose friendship with Mary Beard and her husband Charles had been deepened by their common interest in the Chicago Congress, was immediately drawn into the WCWA, as the Archives plan was usually referred to.

Mary Beard, besides being a scholar and historian of distinction, was also a very imaginative person, but not an organizer in the practical sense of the term. She always had a clear perception of how a project should turn out which she had conceived, but not quite of how to make it become that way. Thus, in trying to bring the Archives project to a head, she relied heavily on Madesin's judgment and experience. Most of her notes and letters directed to Madesin on this subject begin "Dear Chief" and usually set forth some kind of organizational difficulty which Madesin rarely failed to resolve. Although Charles Beard's role was chiefly that of a friendly spectator, he tended to agree with Madesin's suggestions and more than once was induced by both women to put his own weight behind their efforts.

The purpose of the Archives was manifold: to collect original documents and records pertaining to the ideas, interests and achievements of women; to trace the facts concerning their lives and work and to assemble and compile them for public use before the original sources were forgotten or lost; to establish a living center with every facility to serve students, scholars and others wishing to re-create the story of women's work; to restore to the record, through factual knowledge, the names of those women whose labor and leadership had earned them a rightful place in history.

The project suffered numerous ups and downs. At one point, in 1940, its outlook was so discouraging that Mary Beard felt compelled to write sadly to Madesin: "The whole WCWA looks dead to me, despite its potentialities. Sorry. Sorry." Very few years later, instead, a full fledged research library relating to the historical contributions of women had become an accomplished fact. According to Elizabeth B. Borden, its director, "a new impetus for the undertaking came in 1943, with the donation by Mrs. Maud Wood Park (Radcliffe '98) of a Women's Rights Collection, including her suffrage records and those of her co-workers. With the addition in 1944 of important material given by the historian Mary Beard and by others, the Women's Archives was established—a research library devoted to all aspects of women's lives."

How Madesin and Mary Beard ever found time, over the years, to keep abreast of the vicissitudes of the Archives is a question that leaves one wondering; nonetheless they were in constant communication about steps to be taken and decisions to be made. Whenever they could, they had lunch or dinner together in New York and Madesin often spent a weekend at the Beard house in New Milford, Connecticut. While Madesin gave Mary unsolicited help by raising sizable gifts of money for the Archives, Mary reciprocated by providing Madesin with unique data for a series of pamphlets she had been commissioned to write for distribution to women's groups all over the country. One of them—"The Constitution of the United States, a Study Outline"—elicited special commendation from the Beards: "It reaches high up, in our estimation," they wrote. "We shall be keen to know the reaches of its popularity among readers."

While the Archives project was at a standstill in 1934, three international meetings called Madesin to Europe in mid-June: a major conference of the International Labor Office and a Board Meeting of the International Federation both in Geneva, and a Congress of the International Council of Women in Paris. At the ILO Conference, where Madesin represented the International Federation, she was questioned repeatedly and almost exclusively about the New Deal and the NRA, commonly referred to by Europeans as 'The American Experiment." The Business and Professional Women also showed great interest in this particular aspect of American life, concerned as they were with Europe's mounting economic difficulties and the need for reforms, possibly similar to those which the NRA was intended to achieve.

Madesin, presiding at the Board Meeting, started out by focussing attention on the Federation's finances, determined as she was to finally make the organization self-supporting. Having pointed out that total contributions received from the U.S. Federation, including five-dollar associate dues, were the equivalent of ten cents *per capita* of the total U.S. memberships, she proposed that all National Federations assess their members for a similar small amount. If this were done, she emphasized, the International would have a steady income which would increase with the growth of membership. The proposal was enthusiastically accepted, but many years were to pass before it was enacted.

The Board likewise accepted another proposal advanced by its President and one that became a fact without delay. She suggested that a date be set aside for the celebration, every year, throughout the International, of International Night, when clubs would hold a special meeting centering around a given theme chosen each year for its relevance by the Board and circulated well ahead of time. It was agreed that the observance be held in February, the specific date to be decided upon year by year. "The theme, to be developed throughout the International" said Senator Plaminkova who had proposed this particular idea, "would provide one more link between widely dispersed national federations." Instituted in 1935, International Night, later changed to Day, is still faithfully observed. During World War II, Clubs in Nazi-occupied countries, defied police bans to hold the meeting in secrecy. The risk itself seemed to strengthen friendship among the participants, while also giving them a brief but happy illusion that they were not totally cut off from their friends and colleagues on the other side of the battle lines.

The Congress of the International Council of Women devoted its entire attention to world problems and their effect on women, expressing views which the general public of that day, in any of the countries represented, would have regarded as little short of outlandish. One such concept, for instance was 'the right of women to work,' used as the subject of a mass meeting in the great amphitheater of the Sorbonne in Paris, filled to capacity for that unique occasion. Madesin, one of several speakers, had been requested to present "The Underlying Principles of Women's Right to Work."

"Only a Yankee with a sense of humor," she said, "or perhaps a diplomat conditioned in the use of a language designed to obscure rather than express any real meaning, could be entitled to speak on this subject, clothed as it is in the generally accepted egalitarian phraseology: "Women's Right to Work." When has that right ever been questioned? I have seen woman toiling in the fields bearing on her back the burden of a pack horse; I have seen her scrubbing, cooking, sewing, working in poverty in more than half the world—but working from sunrise to sunset. Who questions her right to these and a thousand other labors? Who questions woman's right to the unpaid or poorly paid drudgeries of her society? No one!" Then, having traced the underlying principles from primitive history to the present, she continued: "No, it is not the right to work to which woman aspires and which she is denied. This she has and ever has had. It is her right to equal pay for equal work, to the jobs paying more money for less hard work, her right to full opportunity and power and to their attendant prestige . . . these she is still denied." "The protection of the morals and health of women and of the heritage of unborn generations are set forth as the primary reason for discriminations against women in gainful occupations. If women are too frail in body to work, let us have

127

more tractors in the field, more washing machines in the home. If motherhood is too sacred to draw a paycheck, let us abolish child labor and let us have scientific care for our babies. It is also being said that there are not enough jobs to go around and that men have families to support. But women, too, have families. If need is the criterion, why not limit the employment of those who, because of accumulated wealth, have no need of gainful employment?

"Two theories of government exist in the world today: individualism which conceives of the State exclusively in terms of the individual; universalism, in which the State stands superior to the individual and his rights. Both these forms of government deny equality to women, yet under each, I contend, they are entitled to it. . . Through our own might we women could secure our right. Therefore, let us talk less or do more. The International Council should begin to act and act now."

The International Council had been created in Washington, D.C. in 1888 by Susan B. Anthony, May Wright Sewell, Frances E. Willard and other pioneers of woman's equality. In Paris, that year, twenty-nine National Councils were represented, Madesin being a leading member of the American delegation. Her first impression of the International President, Ishbel, Marchioness of Aberdeen and Temair, then nearly eighty, was of a woman of remarkable physical vigor, coupled with an astonishing serenity of spirit and a cool, logical mind. She had first become President in 1893 and had been frequently re-elected to this office. By 1934 she had served in all some thirty years. A great admirer of Queen Victoria, she bore her a startling resemblance in features as well as in dress, as the Queen had appeared at the turn of the century. In 1938, when Madesin was elected a Vice-President of the International Council, Lady Aberdeen gave her a photograph of herself which could easily have passed for one of Victoria Regina. It occupied a prominent place at *Philsfolly,* where it soon became a classic among many other 'conversation pieces.'

However, the remarkable photograph was not yet ensconced at *Philsfolly* in August 1934 when Madesin launched her first experiment with a large picnic on her grounds. The invitation issued to club members in New Jersey said: "Wear old clothes and your oldest, flattest shoes. Bring your sandwich and we will take care of coffee, cream and sugar. Put on your gayest disposition and tune up your voice for community singing!."

More than a hundred came. The woods were filled with voices as everyone explored the lodge, wandered along the trails, or climbed high rocks for wonderful views. Presently, over a huge wood fire by the brook and with water from the mountain spring, coffee was brewed by the gallon, while the picknickers settled under the trees. Later, in the big living room, they listened and asked questions as Madesin, with a generous sprinkling of humor, related what she had seen and heard abroad that summer.

Finally, with her at the piano, the guests, as Caroline Haslett said "sang together in typically American fashion which was quite a delightful experience."

The success of the first picnic led to its yearly repetition, with often more than twice the original attendance. 'Celebrities,' American and foreign, of which there was always a good contingent, were usually willing to say a few words or lead an animated discussion. Madesin's ability to organize such a 'party' for women only, making it vastly entertaining while giving everyone something serious to think about and take home, revealed an uncommon and useful talent which enabled her to draw together the most seemingly disparate individuals.

During 1934 Madesin had also been working on an article commissioned by *Pictorial Review,* then one of America's leading magazines for women, on the subject of what women thought they would do if war came. She had gathered material in Europe, interviewing ten of the continent's most prominent women. "I always put my question bluntly," she writes. "I asked it of Kerstin Hesselgren, the first, and for a long time the only woman Senator in the Parliament of Sweden. She smiled: 'Just what they did in the last war. Women do not want war but they do not know how to stop it. When husbands, sons and fathers begin going to the front, women will conserve food, roll bandages, work for the Red Cross. . . .' Emilie Gourd, Switzerland's ardent leader of peace and suffrage movements, replied, 'Some years ago I thought the women of the world would stand against another war. Now I am not so sure. . .' From Czechoslovakia's Senator Plaminkova, one of the most politically astute feminists in Europe, came the answer: 'If women thought a war was aggressive they would have nothing to do with it. They would make a demonstration against it—even though it might be at very great danger to themselves. I do not believe women are afraid of guns or of the machinery of war. . . .' I asked the widow of the 'grand old man of Hungary,' Countess Albert Apponyi, a member of the Hungarian delegation to the League of Nations. 'Women would do their duty,' she replied. 'In principle women are pacifists. They would oppose war to the last. But if it came in spite of them, they would do their duty. . . .'

"So the answers went, significantly similar."

A direct result of these interviews was a series of broadcasts on "Women and World Peace," presented under the auspices of the International Federation, that aroused considerable interest throughout America. Speakers included such noted peace leaders as Jane Addams and Carrie Chapman Catt and the presidents of the country's foremost women's organizations.

Introducing the series, Madesin described peace as a "women's cause following in the wake of their struggle for education, suffrage and economic independence." Afterwards, summing up the main points made by the various speakers, she listed them as follows: "Abiding peace rests upon social justice and well-being; the approach to world peace must come through increasing international understanding and goodwill; there must be less rivalry in international trade, an equal participation of women with men in political life throughout the world, recognition of the worth and the rights of the individual, a greater exercise of the rights of citizenship, a world will toward peace and a world prepared to make sacrifices for peace." In the 1970's these have become popular concepts, although still largely unimplemented, but in the 1930's they were new and surprising to most Americans and, coming from the lips of women, "startling indeed" in the opinion of most of the men who heard them.

Towards the end of that year Madesin knew that she would have to decide which of several paths to follow in her own life. She now realized that she could not maintain a satisfactory law practice while also keeping her commitments to the causes she had espoused and had no intention of forsaking. Thus the question she must now answer was: Should she give up her legal profession in order to devote herself entirely to the advancement of women in her own country and abroad? How serious a financial loss would such a decision represent? Although her speaking engagements provided a fairly substantial income, the calls on her personal resources were disproportionately heavy. The cost of traveling to meetings of the International Federation abroad and to the conventions of other organizations in the United States or overseas, which, of course, was never reimbursed, was a major item of expenditure to be reckoned with. In addition, Madesin provided the International with all the financial help she could spare from her own limited resources whenever she failed to raise contributions from other sources. This too was a drain she could not overlook.

The decision must not have been an easy one for Madesin to reach, at fifty-four, and still fascinated by and attached to the practice of law. However, in the early part of 1935, she dissolved her partnership with Barnet Muffs and wound up her own legal cases. The bold step demanded a good measure of faith as well as courage but, very soon and unexpectedly, her investment in both was profitably rewarded. In July, *Pictorial Review* invited her to become an associate editor of the magazine and to create a clubwomen's department designed to cater to the interests of homemakers as well as to the millions of clubwomen throughout the country. Her monthly assignments included the writing of one full-page editorial for each issue and one small text book, dealing with a different aspect of home and club life. The subjects ranged from "how to handle finances" to "how to live at peace with the least congenial member of your club."

The attractiveness of the offer made Madesin's acceptance all but a foregone conclusion. "I count this a great opportunity," she wrote Mary Beard. "You know of my interest in women and that I want to write. An audience of two million is something to conjure with." The job was not only a new challenge which she faced with enthusiasm, but it also brought her into close association with a world she barely knew—the world of writers. In the course of nearly four years, until *Pictorial Review* went out of existence, in addition to the monthly article, Madesin produced twenty-four small books, whose printings ran to an average of 75,000 copies each, while her editorials were read by millions of women every month. She wrote in a light vein, her dry humor flashing between the lines, and, being Madesin, with always a bit of "preachment" thrown in for good measure! Whatever she wrote, her main purpose always was, as she put it, "to combat the apathy, the indifference, the satisfaction with unimportant results, typical of far too many women today. The challenge of tomorrow is a new challenge to woman's thinking and actions, dealing primarily, as it does, with such hard realities as economic security, housing, honest politics, good government, rather than with personal culture or self-improvement. . ."

As a practical guide to an understanding of three of these "hard realities," taxes, the Constitution and the then recently passed Social Security Act, Madesin devoted a short text-book to each, so conceived that it could be used in a series of organized discussions. Her approach was novel and imaginative. The complexities of Social Security, for instance, were presented in the form of a six-act play to be read or recited at six consecutive meetings. Taxation was explained in terms familiar to every homemaker, prefaced by the advice: "We must be as sensible about the nation's pocketbook as we are about the one belonging to the householder." The book dealing with the Constitution, which won praise from the Beards, was a ten-part analysis, designed to be studied and discussed in ten separate meetings. "A study of the U.S. Constitution," she pointed out, "should be of aid in equipping club members for better citizenship."

In no time, the little books, clear and concisely written, brought a flood of letters from women asking Madesin all sorts of advice, chiefly relating to their Club and its problems. *Pictorial Review* was overwhelmed by a response for which it had given Madesin insufficient staff. But Madesin handled the mail-jam by creating what she called a "Club Clinic." Each letter-writer received a four-page questionnaire, planned to reveal enough about any Club to enable Madesin to prescribe a remedy for its ills. Apparently the Clinic worked miracles. Letters of appreciation poured in, demonstrating Madesin's extraordinary understanding of feminine psychology in general and of Club-woman psychology in particular.

Pleased as she was by the results of her editorial efforts, a far greater source of satisfaction to her, in the mid 1930's, was the progress made

131

by American women in the political arena. Under the Roosevelt administration, and undoubtedly with considerable prodding from the First Lady, Frances Perkins had been appointed Secretary of Labor, Josephine Roche, Assistant Secretary of the Treasury and Nellie Tayloe Ross, Director of the United States Mint. Other equally qualified women were placed in executive positions in such government agencies as Relief and Social Security and posted in Washington and in other major cities around the country. Likewise to Madesin's delight, in 1935, only a year away from a presidential election, the National Federation of Business and Professional Women's Clubs decided to take a poll of all political candidates running for local, state or national office, on "issues relating to the progress of women and in particular of self-supporting women." A year earlier, the U.S. Federation had adopted the following Declaration of Principles, largely inspired by Madesin's ideas:

"The National Federation of Business and Professional Women's Clubs is prepared to defend the principles of such economic security to men and women as will assure to each individual the safeguards guaranteed by the Constitution of the United States. We stand for a sound education, for the right to work, to receive rewards sufficient to lift living standards and safety of individuals in non-productive years. We will promote in our communities, state and throughout our national government, economic reforms that will bring about the evolution of Social Justice. Because there can be no economic security for any class or group unless there is economic security for all, we demand for women employment, appointment, salaries and promotions on equal terms with men."

Read today, amid the clamor of the protesting 70's, this document, as timely now as when it was first written, bears witness to the hard reality that the strongest declaration of intent is no assurance of implementation, unless public opinion is mobilized and the citizenry inspired to take strong action to see that the forces in power transform words into deeds.

Another Federation 'first' was a radio program in July 1935 originating in Rome and, by what seemed then a miracle of technology, instantly heard in the civic auditorium of Seattle where the Federation was holding its convention. At the precise moment for which the transatlantic broadcast had been planned, the strains of the national anthems of Italy and the United States, played in the Italian capital, filled the vast hall with awe as well as sound. Across the Atlantic ocean and across the entire American continent traveled the voices of Dr. Maria Castellani, president of the Italian Federation, and of the Countess Mazzitelli, the first woman ever elected to Rome's City Council, carrying a message of solidarity from all the women of the European federations.

Among those who listened attentively to the remote broadcast was the U.S. Secretary of Agriculture, Henry A. Wallace, the convention's main speaker. Already a political figure of note, he later became Vice-President of the United States and, later still, a somewhat controversial candidate for the presidency. That night, in Seattle, Madesin, who had occasion to talk to him at some length, could hardly have imagined that some ten years later she would be running for public office on the Wallace ticket. But before that chapter of her life could come to pass, America and most of the Europe to which Madesin was so deeply attached, were to live through the horrors of World War II, a prelude to which was already developing in the Mediterranean.

During that month of July, while friendly messages from Roman women were reaching the United States over the airwaves, Italian troop-ships were moving through the Suez Canal, carrying weapons and supplies to the frontiers of Ethiopia, a country singled out as the first victim of totalitarian aggression. When the invasion began on October 3rd, its far reaching implications were lost on the general public, and perhaps not recognized even by Madesin. An attempt by the governments of Britain and France to arrange a settlement collapsed in December and the Italian forces, with air power and modern arms, quickly overcame the resistance of the primitively equipped Ethiopians. The League of Nations imposed economic sanctions on Italy, but took no stronger measures to support or defend the victim, a full-fledged member of that presumably peace pre-serving body. By May of 1936 Haile Selassie had fled his capital and his country was soon annexed to a newly proclaimed Italian Empire. Then the sanctions were lifted and the fruits of aggression internationally recognized as valid. For Adolf Hitler this was the dress rehearsal for an attack on his European neighbors which he and his henchmen were turning over in their mind. It would not be long before the "gathering storm," so un-forgettably described by Winston Churchill, would crash upon the western world.

The League of Nations had been morally if not otherwise destroyed. Fascism was triumphant and, in the ominous calm which set in that summer, the European federations of business and professional women were carefully steering clear of political pitfalls. Early that year several of their leaders had begun to consider replacing the Triennial Congress, scheduled for 1936, with a simple Board Meeting, but, in the end and with some misgivings certainly on Madesin's part, the Congress was held in Paris in July as originally planned.

Whatever the reason, it proved to be one of the largest and most notable of many. "Never before and probably not since," wrote Madesin, "have we had quite such a remarkable group of women." Frances Perkins had promised to deliver the principal address dealing with "The Participation of Women in Public Life" for which there was great expectation. Suddenly, the U.S. Embassy in Paris informed Madesin that Miss Perkins would almost certainly not be able to come. Consternation was short-lived, for a cable to Madesin announced her arrival on the eve of the Congress' opening.

As it happened, that evening Madesin had taken three of her most distinguished guests to the Comédie Française and had to leave the theater to meet Miss Perkin's train. Senator Plaminkova went with her. The U.S. Ambassador to France joined them at the platform where he had to lend a hand in trying to hold back a horde of photographers and press reporters. "When the train at last drew slowly in," recalled Madesin, "nobody knew at which end she would be and we scattered up and down the quay. Senator Plaminkova and I were at the wrong end and it was only by running all the way back that we were in time to greet our honored guest. I shall never forget Senator Plaminkova, great in body as she was in soul, gathering up her skirts and trotting down the platform panting audibly and, as we reached our goal, suddenly exclaiming, "I like it!" Presently, at the door of the coach was Frances Perkins, in her tricorne hat and veil, accompanied by her very pretty young daughter. Surrounded and all but overcome by flashing cameras and inquisitive reporters, we finally extricated ourselves from the crush and got back to our hotel, while the Ambassador escorted the Secretary of Labor to hers.

The high point of a totally gala week was the night of Miss Perkin's main speech in the Grand Ballroom of the Lutetia. At the close of it there was also to be a transatlantic broadcast to America, with the major "stars" of the evening participating. At the very moment when the speakers took their place on the platform and the international broadcasting equipment, complete with klieg lights, was all in place, there burst into the hall a noisy platoon of French militant suffragettes, who immediately padlocked themselves to their chairs and could not be removed!

"They had come to protest the presence and speech of Madame Brunschwigg, French Undersecretary of State for National Education who," recorded Madesin, "in their view had failed to support their cause in the fight for equal rights which, at that moment, was before the Chamber of Deputies. As soon as I had introduced Madame Brunschwigg, who was to present the official welcome of the French government, the suffragettes began to shout uncomplimentary remarks which drew strong applause from various other delegations, themselves militant in the fight for women's rights. The confusion and clamor left me puzzled as to what to do next. Madame Plaminkova, having asked me if she might speak to the shouters, came forward pleading, upbraiding and railing in her emphatic French, all to no avail. Dismayed, I stepped to the very edge of the platform and, forgetting that the suffragettes probably did not understand my language, in straight American I shouted words of indignation and loudly demanded fair play. "After all," I stormed in conclusion, "this is our meeting and we have the right to hear our own speakers!"

"The chained protesters, evidently startled by the avalanche of incomprehensible words, were suddenly stilled. As far as I could make out, they even listened to the French translations of all that was said in English, brilliantly given by Mrs. Olivia Agresti Rossetti, a well known writer and a descendant of the celebrated English poets and painters of that name.

Miss Perkins, although totally realistic as to the effect of the economic trends on the employment of women, also sounded a note of faith in the future saying: "The machine, which has created so many problems for mankind, has, indeed, also created a state of society in which it is more possible than ever before to tie all peoples together in a new brotherhood. The struggle is not quite so intense, the humanities become more possible and the ancient idea of the brotherhood of man becomes realizable in our generation. The opportunity for this realization is imperfect unless women are included in it."

"Just before the International broadcast, which we feared would suffer from a renewal of the shouting, several of us lined up around the speakers and the microphones, forming a human wall we hoped would shut off some of the expected uproar. But none occurred. The next morning I received a note and a large bunch of magnificent roses from the leader of the suffragettes. Through it all, I had sympathy for them and understanding and perhaps even a slight sense of envy. For many years now, from time to time I have felt slightly ashamed that I have never been in prison because of the strength of my convictions, that I was not a militant suffragette, never even walked on a picket line or carried a banner, for the cause for which I certainly cared far more than for reputation, comfort or safety."

Perhaps the demonstration did some good after all, for a few days later the French Cabinet passed a resolution in support of granting suffrage to French women, even though the franchise was not actually given them until many more years of bitter struggle had gone by.

Although the German Federation had been disbanded under Hitler, and was not among the sixteen national delegations to the Congress, several women from Germany had come as observers. European federations, including those from Poland and Rumania, and an Associated Club from Lucknow, India, all had to their credit substantial progress and several significant legislative successes whereas the report of the Austrian Federation was of a different nature. The forward looking democratic government had fallen, not without bloodshed. A near-fascist regime threatened business and professional women, and indeed all wage earning women, with the same fate that had befallen their German sisters. With great courage the Austrian women continued to fight for their rights. The chairman ended her report with these words: "Although our activities in all fields are greatly hindered, we refuse to acknowledge discouragement and are prepared to work continuously for the advancement and protection of the interests of our members."

But, again, heart and will were not to prove enough. Before the next Congress Hitler's march into Austria had brought tragedy to a country too small to resist the goosestepping invaders.

Miss Gordon Holmes, an outstanding British financial expert and the Administrator of the National Securities Corporation of London, who had come as a visitor to the Congress, was shocked by the disparity between the work accomplished by the International Federation and the meager financial support it could count on. Thus, with characteristic enthusiasm, she agreed to become the organization's Finance Chairman and immediately started a campaign to relieve the recurrent monetary ills.

From that moment and to the end of her life in 1951, Gordon Holmes was an immensely effective participant in everything the International Federation embarked on. She was, indeed, an amazing person. "No one," said Madesin, "who had ever seen or heard Gordon Holmes could forget the imposing presence, the grand manner, the stately tread, the trenchant phrase, the angle of the long cigarette holder—all were stuff out of which legends grew. Dominant, determined, impatient, sometimes hard to take, unexpectedly tender and always generous, most of us loved her and all were bound to admire her brilliant qualities. Some of us called her the 'General.' "

When Gordon Holmes attended her first Board of Directors Meeting, fires began to crackle. Up to that time the bulk of funds had come from the United States, but the General quickly initiated a discussion of methods for raising money in Europe itself. Before the discussion ended a number of countries had promised at least special contributions. Underlying all this was a problem reaching far beyond the International Federation which Gordon Holmes and Madesin had sensed, each in her own way.

The problem was one of obligations and relationships between the have-not nations—ravaged by World War I—and the United States, relatively untouched by war and rich beyond measure in land, natural resources and high industrial development. The isolationist trend in America found nourishment in the so-called 'ingratitude' of countries which had needed and received help after World War I, while it chose to ignore the long proven fact that it is as uncomfortable for nations as for individuals to be recipients of 'charity.' There were many Europeans, however, who saw some validity in this critical American attitude and, at that time, Gordon Holmes was among them. Madesin Phillips' position and the philosophy on which she had built the International Federation were very different. To her, the human family was one, and the world's goods were for its common use.

A comment made some years later by Madesin, when she was reading Gordon Holmes' autobiography, "In Love With Life," clearly reveals the difference in their points of view. She said:

"I think it is worth noting that Miss Holmes' work with the Federation changed some of her attitudes. In fact, I think the following paragraphs from her autobiography constitute a great, constructive triumph for the Federation, showing what influence it could and did have upon the inner life of one quite unique woman.

"Following a long indictment of several countries for their eagerness to receive American money and for the paucity of their gratitude or thanks, Gordon Holmes wrote: 'Americans may read this. If so, don't attach undue importance to it, the undue importance that I myself formerly attached to it. In fact, don't attach any importance to it at all. It took my new American friends themselves during the next few years to make me realize that, with many kinds of work, it's so much more important that the work shall be done than to argue who is going to pay for it. . . So, my Americans, go on doing just what you have been doing, more if necessary, as seems inevitable in the year 1943. Destiny, fate, has been good to you—Pay back, pay back! Continue to make your material offerings on the altarstone of Humanity as your outward and visible sign of that inward and spiritual grace of gratitude, of that humble and contrite heart, which is the oldest sacrifice demanded of humanity.' "

Today one might well wonder what comment might have flowed from the General's lively pen when the defeat of U.S. policy on the two-China proposition in the United Nations Assembly in October of 1971, let loose in that august hall an unseemly demonstration of high glee on the part of certain nations then still the recipients of American aid. What phrase might she have used, either trenchant or compassionate, to analyze the significance of threats voiced in the United States Congress to cut off all support from the United Nations as a retaliatory measure, even though the impulsive words were not matched by comparable action? Since the mood of the early seventies is so similar to that of the early forties, one may conjecture that Gordon Holmes, aware of the extent to which history does tend to repeat itself, would have repeated her own words, saying to her American friends, "It is so much more important that the work shall be done than to argue who is going to pay for it. So, my Americans, go on doing just what you have been doing and more if necessary. . . ."

12.   The End of an Era

From Paris, as she had planned earlier, Madesin went on to Berlin. Believing as she did, and frequently said or wrote, that, now more than ever before, the hope of the world rested on the rising generation, such a visit had good reason. She had become very concerned about the rising rate of juvenile delinquency in her own country and intended to see for herself the highly dramatized youth programs being carried out in Germany and Italy. With her on the trip were Helen Havener, who had so effectively arranged publicity and much else at the Paris Congress, and Marjory Lacey-Baker, who, relieving her of countless details, had become an indispensable traveling companion.

In Berlin, all was gaiety, music and color. The Olympic Games were in full swing and, incidentally, it was during one of these sports events that Hitler and his henchmen marched out of the stadium when an American athlete, who was black, won the highest honors. In Madesin's words: "The city was a restless splendor of banners; crimson streamers bearing the swastika were profusely interspersed among the flags of other nations; the streets were a moving mass of apparently satisfied humanity. Conspicuous everywhere were large groups of boys and girls on their way to visit historic monuments, museums, public buildings and the like, all planned, I was told, 'to awaken their pride in the Fatherland.'

"Frau Margarete Kaiser, a very active journalist, had made the arrangements for our visit with a car and chauffeur at our disposal. We saw the activities organized for the young. We visited a training school for young leaders under the escort of a girl and a boy, both in uniform, who explained everything to us in good English. We went to see a youth hostel, one of more than two thousand, we were told, used in a year by some seven million young people. Near Berlin we visited a farmhouse which had been transformed into a Women's Work Camp. It was overflowing with older girls undergoing a Spartan régime involving hard work on neighboring farms, daily study, prescribed reading and little recreation. In each dormitory-like bedroom, with its double-decker beds, shuck mattresses and boards in place of springs, we saw small photographs or newspaper pictures of Der Führer.

"I had an illuminating interview with the powerful Frau Scholtz-Klink, in charge of more than eleven million women throughout Germany. She gave me many facts and figures, and in interpreting 'how we Germans see our task today,' she said, 'The work of the individual woman, no matter where, is the expression of her contribution to German life and is an unending effort to strengthen the whole with the best that is in her.'

"Unconvinced by her picture of German womanhood, I went to the impressive Labor Building to talk with Dr. Robert Ley, chief of the German Labor Front and founder of the Strength-Through-Joy movement. I asked him, although I was sure of his answer, if there were any truth in the report that German women were discriminated against. This he denied vehemently and said, 'Come with me.' Leading me down a long corridor with offices on either side he opened every door and wherever he found two or three women at work he went in and vigorously shook hands with them. Each time he said to me, 'See, they work here. They are not discriminated against.' But obviously they were doing just the routine clerical jobs long their special province. As in the Women's Work Camp, so here, I saw no office without its large and flattering portrait of the Nazi leader.

"Our visit was cut short by a cable from Maria Castellani in Rome, saying that she had arranged for an audience with Mussolini and urging me to come immediately.

"Nearly a decade was to pass before I returned to Berlin. By then, a blind and vicious nationalism had brought ruin upon it and death and destruction to a stunned world; the swastika had vanished, replaced by new flags fluttering in the breeze: American, British, French and Russian, a symbol of victory rising with tragic irony above mountainous piles of rubble."

In Rome, Madesin's quest for truth behind the impressive façade, continued in the few days that elapsed before her interview with Il Duce. "I talked with Renato Ricci, attractive and, it seemed, beloved leader of Italian youth. He spoke of his faith in the totalitarian principles established by Mussolini for the education of the young people of his country. He said, 'They should have knowledge of their own health and strength, knowledge of military art, knowledge of their nation's history and political development.' He took me from floor to floor of an imposing building in which Italy's young men received two years of training as leaders, explaining their curriculum. It overlooked the Mussolini Forum with its huge sports arena surrounded by marble athletes of heroic size.

"I had an opportunity to confer with Professor D. S. Piccoli, author of "The Youth Movement in Italy,' who spoke at length of 'the discipline and self-control which prepare men and women for the tasks of peace and for the tests of war.' It had an ominous sound—the tests of war.

139

"One of my most vivid recollections is of a hot Sunday afternoon visit to an encampment of two thousand boys. Their tents were pitched on a pine-clad hill sloping down to the river Tiber, and before them lay the Eternal City. In talking with the boys through an interpreter I recognized how vital was their sense of identification with Italy's great past, but in Rome, as in Berlin, I was shocked by the intense, almost reckless emphasis on nationalism."

Maria Castellani was greatly disturbed by the worsening situation for Italy's professional women. The number of unfavorable government restrictions placed on their employment had increased at an alarming rate. She had worked hard to arrange Madesin's meeting with Mussolini, in the belief that, owing to Madesin's international standing, the encounter might well result in a reversal of this negative trend.

In the late afternoon of August 11, Madesin drove to the heavily guarded Palazzo Venezia. "I felt somewhat nervous," she wrote, "and perhaps understandably so, since I was about to face the world's most talked about man at that time, but the significance of his conquest of Ethiopia had begun to affect me. I felt angered and dismayed as much by his aggression as by the failure of such powerful nations as Britain and France to arrest it. However, the purpose of my meeting with Il Duce was still a valid one. With much ceremony, I was escorted first by one and then by another uniformed guard, finally arriving at my destination, the great Renaissance room where Benito Mussolini received his visitors—beautiful with its inlaid marble floor, Corinthian columns, magnificent ceiling. It was empty save for a massive desk at the far end with a visitor's chair beside it. No more impressive setting for this national leader could have been devised. Mussolini sat against the far wall behind his desk facing the entrance door. In walking, bravely as might be, the length of that sixty foot room, I was aware that he was evaluating the approaching visitor—his customary procedure, I had been told.

"Il Duce motioned me to be seated and at once asked why I had come to Rome in that period of great heat. 'To see you, Excellency, because you are—' But he did not let me finish. Shaking his finger before his face as though chiding me he said, 'Not interested, not interested.' Then he poured out a rapid torrent of questions. He wanted to know about my country, its leaders, the strength of the Communist Party, and he asked me who was the head of it in America. For the moment I could not remember. 'Ah,' he said, 'you do not recall his name. Then it is not important.' He wanted to know about our International Federation—its purpose, membership, affiliated countries. His English was good, his manner courteous but imperious.

"By this time I was talking easily with him, his interest in our conversation seeming no less than my own. After some twenty minutes he rose and walked with me down the length of that stately room. As we

140

reached the door, I spoke of peace. 'Peace without justice is impossible!' he said with vehemence. Then, with a brilliant smile, he bowed ceremoniously, kissed my hand in true European fashion and showed me out."

The audience had been an exciting and interesting experience for Madesin. For Maria Castellani it spelled "complete success." Commenting on it, years later, she said, perhaps too optimistically: "The effect was clearly evident in that thereafter more favorable agreements were made with the labor unions to which all professional workers, men and women, were obliged to belong. I would believe that certain orders were issued from the top. From that time on the rapid development of the Italian federation can largely be attributed to a change in the government's attitude toward our professional women which, I am sure, was the result of Madesin Phillips' brief interview with Mussolini and the account she gave him of the International Federation." On her part, Madesin took this flattering comment with more than a grain of salt, and, at all events, the course of history dragged down whatever gains the women had made, in Italy and in other dictatorships.

When Madesin returned from Europe, having urged the Board meeting in Paris to accept the invitation of the women of Hungary to hold the 1939 Triennial Congress in Budapest, she was determined to follow her natural inclination, which was to prefer hope to despair and to try to see light even in the advancing gloom. Now that her term of office as President of the National Council of Women was coming to an end, she planned to give all possible time and thought to the International Federation, so that, whatever the oncoming years might bring, its structure, at least, would be strong enough to uphold the membership.

The first practical step she had to take the moment she got back to New York was to find new offices for the International, since she would no longer have the use of the rooms in the Vanderbilt which she had arranged for the Council. The London office of the International had been closed with Dorothy Heneker's decision to return to Geneva. The situation looked rather dismal, but Madesin never seemed to run out of "Phillips' luck," or, more likely, she never ran out of ideas that brought it on. Her frankness in asking for favors was one of her assets, and again proved to be such when she called on the manager of the Biltmore Hotel in New York, seeking some arrangement to replace the Vanderbilt.

Declaring candidly that her organization had only a slim budget, she enumerated what she hoped the International might bring to the hotel while stating just as clearly what she believed it could not offer. She made such an impression on the manager that he said: "Every non-commercial organization has told us what an asset its occupancy would mean to us in meals, rooms, functions and much else, but rarely proving their case. You, instead, tell me what you cannot do, as well as what you merely hope you can do. We shall be glad to have you here." The rent for a fairly good-sized room with bath and all services was set at the unbelievable rate of one dollar per day. Why mention the figure? Because it remained unchanged for twenty-four years!

With the renewed vigor of the helpful Co-Ops to support her, Madesin settled down, as much as she ever could, to the detailed work of running the International's machinery. Gordon Holmes had at least relieved her of financial worries for the Federation, and the end of the year had brought a real surprise—Gordon Holmes, sending her a bank statement, said: "This can be regarded as a sort of Christmas present since it shows the famous £400 ($1,600) deficit well covered."

Already America was engulfed in a frantic presidential campaign and Madesin soon found herself in it up to her eyes. Speeches, mass meetings, the din of battle—to all of this she responded as a fire horse to a three-bell alarm. After Franklin Roosevelt had won his overwhelming victory at the polls, after several significant gains for human welfare had been secured, such as the TVA, social security measures or the banking reforms, Madesin, unlike the bulk of the electorate, did not lean back, oblivious to how much still remained to be done. The struggle for women's rights, of course, had to be kept up, since their gains had been minimal. She could pitch for them from the pages of *Pictorial Review* and from the endless number of platforms from which she was invited to speak, but the creation of the Rome-Berlin Axis, dramatically announced by Mussolini in November 1936, had caused an increasing urgency to creep into her words. At home and abroad there was unrest and ever more unrest. *Philsfolly,* where she could always 'unwind' and find refreshment for her spirit, seemed to become more and more inaccessible, because she had less and less time to spare.

Almost against her better judgment, that very fall Madesin had accepted a new commitment. Mary E. Woolley, Judge Florence Allen and others, were organizing a national body of some fifty social and civic leaders to serve as the Women's Cooperating Commission of the Federal Council of the Churches of Christ. She pleaded with Madesin to be one of these fifty members. The Commission's purpose was to bring the viewpoint of lay women to bear on the policies and programs of the Council of Churches. Since girlhood Madesin had believed profoundly in the importance of spiritual ideals and found it impossible to decline the invitation. Starting that autumn of 1936, she served fifteen years on the Commission.

Re-appraised after a few months, and from across an ocean, the images that Madesin's mind had captured and vividly retained of her experience in Germany and Italy were becoming more and more disturbing. The daily headlines only made matters worse. Yet, the great variety of men and women she met with and talked to almost every day in the course of many activities did not, on the whole, appear to share her apprehensions.

142

Thus, she looked forward to the summer of 1937 when the Board of the International was to meet in Stockholm. This was an excellent lookout point, Madesin believed, from which to study the nature and density of clouds in the skies over Europe.

The gathering in the Swedish capital produced one of the Federation's most dynamic programs. The sense of urgency was unmistakably present in Madesin's report when she said: "It is not difficult to understand why so many persons desire women to return to the home. Men want and need the salaries women earn. We are in a changing world where the old order is becoming disjointed. Higher mechanization can produce more of everything than we know how to distribute, yet millions of men, women and children are without adequate food, clothing, shelter or jobs. There is talk of war, as if such a tragedy could provide a solution for this problem, but where there is scarcity, human nature may be expected to reveal itself according to stark and primitive urges. Women must keep their sights high.

"In the daily struggle for a chance to earn a wage, the woman, as the younger and less firmly established economic factor, is obviously the point of attack. Women should not spend time complaining about this. Moreover, the attack is not primarily on women workers; it is part and parcel of the struggle between the strong and the weak, the entrenched and the newcomer, tradition and change. Discrimination, as we speak of it, is a relic of an outworn ideology which men as well as women must now be willing to replace. Far better would it be if thoughts, desires and ideals were translated into realistic and constructive action. We, as gainfully employed women, must find the courage, initiative and will to take the lead."

Madesin then proposed a "Three-Year Objective" aimed at four specific goals: a) the exposure of current fallacies relating to business and professional women; b) placing a larger number of qualified women in public office, c) placing a larger number of women in executive positions; d) making certain psychological adjustments within ourselves. Already from most of the countries represented had come surprisingly heartening reports of advances made in every field and a notable growth in membership. With the acceptance of the objective, the wish expressed in her message of welcome to Sweden by Alva Myrdal was already in part fulfilled. The well known Swedish sociologist had said: "May some working program and ideas come out of this meeting which will strengthen the thousands of anonymous women whom we serve."

Although it is probable that neither Madesin nor Alva Myrdal was aware of it, their encounter in Stockholm was to have far reaching effects because of the very deep friendship which grew between Madesin and both Gunnar and Alva, and because of Alva's later influence on the International Federation.

Slender, golden-haired and very youthful in appearance, it was difficult to believe that Alva Myrdal, in 1937, already a distinguished sociologist and author, was a notable force, not merely in the national politics and social movements of her own country, but one beginning to be noticed abroad as well.

From Sweden Madesin went on to England, to address the Soroptimist Convention at Harrogate, invited by Gordon Holmes. Madesin knew that the Board of Governors of that organization was recommending to its Convention that the Soroptimists assume the responsibility of organizing junior business and professional women's clubs all over England. It was a matter extensively discussed and, of course, of concern to the future of Madesin's Federation whose efforts to attract members in Great Britain might have been seriously curtailed. Madesin was also somewhat worried by the fact that, in her words she "knew how to speak to American women, but had no technique for a British audience." Gordon Holmes solved her problem in a flash: "Forget we are British and talk to us as though we were your own Americans." Throwing away her notes she did as Miss Holmes suggested. She also pointed out very deftly that Soroptimist Clubs only chose one or two members from any category of employment, which then left out scores of qualified women who were not, or could not, be included. She underscored the need for an organization, such as hers, serving all women. The response was warm and the following day, after a pleasant talk with Soroptimist leaders Madesin suggested a "gentleman's agreement": "You go ahead and form your junior business womens clubs. We will stay out of Great Britain for at least a certain period. But if you decide not to organize, you will then help us." It was so agreed and a few months later a message from England informed Madesin, "The ball is in your court." The Soroptimists were leaving the field to the International. It was quite a victory and, as a result of it, the Clubs soon established in Britain became a major stay of the International.

When Madesin sailed for home on the *Queen Mary,* she was accompanied by Gordon Holmes and by the General's charming young secretary, who were to be in the United States and Canada for six weeks. It was very hot in New York and Madesin immediately took them both to *Philsfolly.* To Gordon Holmes this was a very different holiday house from any she had known, lacking as it did, and by intention, the modern conveniences typical of sophisticated city life. She sat in the shade for long hours delighted to read Anthony Trollope, or talking over international affairs with Madesin. "She went with Marjory Lacey-Baker to market fascinated by the quaint country store," Madesin relates. "We enjoyed splashing in our little pool, but not so the General. Twice a day, morning and evening, we drove her five miles to the Puddingstone Inn in the village of Boonton that she might have a cold bath. It was more than the innkeeper could understand, to drive ten miles twice a day, and pay each time for a tub of cold water and a bath towel. Few who stayed at the inn that summer failed to hear the remarkable story of the big English lady and her ablutions. Her tea schedule, too, was a new experience for us. We always had afternoon tea, but drinking it before breakfast, 'early tea' as the British call it, and at ten in the evening—these were an innovation in our household."

After ten leisurely days it was time to return to the busy world. Both the General and Madesin were to address the Canadian Business and Professional Women's convention at Niagara Falls, Ontario, and the United States convention at Atlantic City. Miss Holmes made a great impression at both. Her reactions to the American event, she recorded, graphically, as follows:

"Atlantic City was my first American convention. I was stunned. An enormous auditorium lined with loud speakers. Thousands of delegates. Newspapers featuring the assembly as headline news, its motions, resolutions and amendments, its candidates for office and elections, its reports and programs. Photographers snapping 'the platform' and 'the floor' from all angles. Reporters and interviewers everywhere. . . .

"And the heat. One hundred in the shade, and no shade. And the noise, the bewildering variety of accents and voices. And the crowds, the state breakfasts and the midnight suppers. And the final banquet, two thousand or so sitting with the incredible courtesy of American audiences through hours of speech making. And when it was my time to wind up the banquet with yet another speech at ten minutes to midnight, still giving me enthusiastic applause."

During a business session of the Convention, Madesin presented a resolution which, though international in character, suddenly precipitated action directed at the U.S. Congress, and quickly made newspaper headlines. One such report of it said: "A scene of dramatic intensity developed when Lena Madesin Phillips arose in the rear of the Convention Hall and asked for recognition for the purpose of offering a resolution." This was granted and she read:

Whereas in response to a request from fifteen Governments, the League of Nations has placed on its agenda for the September Assembly of this year a proposal to incorporate in the League Covenant an Amendment for equality of rights for men and women. . . .
Be it resolved, that the National Federation of Business and Professional Women's Clubs expresses its approval of the above proposal and its appreciation of the forward-looking stand of the fifteen Governments which have brought this important and vital subject before the League.

"Her resolution was adopted by an overwhelming vote. Immediately a California delegate was on her feet to propose a second resolution on a subject long debated at conventions, voted and consistently defeated. 'Madam President, I want to follow Miss Phillips' resolution by moving that the National Federation of Business and Professional Women's Clubs express its approval of the proposal now before our own Congress known as the Equal Rights Amendment.' In rapid succession a number of delegates spoke, mainly in favor of the resolution, but some opposed—those who believed in protective legislation. Finally, according to the *Equal Rights* report, "scores of others were on their feet awaiting recognition when a demand was made for the vote. The voice of the convention was raised in one resounding 'aye,' not a single 'no' was recorded. . . . Equality marches on!"

For the women who, in 1938, wanted Equal Rights inserted in the U.S. Constitution this seemed a first step to victory. But the women who were striving for the same victory in the 70's it was clear that the militants of thirty years before had made little headway on Capitol Hill.

Before the General went home she had a long string of conferences with her Wall Street banking associates who sought her opinion on the European money situation. Then she wound up her American visit by driving with Madesin to Hyde Park to have tea with Mrs. Roosevelt. She found her "simple and charming, dispensing iced tea amid secretaries and dogs. I am always too overawed inwardly to get much out of these brief encounters myself, unless there is some immediate point of contact. So I watched Madesin settle herself with easy informality at the end of Mrs. Roosevelt's sofa obviously delighted to have this opportunity to discuss world affairs with the President's wife for whom she had the greatest admiration."

After many leisurely discussions with the General on how to finance the International on an expanding and continuing basis, Madesin was persuaded to send an appeal to all her friends, professional associates and acquaintances—more than a thousand names—explaining the aims of the International and its financial needs. It was a personal message written on her own note paper. "The replies," Madesin commented, "made me feel as if I were dead and flowers were being sprinkled on my grave, but it was the best year financially we had ever had." Later that year 'Phillips' Luck' knocked again at her door. The daughter of Ruth Hannah McCormick Sims, one of the first American women elected to Congress, had once asked Madesin's advice on how to dispose of two inheritances of which she wished to keep only a share. As one on the list of worthy organizations Madesin had included the International, but without underscoring it. In September 1937 a letter from Katrina McCormick said: "First because I have tremendous admiration and respect for you and, second, although I am not completely sold on the cause, because I know that the working women need guidance today and that takes money, I am having my lawyer send you a check for $5,000. I wish it could be larger."

146

Madesin replied: "I could weep for joy thinking of what your $5,000 will do for our program. You are good to write you wished the sum were larger. My dear, nothing in all the world looks quite so big to me as your gift—not the Empire State Building, the Rocky Mountains or President Roosevelt in the eyes of his loyal henchmen." The gift was set aside in a special fund to carry out the Three-Year Objective which was already proving its effectiveness.

Early in 1937 in a speech in Chicago, President Roosevelt had dramatically told the American people that their nation had a "rendezvous with destiny." It was his first effort to make the country realize the serious threat against democratic institutions and against peace already then confronting mankind. Even a cursory survey produced a shocking picture: Mussolini, a despot no longer benevolent, had conquered Ethiopa. The position of Austria was ever more precarious. The Republic established in Spain was desperately trying to defend itself from Francisco Franco and from the German and Italian planes supporting his advance. The Japanese were settling themselves on China's back. The League of Nations was paralyzed by the division of interests revealed in its failure to stand by Ethiopia and by its almost chronic indecision. But Roosevelt's speech awakened only very few to the realities of the situation.

To Madesin the continuing apathy was frightening, yet she could see reasons for it. "Those of us who read and hear of great tragedies occurring in distant countries," she wrote, "are apt to see them as isolated events silhouetted against time's horizon. It is hard for us to realize that even as life goes on, disaster strikes."

With the autumn, relief to Madesin's troubled spirit arrived in the persons of Gunnar and Alva Myrdal, coming to the States for a brief visit which was destined to last almost five years. Gunnar Myrdal, then just under forty, and whose looks could have earned him a living any time as a motion picture star, was a professor of Social Economics, a Senator in the Swedish Parliament and a scholar with a broad international reputation. He had been booked to deliver the Godkin Lectures at Harvard, but while he and Alva were planning this visit, the Carnegie Foundation had invited him to come to New York to direct a comprehensive study of the Negro in American Life. This was the study which resulted in Myrdal's classic work, "The American Dilemma, the Negro Problem and Modern Democracy" published in 1944, later updated by its author and constantly reprinted in English and several other languages. Alva Myrdal was also in America much of the time and, as a Vice President of the International Federation, her contacts with Madesin were frequent, in addition to the many occasions when Gunnar and other likeminded friends joined them for long evenings of soul-searching discussions.

The date of the Triennial Congress in Budapest was approaching, even as the situation in Europe was visibly deteriorating. On March 12th,

1938, Hitler's Brown Shirts had moved into Austria, seized the government, ousted Chancellor Kurt von Schussnigg, stricking terror all around them. The Austrian Federation had been hurriedly disbanded, its records destroyed. A newly formed club in Berlin had ceased to exist. In Czechoslovakia, where Conrad Henlein, the voice of Hitler, had been agitating for the return of the Sudetenland to Germany, fears were widespread and mounting.

Before going to Budapest, Madesin was due in Edinburgh for a ten-day Conference of the International Council of Women of which she had been elected a Vice-President. This was the occasion on which Lady Aberdeen gave Madesin the famous Victorian picture of herself that delighted the visitors to *Philsfolly*. In London, where Madesin made a brief stop, Gordon Holmes joined the traveling party, and over dinner startled the Americans by remarking that England already had a gas mask for every person over two years of age. That was how seriously the international situation had deteriorated. But it was in Vienna that Madesin became fully aware of how bad it really was.

Her short stop there was to see her dear friend, Dr. Marianne Beth, early founder of one of the International's most prosperous Clubs. The Austrian federation had ceased to exist, of course, but this was as nothing next to the fact that, owing to some remote Jewish ancestry, Frau Beth had been compelled to divorce her celebrated and beloved husband. They saw each other clandestinely at considerable risk. "I had not known all the facts," wrote Madesin, "but I did know that all was not well with her. She met us at the railway station. The change in her was startling, now a thin, dark, weary woman, but still full of a high philosophy. She took us for tea to a small inconspicuous hotel. The streets were empty, shops boarded up, Nazi flags displayed everywhere. We who had known the real Vienna felt like crying. In an inner court at the hotel she and I sat at a table close to the wall so that we might talk privately, and my companions at one adjoining. When we were seated the waiters asked from which countries we had come, saying they would like to place our flags on our tables—obviously a device to discover our nationalities.

"In this ominous atmosphere my friend and I talked as best we could. I learned that it was a dire necessity for her to leave the country, even if she must go without funds, for at that time nobody was permitted to take out more than the equivalent of twelve dollars. Her son and her daughter, accused of anti-Nazi student activities, had already escaped. If Dr. Beth could get away it seemed likely that later her husband, a distinguished professor of theology at the University, could more easily leave alone. She told me much of the incredible indignities and hardships which everyone was suffering. She said that 10,000 committed suicide in the first month after the German occupation.

148

"Suddenly I saw something on the wall by my side—a reflected light. It was mid-afternoon and I was curious about it. It danced up and down and around, like some eerie sprite. In reality it was nothing so playful. It was a photographer, taking snapshots of us for the Nazi files, writing down a description of how we looked and what we did, and watching our movements, perhaps even trying to determine what we were talking about. For me, fresh from America where the rumors which we had heard of cruel treatment and atrocities seemed almost unbelievable, this was a revealing experience.

"Marianne accompanied us to the station to bid us good-by and I realized she believed that this might be our last farewell. Gordon Holmes, who writes of this incident in her autobiography, remembers that I said to Marianne, 'I shall see you soon in America. We shall meet again in New York.' Such a farewell, the General comments, 'was almost cruel since Miss Phillips must have realized the impossibility of rescuing a woman of Dr. Beth's known position on internationalism'."

Gordon Holmes was mistaken. Six months later, Madesin was at a New York pier waiting for Marianne Beth. She had done a great deal to get her out of Austria and brave Marianne, ultimately reunited with her family, made a notable career for herself in the world of letters, as an American citizen. But she and her family were far from being the only victims of Nazi cruelty to be rescued and given a new start by Madesin's efforts. A folder, concealed from most eyes, contained letters and forms Madesin prepared and pledged herself to fulfill, in response to heartbreaking calls for mercy from across the Atlantic. Soon, most of her appeals for contributions ceased to be for Federation programs. They were for the survival of women whose faith in those very programs had created the Federation. It was always of the courage of those who finally set foot on American shores that Madesin spoke, rarely, unless it became strictly necessary, of how they had been helped to break away from the bonds that would have destroyed them.

There were many absences from the Budapest Congress. Not only the Austrians and the Germans, but also the usually strong Italian delegation, and others who dared not leave their countries at that time. Registrations at the Congress were only 171, 18 of them members of the Board, but thanks to the ability of the Hungarian organizers the visitors of note were numerous.

Madesin had looked forward to revisiting the enchanting capital of Hungary but, here too as earlier in Vienna, she could not shake off the pall of uneasiness that hung so heavily in the air. The hostess federation, however, accomplished a miracle, allowing no shadow to fall across the meetings or the entertainment. Madesin kept remembering "the masks the Hungarian women wore just for our sakes."

"Whatever the undercurrents," she recalled, "everyone feasted their eyes on the picturesque setting of the hotel where we met. It faced the Danube across from the old city of Buda crowned by the Royal Palace, the Houses of Parliament, the Coronation Church and the Fishermen's Bastion, floodlit at night with stupendous grace. From our windows we could hear the haunting strains of gypsy music floating up from the cafés along the promenade below, but we could also see, chugging slowly past, the river boats flying the swastika."

The beauty of the setting was well matched by the brilliance of the formal evening opening in the hotel's vast convention hall. His Royal Highness, the Archduke Josef Ferenc, honored the ceremony by his presence and by an address, obviously appreciated by the gaily attired audience. Delegates were welcomed by Mme. Lilla Melczer, Member of Parliament and Federation president and by Mr. Karoly Lamotte, the city's deputy mayor, England's Caroline Haslett introduced Madesin who had worked on her speech with unusual care. There were certain points she intended to make and certain ideas she was determined to present, yet she had to avoid anything which might have started a controversy dangerous for the Hungarians and delegates from countries geographically too close to Hitler's Germany for comfort. Concisely but effectively, she traced the factors of social progress through the ages, from the democratic ideas of the Greeks to the Christian doctrine of the Middle Ages, from the humanities of the Renaissance to the demand for individual rights that sparked the French and American revolutions. She pointed to the effects of the machine on society, to the changed meaning of production and consumption and, finally, to the two political concepts gradually dividing the world: the authoritarian system in which individual welfare becomes subservient to the interests of the state; the libertarian, holding that the state exists only as a safeguard for the individual.

While there was attentive silence in the hall, with some heads nodding assent from time to time, the recommendations Madesin set forth, still so strikingly pertinent today, were then probably neither welcomed nor understood by many who lacked the vision to follow her so far.

"In my view," she said, "future safety and well-being depend on our acceptance of the following conclusions. One, that international trade, international migrations, international communication, affecting ideas as well as materials and people, have wiped out national boundaries—the world is now a unit, in which the sanity and welfare of each nation is reflected in every other nation. Two, that well-being and opportunity must be experienced not only by every nation, but by all the people of every nation. Three, that most familiar concepts, traditions and accustomed ways of thought and of action, having lost automatic validity, each must be tested anew in relation to present needs. Men and women must be given, at least,

150

sufficient knowledge to decide for themselves, irrespective of the past but mindful of the future. Four, human life is to be lived in a reasonable expectation of happiness here on earth. Whatever the present power of appeal of church and religion may be, man is no longer willing to think only in terms of future, after-life, rewards. He is asking, indeed demanding, satisfactions here and now. Five, there exists a universal desire for peace. Six, we now have a realization that the advent of the machine, although promising undreamed of leisure and well-being for mankind, makes necessary the re-shaping of the existing order and we have not yet worked out a new pattern. How to achieve bread as well as beauty, jobs as well as justice for all people, is the question with which every nation is struggling today. Peace and the survival of civilization rest upon the kind of answer we may find.

"What, then, is the part of women, particularly business and professional women in finding a solution to the problem of change? I believe it to be twofold: each woman, as a citizen, must bring to the national policy of her own country the contribution of forward-looking and constructive thought followed by determined action. Secondly, each woman must dedicate herself to protect and promote the interests of all other women in business and the professions.

"We invite the women of every nation to participate in this effort, and every man who is in sympathy with it to lend us his moral support. The International Federation stands for goodwill towards all peoples and takes active interest in every problem affecting business or professional women. Even more importantly, it views the present chaotic condition of the world as being the last dark hour before the coming of day and pledges it all—whatever the cost—to the brightness of that day."

Warm applause marked the conclusion of Madesin's speech, but the important reaction to it was manifested later, when men and women in considerable number came to speak to her, raising questions which showed deep concern with one or another of the points she had made. At that moment Madesin no longer had any doubts about the extent to which Hungarians, especially, were fearful of what the immediate future would bring.

But once the business sessions were over each day, "delightful and unique entertainment seemed to fill every available moment, and the lively ways of the Hungarians prevailed. The most brilliant of these functions was a reception, given by the Minister of the Interior and Mme. Fischer at the celebrated *Salle des Cérémonies* of his Ministry. The uniforms of the Hungarian officers with their glittering decorations, the women's colorful evening gowns, and the presence of a large contingent of the diplomatic corps carried one back to a vision of pre-World War I *insouciance*."

151

The most serious note of all was sounded when the Board of Directors met after the Congress, to discuss, not theory or policy, but day to day practice. A new International Treasurer was appointed to replace Mrs. Ellen Libby Eastman, resigning after five years because of the pressure of her own business. Her successor, Miss Isabelle Claridge of the United States, had been a speaker at the Congress and, in her professional capacity, was treasurer of two million-dollar coal mining corporations, as well as treasurer of the United States Federation. After this, the Board being of the opinion that the international situation might possibly deteriorate further in the next two or three years, voted to authorize the creation of an Executive Committee with full powers to act for the International in the event of emergency conditions. The members were Lena Madesin Phillips, president, Mrs. Alva Myrdal, vice-president and Miss Claridge, treasurer; all of them, including Mrs. Myrdal, residents of the United States, the country least likely to be affected by whatever might occur in Europe. It was fortunate that this action was taken in 1938, because by September 1st, 1939, Hitler's armies had invaded Poland and World War II had broken out in the Old World.

Reception and Board Meeting in the Golden Hall of Stockholm's City Hall, given by the city of Stockholm for the International Federation in June, 1937

13.   Freedom Engulfed

All through the winter of 1938 and into the spring of 1939, the mud flats across the Long Island Sound from Manhattan were being transformed into the ironic fantasy of international unity and progress that was New York's World Fair of 1939–40. Imposing structures rose to house displays from nations great and small. Fountains played and banners waved, but on the wall of a fairly inconspicuous white building, the words on a plaque reaveled the futility of all the flags and fountains and brassy publicity heralding the World of Tomorrow. Inside were exhibits from Czechoslovakia, outside, these words: "The Czech and Slovak people are victims of a great international crime . . . an unbearable imposition on their sacred rights. People of the Democracies!—to all right-thinking men and women everywhere I repeat the motto of my beloved country, TRUTH PREVAILS. Eduard Bénès."

The crime against Czechoslovakia had been committed in 1938. On September 29th, Chamberlain, Daladier, Mussolini and Hitler had met in Munich, ostensibly to negotiate Hitler's persistent demand for the surrender of Czechoslovakia's Sudetenland, but in reality, and without inviting Czechoslovakia to the negotiating table, they were prepared to capitulate to Germany's Fürher. No sooner was the nefarious pact signed, than the Sudetenland was annexed to Germany, while Hungary and Poland took their share of the spoils of treason, moving into Czechoslovak territory from their respective boundaries. In March of 1939 Hitler invaded what remained of the proud and independent republic, destroying its hard-won freedom.

September 30, 1938, the day when the Munich Pact was officially signed, became one of the most shameful dates in the history of the so-called free and democratic Western world. Mussolini's take-over of Ethiopia had paved the way for it.

Before the pact was signed and their country's fate sealed, the vast majority of the Czech population had refused to yield to despair or even fear. Women's organizations, better knit than others, immediately closed their ranks and began to fight to retain independence by every means possible. Senator Plaminkova, influential in politics and powerful because

153

of the enormous following she commanded, immediately appealed to Caroline Haslett, then President of the British Federation: "We trust that you, who feel with us in this tragic hour, will use your influence without delay in every way you see fit. It is necessary to act immediately." The British Federation did react immediately, sending telegrams to the Prime Minister and other members of the government involved in the Munich meeting. It also secured the support of other major women's organizations in the country. All proved useless. The crime against decency had been committed in the name of peace: Chamberlain and Daladier returned to their respective capitals to find them decked in flags, as for a victory. The women of Czechoslovakia spoke out again. This time it was not an appeal but a dreadful, implicit indictment of those who had sold them out. They said:

"Czechoslovakia is losing frontiers which have protected her for a thousand years, consecrated by blood and life. . . . Abandoned as we were, we had to follow the joint orders issued us by friends and enemies together, who dictated conditions worse than those imposed on a defeated country. Women of the rest of the world, who are now so happy because peace has been maintained, while you were raising flags of victory in your streets, we were trying to help thousands of children and mothers driven from their homes, trying to find substitutes for their wage earning men and for the security of their own four walls. All of us in Czechoslovakia were ready to defend our country's borders. We were then, as we still are, convinced that we would have saved the peace of the world for a much longer time than has been done now."

Two weeks before Munich, Adolph Hitler, satanically stirring up public anger in the Sudetenland that would later be used to justify his actions, had broadcast a violent denunciation of Czechoslovakia and of Eduard Bénès, its president. "Fearless, in the dedicated spirit of her country's leader," Madesin writes, "Frantiska Plaminkova had refuted his lying statements in an open letter. This was not her only act of defiance. She would say and do much else before the war was over, ready to pay the price. When the Commission to determine the new boundaries of Czechoslovakia was meeting in Berlin, she appealed to statesmen and to organized women in many countries to send protests to influential persons and governments everywhere, hoping to stop the hand moving in Berlin. 'We want our children to live and work in their own country,' she pleaded, 'we want to remain a small but independent nation. We beg you to save our families from having to become part of a foreign nation.' Reading these poignant words in New York, I realized how helpless an individual could be at such a time. All the pleas and all the pressures had not abated the destructive tide.

"Vividly, I saw 'Plam' as if she had been before my very eyes. I saw

154

her passionately in love with justice, with right and with her country. I clearly heard her rapid speech, part Czech, part French, part English, so uniquely hers that we said she 'spoke Plam.' I sensed again her total courage, her total loyalty. We cabled her our loving sympathy, offering whatever help we could give. But I knew that this, again, was not enough. Very soon, however, an opportunity to be of some help came my way."

Brackett Lewis, director of the Masaryk Institute in New York, walked into her *Pictorial Review* office with a request from 'Plam.' Confirming all that Madesin had read of the thousands of families being torn from their Sudetenland homes, he spoke of the serious economic problem created by their resettlement in other Czech regions. They were, themselves, striving to relieve the pressure on their fellow countrymen, by working at their handicrafts and trying to overcome the hardships that made the mere fact of being alive such a tragic problem. Senator Plaminkova, Brackett said, was hoping to find a Christmas market for these goods in the United States. She had appealed to the Masaryk Institute first. Several department stores had been approached, but it was already November and too late for anything commercial to be organized, despite their interest and goodwill. Madesin said she would try to set up a bazaar, somewhere in the city, to sell the work of the dispossessed Czechs.

Day after day, in bitter cold weather, Madesin and Mrs. Ruza Stuerm of the Masaryk Institute, tramped through mid-town Manhattan, looking for a vacant store. At last one was found on Forty-third Street, just west of Fifth Avenue, in an excellent location. They were given its use without charge.

"Enlisting the help of other women's organizations," Madesin explained, "we secured volunteer saleswomen to staff it, while our own Co-Ops took care of countless other necessary details. An honorary committee of very prominent women proved invaluable and included Mrs. Franklin D. Roosevelt. Mme. Mila Vegrova, president of our Czech Federation, arrived on the same long-delayed boat that brought the crates and bales of goods. Excitement mounted as time grew short. Everybody helped. Long tables and other paraphernalia were assembled, brilliant, tricolored posters were provided by artists, announcing the Christmas sale 'For the Homeless of Czechoslovakia, under the auspices of the International Federation of Business and Professional Women.' Buyers from major department stores volunteered to work into the night pricing the pottery, glassware, wooden toys, embroideries, costume jewelry and many other delicate and lovely articles for which the Czech craftsmen were famous.

"On December 14th we opened our doors, with former Governor Alfred E. Smith, an officer of the Czechoslovak Relief Committee, presiding

155

at the ceremony. Between ten and seven every day the dollars rolled in. When Mrs. Roosevelt, coming up from Washington, informed us that she would include the Bazaar in the day's schedule, the place was mobbed by shoppers who reduced the stock to naught. We closed that night— December 21st—ready to send 'Plam' $2,500. I knew it was little enough as compared to the need, but at least we had not failed her, her staunch principles and her stout heart."

"Two or three Co-Ops and Gordon Holmes spent the Christmas and New Year holidays at *Philsfolly*, blanketed with snow. The General had arrived towards the close of the bazaar for a three weeks' visit. Picking her up at the pier, we settled her at the Biltmore Hotel and returned later for dinner. I have never quite gotten over the fact that the Co-Ops and I did not manage to get through that first dinner with her without a violent argument over Munich. Like so many Britishers at that time, Gordon Holmes felt that appeasement was better than war. We could not agree. Too late, she came around."

Anxiety over world tension was reflected in the theme chosen for International Night 1939: 'What Should be the Function of Women's International Organizations in a World Crisis?' Alva Myrdal's comment could well have been written today: "Let women, through all their international relations, work for factual information and clear thinking in foreign affairs. But let their main function be to specialize in that social and cultural progress which everybody else seems to forget. Let them be the caretakers of a democratic tomorrow—in spite of all the threats to democracy today."

That year, and for many years thereafter, an International Prayer, written by Madesin at the request of an American member, was read on International Night in thousands of Clubs in America and abroad:

O God, Thou who dost acknowledge all people as Thy children, grant that we this night and ever after may partake of Thy all-embracing love and understanding. Lift us from the isolation of our selfishness. Heal us of the prejudice born of ignorance. Open our eyes and our hearts to the oneness of mankind. Bless and protect our members who dwell in many far-off lands yet with us are united in a common cause.

Since like younger sisters they follow in our footsteps, teach us with Thy wisdom, for their sakes as for our own. Grant that we may not betray their trust in us. Help us to remember that from their distant shores our own forefathers came and that we have found peace and plenty here. Tell us once again that Thou dost expect much of those to whom much has been given.

Father of all, we thank Thee for the service and the fellowship of our International Federation. Give strength, wisdom and greatness of spirit to its leaders. Drench the hearts of its members with Thine own compassion for the sufferings of all peoples. Make effective our efforts for a better world. Show us the path to peace and in it help us to walk steadfastly and with courage.

Grant that in this hour we may find Thee and each other in righteousness and in the fullness of eternal beauty.

Amen.

Earlier that February, the sudden folding up of *Pictorial Review* brought a drastic change in Madesin's life. It had been a substantial source of income and the millions of readers she had reached had rewarded her generously with their response. Of course she would continue to write, because she loved to write, but without assurance of publication. After her death, in a drawer were found satirical essays, short stories, an unfinished autobiography and the beginnings of a History of the International Federation, on all of which she had worked when time allowed and the spirit moved her. She had been repeatedly requested to write the History, but to someone who asked her when she would finish it, she had replied: "I count it more important to serve the living than to record the past, just now. I'll work on it seriously the day I retire." That day never came.

The demise of *Pictorial Review* coincided with a new set of demands on Madesin's time, energy and resources from European women affected by the war situation. Predominant and urgent were the pleas coming in daily for help in escaping from intolerable political and economic conditions. A long and pitiful story, just beginning to unfold—it was the sort of help that required an infinite amount of careful work, rather than mere money. Madesin added it to a schedule of speaking engagements that took her across the continent in winter and spring of that year, finally leading her to a hospital for X-rays and observation before April was out. The diagnosis was a gastric ulcer which was to flare up for the rest of her life, whenever she was under too much stress or sheer physical fatigue. Her resilience, however, was extraordinary and a period of rigid diet and considerable rest returned her, renewed, to the complexities of that crucial year. In the middle of the war, when she was again obliged to yield temporarily to an attack, she explained to a friend: "Every time Hitler invades another country I go into the hospital for a bout with that ulcer of mine."

Despite such handicaps, she was completing plans for the meeting of the International Board that summer in Trondheim, Norway. Before that, with the plight of the refugees almost obsessively on her mind, she went to the Convention of the U.S. Federation in Kansas City to speak, for the first time, of "the part which members of the National Federation could play in helping to orient business and professional colleagues from other lands who have fled their homes in such appalling circumstances." She recommended assisting them as a definite part of the program of international relations in every state. The American women, shocked by facts they had not known before, or not fully evaluated, and moved by the thought of what other women, so similar to them, were experiencing because of a mere accident of birth, pledged support and went to work as best they could.

A week before sailing for Norway, Madesin went back to Kentucky, flattered and happy to be receiving an honorary degree from her own University, but sad at heart because she could not share the occasion with the one person who would have appreciated it to the full—her father. Twenty-two years had passed since she had been the first woman graduated with honors from that University's School of Law, and many more since the day when a starry-eyed girl from a country town had started off for New York City in search of Tin-Pan Alley. If physical semblance had been altered by the inconsiderateness of time, not much had changed within her. Her old determination to succeed in whatever she undertook, regardless of the cost to herself, had perhaps toughened, although the intimacy she had developed with an infinitely vaster world of ideas and people had mellowed her spirit, adding tolerance to her once reckless passion for justice.

The event at Lexington developed into an overwhelming homecoming affair, with more invitations from old friends and relatives and from new admirers than Madesin could possibly contend with in two days. Requested by Sarah G. Blanding, Dean of Women, she spoke at the luncheon for graduates to an audience of six hundred seniors, alumni and faculty. Later, in the beauty of a southern evening, she walked in the long procession to the platform, escorted by Dr. William James Hutchins, then retiring as president from Berea College, and father of Chicago University's prestigious leader who was among the guests.

"It was a moment both proud and exciting," she wrote, "when the citation was read and the hood, lined with the blue and white of my Alma Mater, was placed on my shoulders."

Looking out over many faces she knew, and later, after the ceremonies were concluded, shaking older hands than hers belonging to simple people from Nicholasville who had made the trip probably, she felt, because they had loved her father, Madesin was suddenly seized by homesickness. For more than twenty years she had been gone from Kentucky, from its hills, its people, its almost primitive simplicity of reaction to events and its warmth—an immense warmth. In that moment, an overpowering need for all this had come upon her, making her want to toss off her hood and gown and rush back to the place where she was

158

born. How thick or how substantial, she wondered, had been the layers of concern with public causes, the walls of emotional self-sufficiency, upon which she had built her life for nearly a quarter of a century? How real was something that could break apart to the roots at the touch of a wrinkled hand, at the sight of a familiar landscape, at the sound of a familiar greeting? Vehemently she gulped down a huge lump in her throat and smilingly accepted congratulations from a little group of New York friends who had come all the way to Lexington for the occasion. The well-built structures that had cracked open went back into place, giving her their accustomed support, but she never felt certain that they might not be fissured again—no telling when or why.

June had been warm in Kentucky; not so in Norway. But the chill she felt in Trondheim was not from the climate. It was a warning from her bones that the gigantic storm was just about to break. It broke on September 1st, when Hitler's armies invaded Poland. It struck Norway, eight months later, on April 9, 1940, when the Nazis came by sea. However, for that International Board Meeting, in June, the Norwegian women, like their Hungarian counterparts, had probably donned masks to make their visitors feel at ease. And to a great extent the visitors did. Voting members present were a bare thirteen, from only nine countries. The other 150 were observers and visitors, mostly from Scandinavia and Britain, with a small group from the United States who were going on a tour after the meeting.

"Mme. Plaminkova was with us," reports Madesin, "but no longer a Senator. We had sent her what she needed for expenses because she could bring no money out of Czechoslovakia. It was comforting and inspiring to have her and I think she drew us all closer together. Looking back on that meeting, I marvel at how much was accomplished in the last year before the war."

The British Federation worked successfully with its own government for changed legislation and great representation for women on all government committees and councils. The Canadian Federation, counting its work with refugees as "a practical gesture in international co-operation" was not only active, but also very generous with funds. A notable achievement of a strictly national character, was a tablet placed at the entrance to the Senate Chamber, honoring the five Canadian women who, gaining recognition for women as 'persons' under the British North American Act, had made women eligible for appointment to the Senate.

The National Federation of the United States was able to reports its largest membership: 1575 clubs with 70,000 members, representing 400 of the 500 occupations then open to women in the United States. It had conducted a successful national campaign to defeat or arrest the onslaught of bills in state legislatures prohibiting or restricting the employ-

159

ment of married women. Finland had conducted a vigorous campaign for women candidates. Its president, Anni Viopio, had been nominated to stand for Parliament. The Swedish Federation had made intensive efforts to increase the number of women in Parliament as in municipal and town councils, scoring a 72% increase in the number of women office holders. In collaboration with other, non-political groups, it had formed a civilian defense committee to organize women for emergency jobs, preparing them for the demands of war. The Stockholm Club has also built a modern apartment house to suit the needs of business and professional women, married as well as single.

Norway, on its part, had forced the withdrawal of a proposed bill in Parliament which would have impaired the status of women in the postal service, and a victory for women was scored in a decision of the Supreme Court which forbade the dismissal of any working person without proven reason. The Polish Federation had been influential in the election of three women to the Senate, including its own president, Mme. Szelagowska. Similar success was achieved in municipal election in Warsaw. The most poignant and perhaps the most comprehensive program of the Polish Federation was the mobilization of women for defense. The Hungarian Federation, in the very heart of the Central European turmoil, had also fitted its program to the nation's most pressing need: all qualified members had trained for air defense or other forms of service.

Italy, where the political situation was totally controlled, had reported gains only in the cultural field, such as the appointment of women as chief executives of the country's two major public libraries, in Rome and Florence. A woman archaeologist had been appointed head of an important expedition sponsored by the Fascist government. Two Australian Clubs had devoted themselves to working for refugees from Europe who had reached their shores. The nucleus of a Federation had been constituted in New Zealand and in Rangoon, Burma, a Club had been formed.

"In the course of my report," Madesin wrote, "I spoke of the great political changes all around us, adding that it was not easy to see the splendid branches which we had in Austria and Czechoslovakia suddenly broken off. 'Plam' jumped to her feet, correcting me: 'The Czechoslovakian branch still exists,' she declared and sat down. I quickly acknowledged her correction, thanking her. I knew that she had wanted to show us all how carefully we had to speak to avoid making matters worse in certain countries, or, even more significantly, to avoid bringing punishment on individual members.

"Referring to the Executive Committee in New York and to its powers, I requested the Board of Directors to authorize its continuance for another year. Tense as the situation was even then, probably none of us quite realized that this simple request would keep the International Federation alive and effective for seven years, until the Board could meet again. At the final session we heard from Mrs. J. Borden Harriman, U.S. Minister to Norway who, in her vivid and stimulating way sounded another note of encouragement. 'I am not discouraged by the allegedly limited progress women have made,' she said, 'nor am I disturbed by what some people call their apathy. Men are much more inclined to take a hopeless attitude about a situation that needs remedying than are women. A woman's slogan is quite likely to be: 'It must be done, so it *can* be done.'

"Earlier, we had had a session that resulted in what was for me, one of the most anxious moments. Alva Myrdal's excellent analysis of the 'fallacies' used to justify lower pay for women had been presented in her behalf by Mrs. Nyblom of Sweden and Senator Plaminkova had led the discussion that followed it. At the end 'Plam' summed up the debate in these words: "Woman can render her best service to her family and to mankind only if she is free, if she is recognized as a human being, privileged to work out her own individual destiny." Immediately after the meeting, greatly agitated, 'Plam' came to my hotel room. She was sure that there had been a spy in the audience who had telephoned back to her country or to Germany an adverse report on her comments. I tried to calm her, but she would not be convinced. Finally, I urged her not to return to Prague, but to go to Britain or America instead. She shook her head with determination and, with one of her characteristic gestures, sweeping out her arm as though to encompass a great number of persons, responsibilities or cares, she said: 'I cannot, too many hanging on me. I must return.'—and left the room quietly, her head high."

Senator Plaminkova said nothing more of her suspicions. She participated in all the remaining sessions; listened to all reports often nodding her approval, especially when Gordon Holmes named Czechoslovakia as one of nineteen out of twenty-five countries which had made its payments to the Federation treasury; she voted to accept Caroline Haslett's invitation to hold the 1940 Board Meeting in London; she attended every luncheon and every tea and, at the final banquet, laughed heartily with the others at an engaging satire, representing a League of Nations of the year 1999, its assembly composed entirely of women discussing the economic status of men.

"The last day," writes Madesin, "standing beside the taxi which was to take 'Plam' to the train, we exchanged a few more words. When I took her hand saying good-bye and looked into her eyes, I saw the clear premonition that this was our last farewell. Her eyes haunted me, intermittently, all through the night. Twice, I got out of bed and began to get dressed, trying to work out in my mind how I could catch up with her, before she crossed the Czech border. The urge to act—to save her—was

161

very strong, but something else within me, that was even stronger, said: 'She will never turn back, never.' The inner voice prevailed. I did not leave my room. A year or so later, in Prague, she was thrown into prison without the knowledge of anyone who might have tried to plead for her."

When the first vague reports of her arrest reached New York but could not be ascertained, suddenly those in the Biltmore office who knew her, could no longer bear to look at a snapshot of her in Trondheim, pinned on the bulletin board. In it, Madesin was shown reading her report from the center of a long table. 'Plam' sat at one end, her face serene but determined and, next to her, the plain felt hat she always wore.

"Fortunately, the Trondheim meeting also had its moments of hilariousness," Madesin recalled. One of them had to do with an unscheduled trip which Madesin, Helen Havener and Marjory Lacey-Baker took because of Gordon Holmes. When the Board Meeting was over these three had spent many hours going over figures and accounts when, finally, Gordon Holmes suggested that they all take a taxi ride with her to get some fresh air and enjoy another look at the old city.

"Presently," writes Madesin, "we were driving along a very dense, dark woodland, beautiful as only such woodlands can be in far northern climates. I remarked casually that one might even see a reindeer lurking between the tall thick greenery. This seemed to put an idea in Gordon Holmes' head. Suddenly she was consumed by a passion to see a reindeer and wondered where we might go on an excursion to find a herd of them. By the time we returned to the hotel, she had convinced us that we must go where we would see reindeer before we left Norway. Upon inquiring, she found that in June reindeer depart into the far north, congregating in the wild woodland beyond Narvik, on the Norwegian coast above the Arctic Circle. That was all the General needed to know.

"Immediately Marjory and Helen were instructed to obtain transportation for the four of us on one of the few small steamers which went in and out of the fjords for mail, passengers and freight, once or twice a week."

Getting accommodations to suit the General proved almost impossible, but whenever she made an appearance, young men in travel bureaus became capable of working miracles.

"It was a wonderful trip," Madesin reported. "We put in at various small towns along those dramatic, indescribable Norwegian fjords. Norway's grapevine system must have been in top form, because all of a sudden, one day as I stood at the rail of the boat looking down on a dock, I spotted a small group of women who, somehow, looked like business and professional women. They glanced up, calling 'Pheelips? Pheelips? Mees Pheelips?' and we were immediately among friends. At Svelvaer that evening, where there was to be a stop of an hour or so, another group of

162

club members appeared, ready to take us to a hotel where rooms had been engaged. Over wine and cakes one of them, who spoke very good English, told us all about the little town, the winter season with the big cod fisheries and fishermen coming from all parts of Norway. 'The harbor,' she said, 'is like a great forest of masts. The boats make a great noise when they go out at six in the morning. You should see them at sea in the struggle for life. You should see them returning in the evening, when a heaven of stars seems to come out of the dark, nearer and nearer!' The long cold winters, the endless nights and the isolation may have been very hard, but these women had captured the essence of beauty and poetry in all that lay around them.

"At last we came to Narvik, where we were to find the great herds of reindeer, perhaps even Santa Claus himself. But they were not there. We must go further, towards Sweden. We traveled by train, looking out of the windows, seeking reindeer or even Eskimos. We crossed the very spot where they should have been, but they were wiser than we. Perhaps from some lofty crag or from the depths of the dense woodland, they were staring at us, strange and foolish creatures coming from our world of artifice to look for them.

"We walked the streets of Narvik at three in the morning under the bright midnight sun. Men and women, many of them sightseers, were everywhere, but reindeer, never! We flew back to Bergen and sailed home.

"On shipboard, in the drenching Northern sunlight, I talked one day with a fearful but exultant American business man. He had just sold enough black-out curtains in Europe to keep his factory running for two years. Merchandising in a civilized world! Even so, how could we have believed that not until 1946—again the mystic seven-year period—would we be able to hold any kind of meeting with our friends across the Atlantic?"

All through September, October and November 1939 the headlines shrieked: GERMANY INVADES POLAND—BRITAIN AND FRANCE DECLARE WAR—RUSSIA INVADES POLAND—GERMANY AND RUSSIA PARTITION POLAND—RUSSIA ATTACKS FINLAND.

At some point, between 1939 and 1943, Madesin noted: "Probably the most significant factor in the record of those Federations which are still free to act, is the growing consciousness that the purposes of our International are warp and woof of the war effort itself. If freedom, equality of opportunity and the rights and dignity of the individual are worth a universal carnage, surely women are justified in defending those rights for themselves. History has taught us, and we can see it for ourselves, that a time of struggle is *the* time for struggle."

In Madesin's vocabulary struggle was a many-faceted word. Some aspects of it she found more dramatic than others, but even the least inspiring she did not shun if the cause were worthy. At the end of October 1939, she jumped at the opportunity to speak before the Annual Convention of the Associated Grocery Manufacturers of America. The title she chose was: "Consumers are People." In that pre-Ralph Nader era, the notion itself that consumers were people was outlandish, while consumer protection was a pledge honored largely in the breach. Who is the consumer? What duties does the industry have towards her? were questions Madesin raised starkly and answered with a remarkable combination of unsparing criticism and logically sound advice. That her audience, unaccustomed to hearing anyone with Madesin's style and persuasiveness, saw merit in what she said, is proven by the fact that the Grocery Industry printed her speech in full, distributing it to its own people all over the country.

On that occasion, as when her subject was international relations or domestic politics, Madesin's warnings of what would occur if some action were not taken, turned out to be prophetic. She foretold the coming of waves of protest from women consumers who, thirty years later, suddenly realized that they were being misled if not cheated by many manufacturers and who found in Ralph Nader, his disciples and others like them, a body of forceful spokesmen and supporters.

"The consumer," Madesin said, "is today's problem child for industry and business. Unfortunately, business and industry have too long ignored consumer questions and demands, have tried too long to laugh them off. The problem has grown until, in my judgment, it offers a major challenge. It is not impossible of solution by business and industry, but neither time nor effort should be spared. The great body of organized womanhood, at least ten million strong, is now the field of much consumer thought, discussion and action.

"As you must know, women talk . . . about pure food laws, advertising, profits and the like. It would be a grave mistake to consider such discussion as mere dabbling and therefore to be casually disregarded. Women exert heavy influence on public opinion. They have become the great carriers of ideas. . . . What does this consumer want, whose number is legion and whose voice is increasingly heard?

"She wants 1) purity of products, cleanliness in preparation, tastiness of flavor; 2) to know what she is buying, with more informative and intelligible labeling and; 3) accuracy of weight, full measure, honesty of appearance in packaging. She resent having been cheated by boxes with false bottoms and deceiving bottles of unnecessarily thick glass. Lastly, 4) she wants to stretch the buying power of her food dollars. Questions of weight, profiteering, expensive advertising, too many middle-men—these have become her concerns. The consumer has asked questions. Business has not answered her. Frustration brings resentment, resentment vindictiveness. It is too late now to talk simply of informative labeling. It is more important to revive confidence."

Anticipating a question likely to be in any business man's mind, 'why have consumers lost faith in us?' she said: "Women's faith is unsettled by the fact, for instance, that while millions were in dire poverty or on relief in 1934, America's productive capacity of goods and services was only 55% used . . . Women do not understand why the administrative genius which has produced big business in America, will let factories stand idle and permit themselves and others to support by taxation millions who should be supporting themselves. It is no answer to shout 'Red!' to honest questions which one will not, or cannot, face.

"Americans are thoroughly committed to the democratic form of government, but I am convinced that men and women will not forever starve even for the Constitution of the United States. For fifty years American industry has increased in power. It has kept a lobby in Washington to protect and increase its profits. It has gone its own way and kept its own counsel. The consumer has seen advertising and other pressure methods used to entice our citizens to purchase things they did not need and could not afford, in order to keep the wheels of business ever turning. She cannot accept all this without question.

"Even the profit system is not a sacred cow to her. The average woman would prefer to feed her family adequately even at the cost of some traditional economic theory. The average American woman loves her country, its liberty, its ideals of equality of opportunity and of justice, and for them she would again sacrifice herself and her sons. But she also believes that a trained and socially-minded industrial leadership could lead in solving these problems which impoverish her family and unsettle her very soul."

If her arguments had carried, Madesin reflected, the next question in the mind of her audience would certainly be 'What can we do now, to cure these ills?' She told them: "Treat women as intelligent human beings with the right to know. They are no longer to be caught with platitudes, flag-waving or attacks on third parties. These are outworn methods. Our noses are increasingly able to detect red herrings. Quit relying on professional consumers, newspaper reports and hearsay, for your knowledge of consumer demands. Look the consumer in the eye. Meet the shoppers face to face. Consumers are people. But if you feel that consumers' inquiries are infringements upon the sacred rights of your business, be ready to take the consequences. For years the platforms of women's clubs of every sort have been open to all sides of controversial questions. Political, cultural, educational and labor leaders have been welcome. Industry, on the whole, has not wished to be bothered. You may take it or leave it, as you will, but you cannot have it both ways.

"Send a speaker who can and will talk. Women will ask questions. Let your spokesman answer them. If he does not know the answer, let him say so, for it will increase confidence if he offers to find out and does send back the answer in the mail. By all means, let your speaker leave the flag and flowers at home. Women do not need to be taught patriotism by any industrial leader, and club women usually know that their brains are more important than their beauty. Don't try to flatter them about their looks. After all, there is no sex in economics. Producers, at the moment, must sell not so much their products as themselves, the system, the intelligence and the integrity of their social attitudes. It is, of course, more pleasant to be on the offensive than on the defensive side. It is usually easier to attack than to justify, but right now, with regard to the increasingly resentful consumer, industry has little choice of position."

As always in her speeches, at the end Madesin looked *up* towards the future, not down, and concluded: "Most consumers, I believe, wish you well, want to go along and wish to be convinced. But they are not robots, or pins to be stuck into a board until you are ready to move them. Consumers are inquiring, talkative and, many of them, financially pressed. If industry can show that it is impelled by a correct and honest social consciousness, it can gain consumer understanding and support. You will have to work at this job. That, after all, is the democratic way and you can also win because, after all, consumers are only people."

Hundreds of men went up to speak to Madesin, once the standing ovation they gave her had subsided. One of them, shaking her hand warmly, said: "I have been in the grocery manufacturing business for years, Dr. Phillips. After all, we make food for people to eat. Yet, today you made me see how much more important people are for how they think and feel than for what we feed them. You have given me a whole new idea of the consumer. I thank you." The comment must have pleased Madesin especially, since she made a note of it in her diary. People! They were all that Madesin really cared about. Women, for her, were people unfairly treated. In areas where men had the upper hand, she defended the women, spoke for them, fought for their rights. But when unjustice, or even mere unfairness, struck at men, or at people in general, Madesin's concern was universal. It was the appalling injustice done to a whole people that had shocked and hurt her so deeply when the Munich Pact was signed, and she agonized over the fact that there was nothing she could do for the people of Czechoslovakia.

Later, in that fateful year of 1939, it was for the people of Finland that she suffered the shock and the hurt all over again. At the end of August, the Soviets had made a pact with Nazi Germany. Publicly, it merely committed them both to non-aggression and neutrality. Secretly, it divided Eastern Europe between them, with the Baltic countries going to the USSR. Three months later, failing to obtain by so-called negotiation what Russia wanted from Finland, the Kremlin launched its troops across the border and sent its planes to bomb Helsinki. Although Finnish resistance was spectacular for skill and courage, by March 1940, the devastating Winter War, as it was called, had ended, inevitably, with Finland's surrender.

By Christmas, however, the tragic plight of the Finns had already brought immediate and generous response to Madesin's appeal for help from Business and Professional Women's Clubs all over the United States. "Thousands upon thousands of winter garments were shipped to the Helsinki Club," writes Madesin, "and along with the packages, to the distribution center organized and supervised by Anni Voipio, went many unsolicited gifts of money as well."

Regardless of how delighted she was by the rapid and overwhelming support from her fellow-citizens, nothing could offset the sickness that gripped her heart over the dastardly act of aggression, "an escalation of the disgrace of Munich." In a letter to Anni Voipio she laid bare her feelings: "All my life I have had a certain pride. Now I am ashamed, ashamed for humanity, ashamed to be a part of the human race. . . . If I do not write words of sympathy, it is because I cannot. Finland deserves more than sympathy. Magnificently you have done your part in defending your country. It is the 'rest of the world' that once more has failed, as in the First World War. I cannot forget that I am one of that 'rest.' "

14. *Apple Acres*

The Soviet invasion of Finland had hurt Madesin as deeply as if her own family had fallen victim to it. All her logic and realism, all her innate optimism and hope, failed to rid her spirit of the pall of depression that had settled upon it. She went about her business as usual—and at this point it was almost entirely International Federation business—but, sitting at her desk in the Biltmore, she had been incapable of putting together the short editorial for *Widening Horizons* that the issue still lacked before going to press.

Finally, very late one afternoon, when everyone had gone home, she found herself writing it, almost unconsciously, and it turned out in the form of a prayer: an act of contrition and a plea for courage. From the house organ that was *Widening Horizons,* it sailed out into many other publications which requested her permission to print it. Millions of Americans, men as well as women, realized that Madesin's words were speaking for what was in their own hearts:

God help me pay the price—for slothful days,
For selfish ways, for all my ignorance.
We did not care enough when Chinese children died,
Long since when German sisters bowed in shame,
When strong Czechs wept, laid down their arms, betrayed.
We did not really care those long, long years
When greedy men of power forged hidden chains
To bind the poor and weak through ignorance.
Each only tried to save his own, giving such drop of pity
As could conveniently be spared.

Now sorrow comes my way. I pay my share of misery.
Another's too. Let it be so, Some have paid for me.
But give me courage to endure, yet still to love and hope and pray.
Help me to know that this dark day, however long, must surely end
In a new dawning bright with faith
When men shall know in time, will pay the price

That all may live as mankind should.
I ask no more.

Now, with the end of the year approaching once more, it was also time for Madesin and the small Executive Council of the International to think of a theme for International Night, 1940. At that moment, they still found it possible to select a theme expressed in the following words: "Looking Forward to the Peace." Yet within the next six months, even the hope of peace had receded into the distance and was scarcely visible. Denmark, Norway, Belgium, the Netherlands and Luxembourg had fallen before Hitler's blitzkrieg. The Nazis had pushed their way across the French borders and, with the swastika flying over Paris, in June 1940 France had capitulated. One certain Frenchman, claiming to speak for the spirit of a nation that 'had lost a battle but not the war' and of a Europe which would not remain cowed, had taken refuge in England. From London and against incalculable odds, Charles de Gaulle carried on his fight for freedom. Presently, Britain became the target of merciless bombing from Hitler's terrifying *Luftwaffe,* and President Roosevelt undertook a number of bold initiatives to give England "all aid short of war."

In 1940, shattering precedent, FDR ran for a third term in the White House and won, though with a smaller majority than in the two previous campaigns and committed to keep America out of the war. After the campaign, in which Madesin had done her share, it was again necessary for the International to select its annual theme for what, in 1941, would be International Day, instead of International Night. Bravely the Clubs on the embattled continent of Europe, continued to make every effort to stage this annual reunion as best as they could. Theoretically nonbelligerent, the United States was still able to communicate with most European countries and, at year's end, a theme went out from the Biltmore office. Incredibly optimistic, "The International Federation's Responsibility in a Post-War World," it was actually intended to inspire hope for peace in those who, by that time, had lost all reason for having any.

A steady stream of packages with food, clothing and medicine was also going out from the Biltmore daily to the neediest federation members overseas. The cramped quarters became a storage house and shipping center, with the always faithful Co-Ops devoting nights and holidays to whatever service Madesin asked them to perform. In Madesin's mind, however, even more important than the packages was the effort to keep in personal touch with as many women in the occupied countries as was humanly possible. She was obsessed by the darkness of spirit into which she feared many of them might have been plunged by the extinction of the lights of freedom. The dreadful fact of the Nazi presence in so many countries she knew could not be altered, not for some time. But she was

169

determined to do her best to alleviate at least the psychological impact of it.

Almost miraculously, throughout the war, most of her personal letters and a general one called "Family Letter," which she sent to a carefully selected list of women likely to receive and able to pass it on, actually reached its destination. Every word was written guardedly, for there was censorship everywhere and caution was needed even if recipients were in Sweden or Switzerland. Many years later, Madesin learned how widely the Family Letter had been circulated and how much comfort it had brought, not merely to club members, but to many other people around them. Occasionally a letter managed to find its way to Madesin's office even from an occupied country. One, from Norway, riskily told her about a club meeting, held despite the dangers involved, saying:

"We met high up in the loft of Mrs. Blank's brewery. Outside, a terrible snowstorm, but everybody was in high spirits. We blamed it on the strong smell of beer. You understand, we aren't used to much anymore. We brought our own food and our hostess had made a layer cake —the first cake we had seen in a long time and maybe the last one, too. . . . Our club keeps up its monthly meetings, which this year have been especially enjoyable because of the solidarity and fellowship which distinguish them under the unusual conditions in which we are now living."

A letter from France was in a different vein: "We did our best, but we could not do it alone. The world did not understand this, but may it never repent it. Let all women of America pray with all their hearts and faith that such sorrow and hardships may be spared their country. It is the only wish and message that the French women send to their free sisters of America . . . And think of us sometimes. We don't know what tomorrow will bring. We know, anyway, that it will be a hard future and that it will be bottomless in pain. We will face it with dry eyes, head high and with fearless heart . . . Maybe I shall never write you anymore —any one of us may meet death the next hour and this thought makes one free of so many things . . . I send you across the beautiful everlasting ocean my most respectful thoughts and wishes."

By the middle of 1940 two events occurred which affected Madesin's activities in a positive way. One was the marriage of Isabelle Claridge, owing to which she would be moving from West Virginia to Philadelphia, therefore much nearer to New York. As Treasurer of the International and one of the three members of the Executive Committee, her financial ability and her always carefully thought-out counsel were of increasing importance to Madesin. Having her closer at hand delighted her. Isabelle Claridge's husband, Elbert J. Taylor, a distinguished consulting engineer who specialized in designing city water supply systems, soon became one

170

of Madesin's particular friends. Isabelle, who was English born, had lost both her parents in the U.S. by 1940, and pleased Madesin by asking her to act as hostess at her wedding. Her two children, Bronwen and John, were added in due course to the list of those whom Madesin regarded as her own 'grandchildren.'

The other event was a change of surroundings. She decided to give up *Philsfolly,* leave the New York apartment, and, purchase instead a lovely old house in Westport, Connecticut, baptized *Apple Acres,* in honor of its beautiful orchard. For some time, Madesin had been finding the noise and confusion of Manhattan increasingly unbearable as a steady fare. *Philsfolly,* on the other hand, was too far to be used for more than week-ends. These brief interludes did not provide enough relief, enough time to think things through. The earlier yearning for 'a bit o'land' had become a stronger yearning for a place in the country to call home year-round, with a garden to work in before breakfast, if she chose, or before supper if she returned early enough from New York, a sky uncluttered by tall buildings, the sweep of stars at night.

She was never quite sure why, when someone asked her, once, where she would like to live, she had immediately replied, "In Connecticut—in Westport." Perhaps it was the rolling hills, not unlike those of Kentucky. Perhaps because it was a non-commercial village just an hour by train from Manhattan. Perhaps because she had friends in that area, including Charles and Mary Beard in New Milford, within easy driving distance. Whatever the reason, the search began and ended very soon in the purchase of an old Colonial house, standing graciously in the midst of a hundred old apple trees, a pink cloud of beauty in the spring. The house and the setting had equal charm. Madesin's intrepid skill with tools and Marjory's housekeeping talent, soon made it as inviting as *Philsfolly.*

Philsfolly was sold, but not before it was the scene of a final picnic in the tradition of its predecessors. Nearly a hundred friends signed the guest-book, for the last time in New Jersey. Another would be started in Connecticut. Just before she started dismantling the house, a well-known journalist from Illinois, Dorothy McLean, came to interview her for an article she entitled "Women's Club Leader Views the War" which covered four columns of the *East St. Louis Journal,* whose circulation hit the heart of the industrial areas on the Mississippi river. "The greatest enemy of America at the moment," Madesin told her, "is not so much Adolf Hitler as the 11 million unemployed whose spirit is being broken by made work or the dole. I believe in giving them land, in teaching them to support themselves by their own efforts, by the soil. We have lured people to the cities, a bad mistake, and away from the land, a tragedy. That is only one step in the process. Every man has a right to an honest to God job in industry. Unless we see that he has the chance

171

for such a job, we are going to regret it. And we are terribly late already."
Then she elucidated her point by adding: "When I was in Rome four
years ago, after I talked with Mussolini, a very rich American, on the
Embassy staff in Rome, called me aside and said 'Go back to America
and tell the big fellows for God's sake to give up something.' What did
he mean? He meant all the big fellows, labor and capital as well, should
have got together then, each giving in, in some way, to the other. Instead
all the big fellows on both sides have spent their time trying to thwart
the government and trying to live up to the great American delusion
that the more money you have, the more successful you are." About the
war she declared: "The English will hold out, the war will continue for
several years, and, at the end, there will be profound changes all over
Europe and England too, but from the ruins will rise a new social order
in which liberty, equality and fraternity will be more than words to
people for whom, up to the present, they have been only words. And
they will mean much more to the next generation than they have meant
to us."

While accepting as many speaking engagements as she could all
around the country, being interviewed on the radio as well as by the
press, Madesin was also writing articles. *Good Housekeeping Magazine*
had commissioned her to write one on "Women and Defense" interviewing Dr. Harriet Elliott, the first woman appointed to the National Defense Advisory Commission. Nothing could have been sweeter music to
Madesin's ears than what she learnt from Dr. Elliott: "This is the first
time that the government has placed human welfare on a par with
military preparations for national defense . . . The ideas of women have
now become the ideas of government. Total defense is democracy's answer to total war. It is intended to safeguard our way of life from enemies
within as well as enemies without. Hunger, malnutrition, ignorance and
misinformation, lack of adequate housing, clothing and warmth—these
are the enemies within our gates. They make men wonder 'what is there
to defend, what have I to lose or gain.' "

Unquestionably, it was a victory to have a woman placed on the
National Defense Advisory Committee upon an equal basis with the
representatives of industry, labor, the military and business. Unquestionably, likewise, the women of America did their part unstintingly and
well, in paid and unpaid capacities, but the enemies within were not
destroyed then, nor have been since. Dr. Elliott had stressed the fact
that one very important service which the women could render was to
draw together their communities; organize them against the temptation
to hoard when some item became scarce on the market, against the acceptance of rumor as fact, against ignorance by teaching them how to
become informed; make an inventory of available skills. By and large

all this was done but, as Madesin saw it looking back on the war years, women should have taken the opportunity when they were needed to make their way into politics. Not only should many of them have run for office, at any level, but they should have finally learnt the necessity of supporting those who ran. "The social reforms we needed then to keep at bay the enemy within our gates, as Harriet Elliott so aptly stated," commented Madesin, "could only come through legislation, and legislation involves political power."

The arrival of autumn found Madesin and Marjory Lacey-Baker settled in Westport. In 1940 the Connecticut countryside was still rural, with unspoiled woodland and open fields, little-traveled roads and winding lanes, inviting exploration. After twenty years of apartment living in a city which seemed to become more noisy and more congested with each passing day, a house in the country to be called home—not merely a week-end refuge—gave Madesin a new lease on life. Commuting to New York did not disturb her until a bad winter came, with heavy snows and icy road which made difficult even the short trip to the railroad station. Then, very sensibly, she took Marjory's suggestion and, closing the house after Christmas, they made the old Murray Hill Hotel, a stone's throw from the Biltmore, their headquarters, but never for more than three months.

In late March, as soon as the ice had gone from the country roads, they moved back to *Apple Acres,* in order not to miss a moment of every recurrent yet ever-different miracle of Spring. The apple blossoms, bursting out all around, the grass coming up in carpets of tender green and glittering underfoot, the birds returning to their feeding stations and to their bath near the stone house—the delicious scene moved Madesin almost to tears. Quickly, before the brief moment of the apple orchard's fairy-like beauty could vanish, she mobilized Marjory to invite their closest friends to come and see it. This time, it was not a large picnic of the *Philsfolly* variety, but a Sunday gathering of not more than a score, some single women, some with their husbands, who came to 'housewarm' the place with that unique kind of informality always prevalent at Madesin's parties.

Although it was Sunday, the four 'apple men' appeared from among the trees and Madesin joyfully introduced the old Italian farmer and his three sons whom she had engaged to care for the orchard, as they had done long before she owned it. They pruned and sprayed and, come time, picked and marketed the crop of luscious Baldwins. Although when the apple men saw that Madesin had guests, they started to turn back, she insisted that they remain, take some refreshment with her guests and do whatever had brought them in the first place. The winter had been hard, the old man said, and he feared some of the trees has suffered.

173

The best way to tell was when they were in full bloom. He gave them all a good bill of health. "This," Madesin commented, "made the day a complete success."

Suddenly, on June 6, 1941, Germany attacked the Soviet Union, breaking the non-aggression pact, swept through five major· cities and laid siege to Leningrad. With his forces now engaged on two fronts— though the Western one was quiescent—Hitler turned the screws ever tighter to keep well under control the peoples he had already subjected. Tales of crimes committed by the Nazi in vast concentration camps began to seep through the sealed borders. The little that transpired was sufficient to fill any decent heart with horror, but no one could then suspect the abominations that were actually being perpetrated. A very few individuals were still able to escape to freedom, while others who had already found refuge in neutral countries struggled to reach America. Trying to help some of them to get into the United States was a monumental undertaking at that time; trying to provide them with a livelihood was only slightly less difficult. Those who appealed to Madesin, directly or indirectly, were highly specialized professionals who had a long record of achievements in their own countries. Among these were Dr. Maria Munk of Germany, Essy Rasmussen and Marie Ginsberg who had held important positions in the League of Nations. Dr. Marianne Beth, with her husband and daughter, went to the University of Chicago, and was among the very fortunate ones. Many families were inevitably separated. Suitable work was hard to find for those who were no longer young— and few of them were. In many of the refugees, the emotional stress of their experiences was heightened by an inner anguish they seemed unable to overcome: the anguish of having been rejected by their own country only because of their Jewish faith or ancestry.

From the outset of the war, in 1939, the International Federation, thanks to Madesin's enormous range of friends, associates and acquaintances, had made it a practice to frequently sponsor a luncheon, a tea or a dinner in the Music Room of the Biltmore, at which some woman of international standing, or several of them together, addressed increasingly numerous and increasingly sophisticated audiences of men and women. The list of those who spoke at these gatherings is impressive. Among them were, at one time or another: Irene Joliot-Curie, famous daughter of famous parents; Isabel de Palencia, one-time Minister from the Republic of Spain to Sweden and Finland; Maria Cristina Marconi, widow of the inventor; Jennie Lee, wife of Britain's Labour Leader, Aneurin Bevan and a leader in her own right; Marie Helene Lefaucheux, noted French industrialist, later a member of the French Constituent Assembly; Kerstin Hesselgren, first woman member of the Swedish Riksdag; Lady Astor, Edith Summerskill, Irene Ward and Lady Davidson, all Members of the British Parliament; Laure Albin Guillot, Director of the Photographic Archives of the French Ministry of Fine Arts; Judith, Countess of Listowel, Hungarian-born lecturer and journalist; Cairine Wilson, Canada's first woman Senator; Madame Pierre Cassegrain, wife of Canada's Secretary of State and president of the Equal Rights League of Quebec; Mrs. Franklin Delano Roosevelt who spoke from the White House; Mrs. J. Borden Harriman, Minister to Norway; Nellie Tayloe Ross, Director of the U.S. Mint and first woman State Governor; Hattie Caraway, first woman to gain a seat in the U.S. Senate. Writers were numerous: Pearl S. Buck, Fanny Hurst, Mary R. Beard, Inez Hayes Irwin, Jan Struthers, Eve Curie, Dorothy Thompson, Anne O'Hare McCormick, to name only a few.

In the fall of 1941 Alva Myrdal returned from a stay in Sweden to lecture in the United States while her husband was putting the finishing touches on his book, *The American Dilemma*. In December, Madesin had one of the international teas in her honor. Before a capacity crowd, Mrs. Myrdal spoke brilliantly on "Woman's Part in Defense," holding the public's attention so firmly that only a few persons noticed a messenger who twice delivered notes to Madesin at the speaker's table. The address was just over, when the messenger appeared a third time. Madesin rose from her chair, motioned for silence, her face suddenly very pale. Slowly she said: "I have a very important announcement to make. The Japanese have bombed Pearl Harbor." The day was December 7, 1941. The following day, the United States declared war on Japan and within hours Germany and Italy had declared war on the United States.

Very soon thereafter the Myrdals decided to return to Sweden with their children. Conditions in Europe were becoming more and more ominous and it no longer seemed impossible that even Sweden might be invaded. If this were to happen, the Myrdals intended to stand with the rest of their countrymen "Well do I remember the day they left," writes Madesin. "Gordon Holmes happened to be here at the time and she, Helen Havener and I went to some obscure dock to see them embark on the small freighter loaded, as we learned later, with explosives. Gordon Holmes, in her usual direct way, chided Alva for taking her three children back to Sweden at such a time. In fact, as I remember it, the probability of invasion was the immediate occasion for their departure. 'How can you,' the General said, 'take your little children back to so dangerous a country when you could remain here with them in security?' 'But there are two million children like them in Sweden who must face the danger,' Alva answered, 'and why should my children, who are Swedish, be spared what others must undergo?' With those words she bade us farewell smiling and gay. They steamed away on the little vessel which was to land them at a foreign port. After that they had

175

to travel many miles across a country not their own to share the responsibilities and the dangers with other Swedish citizens. It was the kind of gallantry one does not soon forget. I missed them greatly."

In a while Alva wrote Madesin of a public meeting organized in Stockholm by the Swedish Federation, in co-operation with twenty-one other major women's groups: "We felt it was time that we solemnly declared our faith in the Scandinavian heritage and in the democratic values. That was a demonstration. We know exactly where we stand. We know that this vacuum of semi-peace is given to our country and to the Swedish women in order that they shall formulate the line of defense also for the many who cannot talk. A Scandinavian Union must be prepared now—and we are the only ones free to prepare it. The women in the democratic countries must prepare the peace platform now, if they are to be able to demand inclusion of their ideals, and there are only you and we to prepare it. I definitely believe that the International has a great potentiality to build up something after the war. But this rests on how carefully we now keep above the battle lines, on how good a care we now take of the belief in true internationalism vested in us. I believe we can make it our motto to state: *"We deny that there is war between the women of the world."*

Madesin fully shared Alva Myrdal's belief that the International Federation was the repository of a faith in 'internationalism' as a working and workable force and, among other ways, showed it by her invention of the Candlelight Ceremony. This was a kind of ritual for use on International Night or International Day meetings. Each Federation had a candle. Blackened candles stood for Federations blacked out by the war. The narrator snuffed out each one as she related the events affecting that country. At the end the only lighted candles belonged to Federations still operating and free. Eventually the ritual was used in many parts of the world, but during the war it proved enormously effective in America, to remind people of what had happened abroad, while in countries such as England it gave people renewed courage to carry on the struggle.

It was at the height of the bombings, in Sheffield, England, that the performance of the ceremony at the local Club, meeting in a shelter, was colored by a moment of unexpected drama. The speaker, addressing the meeting after the short ritual, was a refugee from Austria. On the table, at some distance from where she stood to speak, were the candles, all bearing name tags, many snuffed out, including that of her own Federation. She had been asked to tell the story of her own, harrowing flight. She had reached the most gripping moment of her account, when one of the blackened candles suddenly toppled over, missing by a hair's breadth those around it and several others, all of which remained perfectly steady, some lighted, some black. A Sheffield member wrote Madesin about it and concluded saying: "Everyone saw the inexplicable accident and you can imagine the electrified silence when the Club President announced, as soon as the speaker had finished, that it had been the German candle which alone had fallen while the others stayed unshaken and upright."

But Germany too, like all other nations, had great women who did not fall. One of them was Alice Solomon, famed in those days as the 'Jane Addams of Europe' and who successfully reached the United States. Early in 1942, both countries were at war with each other, six major women's organizations, the International Federation among them, joined to pay a tribute to Alice Solomon. Doing the honors on that occasion were Mrs. Carrie Chapman Catt, then already in her eighties, and Dr. Samuel McCrea Calvert, General Secretary of the Council of Churches, while Adolf Busch and Rudolf Serkin spoke to her with their music. But fate does not bestow its favor equally on those who deserve them. In January of that year, Madesin rushed to Washington in behalf of Senator Szelagowska, of Poland, who had fled her country, narrowly escaping death, but all efforts to locate her whereabouts had failed. "During a quiet luncheon with Mrs. Roosevelt at the White House," Madesin recalled, "I was steered in several helpful directions. At first my conferences with the Department of State, the American Association of University Women, the Embassy of Poland and others seemed destined to remain fruitless. But one had to keep on trying, first this way and then that. Finally, Mrs. Szelagowska was found and made safe. Happy as I was, I could not take my mind off Frantiska Plaminkova. The reports were still impossible to track down."

She had barely returned from Washington, when a letter from Gordon Holmes gave her spirits an enormous lift. It was written from bombed-out Coventry: "Coventry and our National Federation have marked another milestone. Our 50th Club! Did that desperate little gathering of seven small new clubs which met at Halifax on September 9, 1939, a week after the outbreak of war, see this milestone shining through the bitter years? One new club for every three weeks of the war, and our 50th Club on February 7, 1942, in an old and famous city blitzed to tragic destruction such as we could not have conceived in September 1939, except in a nightmare? No, but that day, we, who were there, desperately clung to all we had to face the future with—courage, faith and idealism. And so Coventry has war wounds, but no defeat, because it has these three basic forces vitally alive within its shining soul."

In that vibrant letter the General enclosed the text of an old inscription she had noticed on a little church in Sussex: "In the year 1653, when all things sacred throughout the Nation were destroyed or profaned, this church was built to the glory of God by Sir Robert Shirley, Baronet,

177

whose singular praise it was to have done the best things in the worst times and hoped them in the most calamitous."

Madesin's eyes sparkled as she read it. It was a good omen, a very good omen for America whose people, like the English Baronet, would also do "the best things in the worst times, and hope them in the most calamitous." Of this she felt absolutely certain.

It would be a long time before the tide of war was turned in Europe and even longer before the United States could open the yearned-for 'second front.' America, that summer, would face enormous losses of men and material in the Pacific. There would be the Battle of the Coral Sea that year in May, and the U.S. Marines' assault on Guadalcanal would cost a tremendous price before a victory in the following year. The experts were forecasting bad times in the immediate future for the nation at war. The mood of the people had to be uplifted, Madesin reflected, and the women inevitably had a vital part to play in doing so. The issue of *Widening Horizons* for April was in the making. She decided to include the General's account of Britain's 50th Club in her own editorial entitled 'Testament of Faith.'

She concluded it with these words: "Let us no longer wonder or weep. Rather let us rejoice. For these heroic deeds are humanity's testimony of Faith in the Brotherhood of Man, in something more precious than life itself. And a bright legacy, a reprieve and a command to us, the living."

Apple Acres

15. London's Ghostly Silences

With America at war, Madesin began to follow Harriet Elliott's advice to women: make your own community aware and concerned. Soon involved in Westport's efforts to organize for action and for a better understanding of the world situation, she made time to speak to PTAs, Girl and Boy Scout Troops, Rotarys and many other civic groups. Norman Cousins, then editor-in-chief of the *Saturday Review of Literature,* had just founded the Town Hall Association of the neighboring town of Norwalk and drew her into its executive committee, while also having her as a frequent participant in his highly successful forums on public affairs. Politics still fascinated her, even at the local level. As Chairman of the Legislative Committee of the large Westport Woman's Club, she sparked considerable action and for a couple of years, also chaired the Connecticut Committee for the Equal Rights Amendment. From this she resigned because "it was too significant a program to be undertaken only in her spare time." She remained Honorary Chairman, however, until her death.

While all this went on in her home surroundings, she could not resist requests to sit on the most relevant of the numerous Committees, Commissions and Boards, springing up all around the country to meet the requirements of a nation suddenly engaged in war. Little wonder, indeed, that she was complaining constantly of the shortage of hours in which to pack everything she felt was too significant to be set aside. Once, at the Westport County Fair, a fortune teller, looking into the palm of her hand, exclaimed: "Good gracious, lady, why are you always in such a hurry?" Madesin often wished she could answer that question herself.

Alva Myrdal's absence of many months in Sweden had reduced the Executive Committee of the International to Madesin and Isabelle Claridge Taylor, which was not enough to handle everything that poured into the Biltmore office, requiring serious attention: new clubs being formed despite the war, financing, pleas from refugees, the search for jobs for members who had reached American shores, the U.S. Federation eager to find ways of helping to keep the International alive and active, there seemed to be no end of decisions to be taken without delay and of mountains of paper work.

By a mail vote of the Board of Directors, or at least of those who could be reached, it was decided to add to the Executive Committee, now renamed Emergency Committee, all Board Members within geographical access to New York. This included the presidents of the U.S. and Canadian Federations and, at that time, the two American Committee Chairmen, Helen Havener, Publicity and Zonola Longstreth, Membership. Miss Longstreth herself was constantly amazed by the continuing growth of business and professional women's clubs overseas in that period of mounting anxiety and danger. An encounter in New York, in 1941, with a purchasing agent from South Africa, Mrs. Juba Sugden, eventually and unexpectedly produced a new Federation in that country, while a stop which Mrs. Sugden made in Brazil, for business reasons, on her way home, sparked the first club in South America. Dr. Bertha Lutz, a well-known biologist, inspired by Mrs. Sugden, organized a club in Rio de Janeiro, of which she was elected president.

Meanwhile, the efforts of a U.S. club in Miami led to the establishment of three clubs in Cuba and a national Federation, headed by Dr. Gilda Peraza, a professor at the University of Havana. But the most remarkable growth continued to occur in England against the worst possible odds. Gordon Holmes, President of the National Federation of Business and Professional Women's Clubs of Great Britain and Northern Ireland was the counterpart of Caroline Haslett, President of the British Federation of Business and Professional Women. The latter headed up women's groups and associations, some of them long pre-dating Madesin's International, organized on strictly professional lines. As a body this Federation was also affiliated with the International, a pattern later followed also by Sweden, but not developed anywhere else. Gordon Holmes' clubs, instead, like those in the U.S., Canada and elsewhere, built their membership from all business and professional women in a given geographical area. In Britain these two Federations were of enormous stimulation to one another and, together, of very major significance to the International.

Not content with her 50th Club in Coventry, Gordon Holmes flanked by Nancy Anderson, the professional organizer who did her work in defiance of serious risk to her life, continued to increase the number of clubs, making superhuman efforts to preside at every function to open a new one. One night the headquarters of her Federation were completely bombed out and the following week her own house in Chiswick was struck. Every window pane was shattered and every door in the house was blown off its hinges. Like other British women, whose gallantry became legendary, the General carried on.

"Often very frightened," she wrote Madesin, but always unfaltering as the results showed, Gordon Holmes, no longer young, made light of heatless trains and hotels, of poor or non-existent food, of endless blackouts and of bombing raids that cut gashes of hideous light in the ominous darkness, filling the air with fire, smoke and the appaling sound of crashes. "In Birmingham," the General reported, "the house was packed for the opening, some members standing on their feet for hours. Late that evening, when Nancy Anderson and I finally arrived at our hotel, nothing having passed our lips for hours, we collapsed in the lounge, had tea—milkless and sugarless—and gorgeous Spam sandwiches! That was the only food to be found in the hotel larder, but never was your American specialty more appreciated! In spite of it all, I feel, as hundreds of others have said to me of themselves, that I hardly know how I could face life at present, if it were not for this intensively constructive club work, which is coming to mean so much to thousands of our British women."

Madesin, feeling ashamed of the security and comforts of America, read these and many other comments which kept reaching her even from countries occupied by the enemy. She marveled that in such dreadful material conditions, the link with the International, which by now was largely ideal, could prove so comforting to so many women. Excerpts from letters, their authors intentionally made anonymous, were circulated through *Widening Horizons,* the Family Letter and in any other way possible.

A Finnish member wrote: "Working through the Club arouses our morale, our courage and our hope. It has helped us to carry through one bitter war winter and will carry us through all the others, if go through them we must."

From Holland: "It means much to feel close to members in other countries, even if one cannot communicate with them."

From Norway: "I think a Club is a real expression, a thing built, well or ill, with material furnished by its members. It is not yours or mine but ours, and whether we value it as a means of escape or self-expression, or as a vehicle for community service, we would be immeasurably poorer without it."

One French woman could hold her head high enough above the misery of her country's circumstances to peer into the future, saying: "I rejoice in all that our International Federation can mean as a world link between women, both now and for our work in the peace that must come."

This looking out beyond the present fitted admirably with what President Roosevelt had said in his New Year's message to the nation in 1942: "In this war, as in no previous one, we are conscious of the

181

supreme necessity of planning what is to come after, and of carrying forward into peace the common effort which will have brought victory in the war. We have come to see that the maintainance and safeguarding of peace is the most vital single necessity in the lives of each and all of us." Even though the military situation was far from having turned in favor of the Allies, groups and individuals, conscious of the necessity to plan for peace and its aftermath, were already getting organized within the United States. Abroad too, and not merely in the neutral countries, such terms as world organization and world government were beginning to circulate effectively.

In her fairly frequent visits to Washington, Madesin was particularly active in the *Institute on World Planning and on the Future of World Organisations* and in Carrie Chapman Catt's *Conference of Women on Post-War Problems*. In one of her many nation-wide broadcasts Madesin said, at that time: "What we shall need is a people's peace, not a politicians' peace. It is the people who give their sons, their efforts and their property in war. They pay the price and are entitled to make the peace. We should be educating them now in the problems of the peace table." Words such as these had drawn surprisingly positive response from men and women all over the country who expressed not merely their personal reaction to the broadcasts, but took the trouble to relate what they knew was being done along these lines in their area.

Presently Madesin conceived the idea of putting together a clear and cogent digest of all peace plans and post-war reconstruction plans already being advocated both in America and abroad. Emma Gelders Sterne, author of *We Live to Be Free,* an immensely popular history of democracy just then published, volunteered to edit the brochure from Madesin's material. Issued in summer of 1943 it went out accompanied by a questionnaire designed to elicit opinions and proposals from the readers. The device proved so fruitful of ideas and projects that, again edited by Emma Gelders Sterne, it was published under the title *A Common Denominator in World Thinking.* Both brochures went to all delegates to the United Nations Charter Conference in San Francisco in 1945 and to all women attending as advisors. The effort was rewarded. The press noted the brochures and several delegates mentioned their content approvingly.

Before Alva's return to Sweden, Madesin had explored with her the possibility of going overseas herself. The Atlantic Ocean, lying between herself and where the action was, gave her a sense of frustration she wanted to allay. Alva immediately sparked at the idea and offered to see if a speaking tour all over Sweden could be arranged. Madesin hoped that, as head of an international organization, and if invited, the U.S. government would let her go to Britain as well. Wondering if she were over-estimating her own ability to add anything to the morale of women whom she saw as so much stronger and more gallant than herself, she tucked the project into her mind, firmly believing that, if the idea was good, at some time the usual finger would point to that turn on the road and she would be off.

Meanwhile, the U.S. Congress had passed a bill establishing a Women's Army Auxiliary Corps. The plan had been under consideration for some time. Women's organizations had been invited to submit reactions and suggestions to its congressional sponsors. The public was not unanimously for it, by any means. Even some of the more active feminists disapproved of it. The whole concept was a new one and not easy to put over in a country which was not really feeling the pinch of a distant war.

Some people, who regarded Madesin as a pacifist because of her openly professed abhorrence of war and her unceasing activity to bring about interest in plans for peace, were surprised that she favored the bill. Those who knew her better, of course, were not. They saw no ambivalence or contradiction in being opposed to war and seeking peace, yet feeling it was the duty of every citizen to serve the country in some capacity, once the country was drawn into war. Madesin believed, as did many other tendential or convinced pacifists, that all wars could not be herded together into a single flock. There were wars of aggression, such as Hitler's invasion of Europe, designed to destroy the sovereignty of nations and the rights of individuals, completely different from wars fought to protect that sovereignty and safeguard those rights. Not to engage in the latter once the former had been unleashed, signified total surrender not merely of national entity and national boundaries, but also of the very principles that were at stake. The betrayal of freedom committed at Munich and the deal between Hitler and Stalin for the partitioning of Eastern Europe, were scars that still festered in her conscience. Pearl Harbor had capped the situation, irretrievably. If women were demanding equality with men in time of peace, she argued, they could surely not refuse it in time of war.

Madesin traveled from coast to coast, explaining to vast and varied audiences why the new law deserved public support. The bill provided for a corps of 150,000 women between the ages of 21 and 45 to serve with the army in non-combatant posts anywhere in the world. Enrollment was to be voluntary and limited to citizens of the United States. "This is a new departure in war service for our country," she said. "Nor has it come, as women nurses came to the battlefields of the Crimean War, through the stubborn insistence of Florence Nightingale, whom even the British generals could not disregard. Today, instead, the War Department *wants* a corps of women. I can think of no greater proof of its necessity. They will be assigned to duties now being performed by

183

the Army and will thus release an equivalent number of soldiers for fighting."

"Are we women so much weaker or more precious or less patriotic than men," she asked, "that we cannot stand side by side with brothers, sweethearts and even sons, when our country calls? If they face death, cannot we face hardship? If they must give up a business or a profession, can not we?" With a sharp edge to her tone, she reminded her audiences, time and time again, of what the women of other countries were having to face, merely because of an accident of birth. At the same time, however, she awakened in people a sense of pride in their country and in themselves using the words she knew would inflame their dedication. "The women of America have all the courage they need, superb abilities and they love their country. War work is hard, poorly paid and, for most of us, without appreciation or glory. But you will find the reward in knowing that you, too, have done your part." It was on occasions such as this that the poet in her suddenly surfaced, touching even those who did not want to understand: "I am calling the women of America— from the teeming cities, the rural towns, from those deep and silent places lost behind the hills, I am calling you from the states which knew the Pilgrim Fathers, from the midwest's plains of greening grain, from the young lands on the Pacific and from my old, old South."

As history has recorded, when the women of America were called, they did not fail to answer.

September of 1942 brought political campaigning once more to the American scene. It was an off-year election, but in several states and towns the contests were hot and heavy. Although Madesin knew the predictable outcome of the race for Representative from Westport to the Connecticut Legislature, the town being a Republic stronghold, she accepted the nomination of the Democratic Party for that office and tossed her hat in the ring.

Campaigning, which was done mostly in the late afternoon and evenings, put a strain on her physical energy which she could not resist. A neglected cold developed into a near-fatal case of pneumonia. Three weeks in the hospital were followed by a long convalescence. "Of course, I was not elected," she wrote later, "Democrats rarely are in Connecticut, but I pulled a sizable vote nonetheless. And, at least, I practiced what I preached!" At the Biltmore, where mail was piling up, problems were waiting to be solved, endless invitations to meetings or to make speeches were going unanswered, Isabelle Taylor who had been made Acting President, stepped into the breach. Quickly, she rallied the Co-Ops who, in turn, brought in other willing hands, established a system of communication with the other members of the Executive Committee by telephone, so that urgent decisions could be taken and, on short notice, had brought order out of chaos, with Helen Havener and Marjory Lacey-Baker coming to staff the office whenever they could.

When Madesin was still in the hospital she had received a cable from the Swedish Federation pressing her to undertake a lecture tour in that country. The British Federation had followed with a similar invitation. A letter from Alva Myrdal arriving hard on the heels of the cables, spurred her determination to find a way of making the journey. Alva wrote: "This is just a chat at your bedside, intended to cheer you up. Please tell Marjory to take good care of you and pray that we may meet here in the spring, laying some ground work for the Federation's activities after the war. It would make me so happy to see you here. It would be a sort of symbol of new times beginning. Everything would start to move upward, we might also have some good tidings for you. I have laid plans and got them half endorsed, for a gigantic merging of isolated professional groups into our Federation. If this succeeds we shall become the strongest women's organization in the country. You can help mightily by your appearance."

No sooner was Madesin out of the hospital than she began to pull wires. She took her invitations from Sweden and Britain to the Outpost Service Bureau of the Office of War Information and explained her plans. Despite the several friends she had in the Bureau, it must have appeared a risky thing to do to allow a woman in her sixties just recovering from a very serious illness, to fly to Britain at the height of the blitz and even riskier to send her on to Sweden. But Madesin would not allow herself to be deterred from her decision to do everything possible to go abroad. In Washington she talked with Mrs. Roosevelt, but the answer was not too encouraging. The editor of *Good Housekeeping,* formerly her editor at *Pictorial Review,* offered her any kind of assignment which might help her to be sent overseas. Finally, the OWI consented to send her as far as Britain, with the assurance that assignment to Sweden would follow if it were at all possible.

In April of '43, while Madesin was still following lead after lead to find a way of making her trip, news reached her from Switzerland that Frantiska Plaminkova had been executed. The details of the brutality with which she had been tortured made her so sick that she was like one paralyzed. Half a day passed before she was herself again, able to look ahead. Then, she was more determined than ever to go abroad. Plam had died before a firing squad because she would not forsake those who counted on her presence. If the call from the women of Britain and Sweden meant that she, Madesin, could help them in some small way by her presence, that was where she should be. What Plam had stood for to those who really knew her, how she had served her country and how she had given of herself to whoever sought her help, the unique sort of person she was—were thoughts that tumbled over each other in Madesin's mind as she worked in her garden at *Apple Acres* to relieve the tension that still gripped her. With her hands buried in the cool earth, her knees on the ground where new shoots were beginning to push upward, she also prayed.

The next day, grieved but serene again and with a feeling of certainty in her mind that before too long she would be starting on her journey, she wrote her tribute to Frantiska Plaminkova for the issue of *Widening Horizons* that, once more, awaited only her front page piece before going to press:

"They say that she is dead. The passion for justice, the love of humanity, the tough courage, the gay vivacity and humor—gone. It is as unreal as for a familiar mountain to have dropped beneath the sea.

"Europe's 'Plam,' known and beloved by the women of many lands. *Our* 'Plam' who by precept and example has taught us so much. Always present at International meetings, always articulate, determined, fearless, wise with the seasoned wisdom of an old race. Words tumbling forth in tangled French or halting English, the gestures, the quickened foot-step; the big hats by day, the decorations bestowed by governments across a black evening gown; the power and fire and lift of spirit when she spoke. Ours no more.

"When she said good-bye to me at Trondheim, Norway, in 1939, I saw clearly the last farewell within her eyes. It was the tender, yearning look of one who knew she must leave to others unfinished tasks long the purpose of her life. Some of us realizing that so passionate a patriot, so powerful a leader could scarce escape begged her to accept one of the invitations to England, Canada or the United States. But always she shook her head saying, 'Too many people at home hanging from me' while her gestures pictured the heavy pull made by the tragedy of her country.

"These four years I have remembered many times that look. But still, I cannot think of her as dead. If it is true, it happened as the report says—before a firing squad. Her spirit was too tenacious to let her body go in any other way in times like these. And such an end is not death —but immortality.

"Her hand will rest upon the gun of every Czech soldier, will lift the wing of each Allied plane and soothe the hearts of all her troubled people. And when at last the guns are silenced and women of all nations meet again, a flaming spirit will arouse, sustain and guide them. That, in part, will be Plaminkova, come again where her heart and purpose were.

"Hail, but not farewell, stalwart soldier, who even in death need not know defeat. As long as we are able to remember, we shall remember you."

The summer was spent largely in preparation for the journey. She begged off from meetings and speech-making, unless they were commitments of long standing, seized by an urgent hunger for the country, for open air and for the nearness of growing things. She stayed at *Apple Acres* as much as she could, engaging in what she described as "an orgy of domesticity." She spaded and hoed and planted and harvested the produce of two large vegetable patches. In a letter to Alva Myrdal, assuring her that she would be in Sweden by the end of October, she said:

"We are putting up about everything that can be squeezed out of our Victory Garden. There is so much talk about next winter's food shortage, that everybody counts it a patriotic duty to have one. We have bought a quick-freezing outfit, which will give us the equivalent, we hope, of Birdseye frozen foods. The operation is extremely simple and suits our lack of experience. It remains to be seen how good the output will be. At any rate, we have already quick frozen about forty pounds of vegetables and will wind up, we hope, with two or three hundred pounds of vegetables and fruit. This is quite a new adventure for us, but we get a lot of fun out of it. Perhaps it is an earthy kind of excitement, but I am surprised to find how important it can become that beans boil only three minutes and then be cooled and packed quickly, or the sense of accomplishment in annihilating a few corn borers or cut worms. I hope I am not becoming bloodthirsty . . ."

September frosts put an end to the adventure in domesticity and, at long last, the permission to travel came from Washington, in a letter from the Outpost Service Bureau: "The idea of your going to Sweden to give a series of lectures fills us with enthusiasm. This is not a complete guarantee that we will be able to send you, but the chances look very good. We are investigating the possibility of a sojourn in England for you and I will let you know as soon as I hear anything definite." Now, all that was left for Madesin to do was wait, the most difficult of all things. She had already filled out long questionnaires, been investigated by the State Department and the Federal Bureau of Investigation. She had had all the innoculations. She had written the basic speech for her Swedish lecture tour.

Finally, on October 10th, the final word came. She was being sent as "a special representative of the Office of War Information assigned to duty overseas." She had become a government official, serving without compensation. Eight days later, on a brilliantly sunny morning, at New York's La Guardia airport Madesin was on a clipper that would take her to Sweden, but with a stop in Britain first. The flight was by a route that covered nine thousand miles, instead of the usual three. Her fellow-travelers were very few and all men in the foreign service. With frequent stops the plane first went to Bermuda; then to Puerto Rico; south to

187

Trinidad; down to Belem and Natal in Brazil and to a change of planes. Then across the Atlantic through southern skies to Fisherman's Lake in Liberia. North again to Portuguese Guinea, to Lisbon, to Foynes, Ireland, to Poole, England and, nine days after leaving New York, London, on a cold morning, wrapped in fog.

While she was on her roundabout flight to London, the last civilian plane to take off from England for Sweden had been shot down and all the passengers killed. The OWI had considerable doubt as to whether she could or should go on. Ambassador John Winant, "whose warmth and sympathetic understanding can never be forgotten" advised her to wait a little while until the situation was less fraught with danger. The little while became seven weeks, but Madesin did not mind waiting—had she not waited ten years to bring to life her International Federation?— and the unexpected stay in London became a memorable experience. Not only for her, was it memorable, but also for the thousands of British women with whom she came in contact. For five weeks she traveled all through England, Scotland and Wales, "speaking many times to all kinds of gatherings and always learning much."

Her first letter home was from London: "One expects to stand aghast at a blitzed London and its awesome blackouts. Actually, however, I am more impressed by what has happened within people than by what had happened to things. While there have been inestimable material losses there have also been great spiritual gains . . . The women of Britain are drab in appearance and very tired. They have few, if any, new clothes. Well-brushed garments have been turned, darned and made to last. Their homes are cold and the monotony of the food depressing. The brussels sprout is a mild, benign vegetable, but to face it daily for a long time cheerfully and gratefully requires a certain morale. The frequent air raids at night sap the strength for the demands of the day. Everyone has war work in addition to a job. But with it all, the spirit of the British is magnificent as they live and work under difficulties beyond our comprehension."

There were many Americans in Britain during the war, sharing the dangers and hardships, doing their jobs and doing them well. But because Madesin was not on a military mission, her visit aroused unusual interest. Her press conference, on the morning after her arrival, was crowded with British and foreign correspondents eager to learn from her the facts and information that were far more available in America than in England. In London, Caroline Haslett arranged for her to stay at the Forum Club, on Grosvenor Place, where she became acquainted with its president, the Princess Marie Louise, an aging niece of King Edward VII, who invited her to call and meet her sister, Princess Helena Victoria. "Sitting by a small fire," writes Madesin, "in a high-ceilinged bitterly cold room at 78 Pall Mall—they in hats and fur collared coats—we had an animated conversation about the course of the war and our two countries."

Caroline Haslett had also organized small meetings of especially active women, such as all the women MPs on the Womanpower Committee, whom she addressed at the House of Commons, the Campaign Committee for Equal Compensation for War Injury, and the Committee on World Status of Professional Women. What she enjoyed most, and was most deeply moved by, were her visits to scores of Clubs all over the British Isles. Wherever she went, partly because of her age and more so because of the magnetism of her personality, she drew large audiences and elicited enormous response. It so happened that in the very limited luggage allowed her, she had brought a very warm, tomato-red dress to wear for her speaking engagements. To clothing-rationed women, Madesin's red dress became a sort of symbol—"a red badge of courage" as one newspaper reporter labeled it—evoking visible pleasure in thousands of faces.

Reunions with British friends were bright interludes, and of real value were a few meetings with officers of the International, including Gordon Holmes and Dorothy Heneker, with whom a number of questions were thrashed out and solved. All were concerned about the rebuilding of the International the moment the war was over, about how to retrieve members and organized structures shattered by war. Constructive plans were laid and shared with many of England's most prominent women in and out of public life. She was constantly amazed by the confidence with which everyone spoke of the post-war days, with a total certainty that freedom would, of course, be restored all over the continent because the war would end in victory for the Allies. This confidence coupled with the extraordinary gallantry with which people went about their daily business between raids, as if this were entirely normal, came back to fill her thoughts at nights in rooms too cold to attract sound sleep. "The streets," she wrote, "are unbelievably dark. There is mystery and something quite unsettling in the shuffling footsteps which echo in the night, a sound of ghostlike things not seen."

As she visited Club after Club in Gordon Holmes' National Federation, her practical sense was again to the fore, assessing their size, the caliber of their membership, their seriousness of purpose and their program, against the financial investment which the International had made in helping to set them up. She quickly realized that the investment was highly profitable and would yield benefits far into the future. What impressed her especially was that, regardless of what happened all around them, British women throughout the war never put aside their efforts for an equality of status.

"British women," she noted, "are afire with zeal for women's place

189

and influence in the new world to come. Like one who has seen her own house blown down they have no question that there is to be a new structure. No time is lost on 'ifs.' Efforts are concentrated on the 'what' and the 'how.' "

Early in the war, when refugees from the continent had made their way into England, Caroline Haslett had drawn most of the women into a new organization she had called The International Women's Service Group. In 1943, when Madesin saw its workings at first hand, it had 600 members from twenty-eight countries. The women worked closely with the Governments-in-Exile, took all sorts of jobs to support themselves and made their experience and skills available to the country that had given them haven with unstinting generosity. The I.W.S.G. was an impressive group which bore the imprint of Caroline Haslett's immensely practical approach—she was, after all, a skilled electrical engineer by profession—combined with her endlessly patient understanding of human problems.

It was December 10th when Madesin received from Robert Sherwood, then Director of Overseas Information, the word she had been waiting for. She was designated "a Special Representative of the Overseas Operations Branch, with temporary duty at Stockholm, on the staff of Karl Jensen, Special Minister and General Representative of the Agency in Stockholm."

That night, even the cold and the ghostly noises in the deadly black night outside did not prevent her from sleeping as soundly as a child. She was so relieved to know that at last she would be on her way to Sweden, that even the excitement of it did not keep her awake.

16.   Mission to Sweden

Robert Sherwood's letter was the precious document that would enable Madesin to go to Sweden, but getting there was quite another matter. A few military planes made the flight carrying only persons in the British service and the diplomatic mail pouch. The stripped bombers flew at an altitude of about five miles over the Norwegian war zone, but could be shot down by the Nazis only with the expenditure of a great deal of gas. None, to date, had been lost. It was not long before Madesin was informed that if she still wished to go to Sweden, she should report at a certain point in Scotland.

"In a little hotel with one smoking grate fire to warm the lot of us, we four would–be passengers—three men and myself—waited. Every day we were told to be ready to leave, only to be advised almost at once of further delay. In nine days I paid my hotel bill and checked out five times. Finally, the pattern changed. As soon as we arrived at the airport, two trim young women in uniform took me in hand.

"Over my slacks and flannel shirt they drew a silk flying suit and over that, another of canvas. Around me was strapped the much publicized Mae West life preserver. A red electric bulb was clipped on my shoulder and attached to a battery in my pocket. The other pocket held a whistle on a cord. These were for attracting attention if I found myself unexpectedly in the North Sea. Next came the parachute harness, wool lined boots, two pairs of gloves and an oxygen mask. Stiff from such swathing, stiff also with nervous excitement, I was strapped in my canvas chair on the plane and we were off. One travels mostly in the dark and altogether in the cold. Over the dangerous water and afterwards across Nazi-occupied Norway, we flew hour after hour, wondering, thinking, remembering and praying. I hoped that we would come through safely, but if not, that in dying I would not be ashamed of myself.

"At last the dim form of a pilot leaned over me shouting 'We are over Sweden now' Most beautiful of words! for they meant safety! Lights came on, my three companions opened their thermos bottles of coffee. Mine had frozen. In a little while we could see beneath the closed blinds the fairy necklace of bright lights which encircled Stockholm. We had made it! One more plane had crossed intact."

The lights made her blink, the sound of traffic and of people took her by surprise, the warmth and comfort of Gunnar and Alva Myrdal's home where she spent the first few days, the abundance of food—falling into all of this, straight out of battered, pitch-dark, hungry England and the incredible flight wrapped in mystery and peril, made her wonder if she had awakened from a nightmare or, instead, was now having a lovely dream. It took all of a week before she could prevent the graphic memories of Britain from dominating her mind, and pack them away in a corner, leaving room for other, less gruesome, pictures.

Presently, established at the Grand Hotel where there had been no vacant rooms earlier, she sent home her first impressions: "Stockholm is too lovely, crisp and cool and flooded with sunshine! And there is warmth. Vacant lots and parks are piled high with wood for winter fuel. There seems to be an abundance of everything, rationed of course, except coffee and cigarettes. The coffee I bought in Lisbon and my American cigarettes are prized gifts. The city is over-crowded with people from everywhere, diplomats, foreign correspondents and refugees. Our American Legation, thanks to Minister Herschel Johnson, every day sends me press releases on the news from home, on the war, the Swedish editorial which a kind club member translates for me. I am quite overwhelmed with many thoughtful attentions and much hospitality."

The variety of persons she met and could talk to at length was astonishing. They included the Prime Minister, Per Albin Hansson, with whom she had lunch at his daughter's house, and the Ministers of Social Affairs, Commerce and Finance. Kerstin Hesselgren, MP, gave a dinner in her honor inviting the nation's leading feminists. The Swedish edition of *Time* magazine was launched at a huge cocktail party where the nation's leading political and literary figures crowded around her, asking questions about America, Britain and anything they hoped she would know which even a neutral country could not easily find out. Finland's Minister to Sweden devoted several hours to a meeting with her, and a luncheon at the Russian Legation gave her the opportunity to talk about Russia with the Soviet Minister to Sweden, Mme Kollontai, who was later to prove helpful to her. King Gustav's brother, Prince Karl, President of the extremely active Swedish Red Cross told her much about the work he was heading up, with American-born Countess Fokke Bernardotte acting as interpreter. The Crown Prince and Princess invited her to tea at Kungholm: "There were just the three of us," Madesin recalled, "and I forgot my practiced curtsey as the tall, good-looking man strode quickly forward with outstretched hand saying, 'How do you do, Dr. Phillips? I am the Crown Prince and here is my wife.' Here too,

I was asked many questions about the United States. Later the Crown Prince sent me a message to deliver to President Roosevelt."

The newspaper people found her fascinating as well as challenging to be with. "They are a grand group and I am quite spoiled by all these nice men. John Scott, son of Scott Nearing, the economist, is a delight to talk with on any subject. Cole, of Duke University is my special 'son' who does odd jobs for me when I am in a pinch. He brought his van Gogh and Monet prints to show me, the other night, when I had broken my wrist. I frequently have dinner with Karl Jensen, the young Danish-American chief of the Swedish Office of War Information, who is out-witting Goebbel's propaganda machine in Sweden in a remarkable way. Nazis are using, or trying to use, the strategy of terror that proved fatal to other countries."

The more she met men and women from all walks of life, the more she traveled over the country, the more she realized that to be an ambassador of goodwill for the United States posed no difficulties, but that to interpret Sweden to American audiences when she got home, would be a different matter. Sweden was no longer the country she had known before the war. The response of this traditionally neutral country to the scourge of war was an eye-opener to her. For instance, some 300,000 refugees were being cared for with a government appropriation of twenty-four million dollars, in addition to generous contributions from private sources. This figure, incidentally, was vastly increased after the war, when Sweden extended her relief work to countries far beyond Scandinavia itself.

Every Club in the country had initiated a relief activity of its own, even as it struggled to help preserve the nation's neutrality and to combat all of Hitler's efforts to break down this wall. Out of their rations they managed to send thousands of packages to Norway and Finland. The clothing was shipped in mountain quantities. Gifts were organized intelligently, so that not a particle of the thoughtfulness behind them was lost.

The long Christmas season was underway shortly after Madesin reached Stockholm, thus her tour around the country could not begin for a month or so. Madesin witnessed the festivities, participated in many of them, was treated as one of the family on Christmas Day by Mrs. Celie Brunius with whose children she played games under the tree, and later was among hundreds of Americans drinking egg-nog at the Legation. The long day ended with a dinner for twelve outside Stockholm as the guest of Dr. and Mrs. Stenberg, both highly regarded public figures and scientists. No wonder Madesin wrote home: "When I finally collapsed into bed I knew that my Christmas in Sweden was one that I could not soon forget!"

When she finally set off on her trip the new year had come in, marking the ninth year of the existence of the Swedish Federation, a strong and articulate organization wielding an influence in government that left Madesin enormously surprised, and most delighted of course. The number of Clubs was relatively small, only a score, but each had at least one hundred members, with the exception of the club in Stockholm, with well over a thousand and a long waiting list. Thanks to Alva Myrdal's eagerness to share Madesin with as many groups as possible, even during the holidays her calendar showed many speaking dates in the city. Among them was a special meeting called by the Social Democratic Party to hear her views on America, the war, the present and future social problems. That day she had fallen on the ice and broken a wrist bone. With her arm in a cast, she tried to show no sign of pain when she spoke. She felt as proud as a child winning a prize when a huge bouquet of flowers entered her room the next morning, with a note saying: "The Club was deeply moved, not only by your brilliant speech, but also by your courage in ignoring the pain you certainly must have felt, even though you succeeded in not showing it . . ." The arm was a handicap for a time, but the excitement of the tour helped her to overcome it. The refugees from Norway, Denmark and Poland also took her mind off her own difficulties. "There are some 30,000 of them from Norway alone," she wrote, "and though they have lost so much and faced the loss of themselves, they seem able to live each day in usefulness and with a strange sort of happiness." The Danes, in their thousands, had come across the narrow waters, and their story, like that of the Norwegians, was the same, a story of terror and tragedy.

In Sweden's large ports on the southern coast, Helsingbörg and Malmö, she saw more of them and again her "heart was wrung with their tales." The BPW Clubs had taken on a large share of the resettlement of refugees in these towns, in the countryside, wherever feasible. In Göteborg, major of all Swedish ports, the Club had attracted to a dinner and meeting all of the city's leading business and professional men as well as women. The American Consul, Mr. William W. Corcoran, reported later to the Minister in Stockholm that "Dr. Phillips' lecture here was the most successful given by anyone promoting our cause since the beginning of the war, not excepting such celebrities as Sir Walter Monckton, Dr. Malcolm Sargent, Thomas Eliot. The press was unanimous in praise of the American speaker."

Every town had something to display and every club saw to it that Madesin missed nothing that could interest or entertain her. "In Lulea near the Arctic Circle," she writes, "I saw, for the first time, the sparkstötting of the snow country. It is a cross between a sled and skates and is the common conveyance when the streets are too icy to permit walking. It is a chair on long runners. With one foot on a runner and holding on to a bar, you paddle with the other foot and fly through the streets 'with the greatest of ease.' In my fur-lined coat and close fitting hat, feeling like a one-legged duck, I paddled to a high-tea and home again. In Umea, also in that region, the press reported that 'never have so many men been seen at a meeting organized by women.' At Sundsvall, I visited the county hospital and learned that a private room and nursing care cost the equivalent of two and a half dollars a day, under Sweden's socialized medicine. At Gävle, as the house-guest of the Provincial Governor and his wife, I slept in the royal suite, underneath a three-foot Vasa crown. Governor Rikard Sandler was one time Sweden's Minister of Foreign Affairs. The meeting at which I spoke provided a wonderful audience. In Gävle I also spoke to some three hundred English-language students at one of the high schools. Both audiences were most responsive. The interest in America is widespread. Among women the interest in the post-war future of our International Federation was likewise constant and therefore very encouraging."

When the tour came to an end, Madesin was ready to go home. She had expected to spend Christmas in Westport and it was now springtime. In Stockholm, at her farewell cocktail party she heard from the Legation that there would be some delay in getting her back to England. With hotel space at a premium, the Myrdals moved her back into their home and Alva immediately proceeded to make engagements for practically every hour of Madesin's days.

"I went to Vinäkar," Madesin recorded, "to see for myself the receiving camp for those escaping from the Gestapo net. They were coming across the Swedish border at the rate of sixty or more each day. One does not ask how they got away, nor about those who failed and were tortured to make them reveal the names of their accomplices. They did talk of their acts of sabotage, or of harassing the Nazi invaders, or getting up in the dead of night, in the dark, to listen for news from BBC or to a speech by Roosevelt or Churchill. A digest of Wendell Wilkie's 'One World' had been circulated through underground channels and widely read.

"The delayed departure gave me time to meet with several leaders among the Norwegian refugees who had two major concerns: one, to know how to retrain their children in the moral standards sacrificed for the protection of family and friends in the years of lies and deception under enemy occupation; the other, to restore a full democracy to their country and the fullest of freedoms. Sitting around a tea-table with a small group of Polish refugees, I realized how heavily they were relying on America for their future. They had complete faith that their independence would be restored. They gave me a little bouquet of five red and white carnations, the colors of Poland, to remember them by. I pressed them among my papers to take home."

Suddenly, one evening, after waiting nearly a month, Madesin was

195

notified that she would be leaving in three hours. "It took about all that Alva and Gunnar and the Legation staff and I could do to get me off by midnight. The flight was uneventful, but the arrival in London was not. The city was undergoing one of the worst air-raids of the entire war. How we got to the Forum Club, I shall never know. The streets which I had known black beyond all conceivable blackness, were now light as day. The sky was filled with exploding bombs and streaming flares, the air loud with the comforting sound of anti-aircraft guns. In my few days in London, I went through other raids,—five on five successive nights. One comes instantly wide-awake at the wail of the siren, dresses hurriedly, grabs tin hat and pocketbook and rushes downstairs to where others are gathered. They sit quietly, talking as though at a teaparty these British women, until the lights go out, the blast takes a window pane or a bomb crashes very near. Then they rise, stand against the wall, or move toward the door in the hope of escape if the worst happens. As death hangs poised overhead, nothing seems to matter except the yearning to remain alive and, also, the hope that you will meet your fate with dignity and courage."

Before returning home she was asked to call on the Crown Prince of Norway, self-exiled from his country. She promised to deliver messages from him to his wife, Princess Martha, in Washington with the children, and to President Roosevelt. She was boarding the clipper that would follow the same roundabout route—Africa, South America and the Carribean—when she suddenly recalled "my father's admonition when, in 1927, I wrote him that I had been in an airplane: 'I hope you will not be so foolish as to take to the air again.' The thought of my current monumental disobedience made me smile as I strapped myself into the seat."

She had been gone five months and she was tired, but she did not go immediately to *Apple Acres*. She stayed with Marjory Lacey-Baker at the "shabby old Murray Hill Hotel in New York" and planned a closely packed swing around the country, to tell Americans what it was like on the other side of the Atlantic. Presently she went to Washington to report to Elmer Davis, chief of the Office of War Information and to try to see the President.

Nearly two months elapsed before he could receive her. When he did, like so many who saw President Roosevelt in those days, Madesin was shocked. "He looked worn and weary beyond words. This disturbed me a good deal." But she had delivered the messages from Sweden and from the Crown Prince of Norway, and briefly, had given Mrs. Roosevelt the highlights of her trip and the gist of her own observations.

In April, the International Federation sponsored one of its large teas, in the Biltmore Music Room, in Madesin's honor. In spite of the pouring rain, that Sunday afternoon, the room was packed, with many U.S. and foreign government officials in the audience. She presented a vivid picture of what she had seen in embattled Britain and neutral Sweden. She described, as best she could, the extraordinary spirit of the British people under fire, of the Swedes trying to keep their doors open to the victims of war yet not leaving room for Hitler's spies to penetrate as well. Then, gravely, she cautioned her own fellow countrymen: "The United States is considered the keystone of the future because of its power, resources, ideals. Europeans understand this more clearly than we do. If, as I forsee, when war ends the two strongest powers will be the United States and Russia, I ask myself, are our leaders and our people ready for the great responsibilities awaiting them? The peoples overseas need our financial help, of course. But they crave the spiritual leadership which they have a right to expect from American idealism. If we fail to give it, then Russia is next in line. The United States must make its choice. It must either vigorously promote an order of international social justice or lose its leadership." She was not, that day, talking about the rights of women or their equality, but of the course of world affairs, yet the same prophetic quality so clear in her demands for women in the 30's was evident in her demand for American statesmanship in the 40's.

After her call at the White House, in May, she had been to see Princess Martha of Norway who, having read an article by Madesin on the women of Norway that had just appeared, had invited her to come and tell her more about her trip abroad. Madesin wrote: "The Princess had been in America since 1940, when her country was invaded, and President Roosevelt had invited her to come with her children to the United States to insure their safety. I was able to give her news of situations in occupied Norway—certain facts that she could not receive through diplomatic channels—and, happily, about people she was concerned about in Stockholm, and of course, about my audience with her father, Prince Karl. She told me she had taken a house for the summer in Connecticut, outside Westport, and invited me to come and see her there."

In Madesin's absence, as once before when she had been so critically ill, the office of the International had been admirably carried on by the treasurer, Mrs. Taylor and those who had rallied to her call for assistance. Now Madesin set to work to compile a report on the International and its affiliates in wartime. It was a four-year statement, starting in 1939 and covering every phase of the organization's activity, including its finances. The major fact to be conjured with was that, of the 28 countries originally part of the International, in 1943 contact had remained possible with only 11. The other Federations and Clubs had either been liquidated by totalitarian regimes or had had to become inactive.

In common with the leaders of other women's organizations and movements, Madesin held to the conviction that there might be an antifeminist reaction once war was over and men returned to seek their jobs. "The war had pushed women forward," she wrote, "thrust new opportunities upon them in hitherto untried ways, gains that must not be lost. In view of this situation, the Emergency Committee of the International Federation of Business and Professional Women has circulated a resolution hoping it would reach all member groups in each country."

The gist of it was a request to governments and to international bodies dealing with post-war problems to appoint qualified women as delegates to national and international commissions, or conferences or other bodies, created for this purpose. National Federations, the resolution assured, will be prepared to supply lists of women with their specific qualifications.

Another concern was being shaped in Madesin's mind by the very fact of looking ahead to when war would have ceased. She began to worry that the hostility between nations might survive the fighting and that, even within the Federation, nationalisms might replace the traditional fellowship which ignored man-made boundaries. Some time before Italy surrendered to the Allies, detaching herself from the Axis and eventually declaring war on Germany, Madesin had received a cable from Maria Castellani in Italy, that had been held up one year by the censors, first on one then on the other side of the Atlantic. A letter arrived, which was six months old, from Antonietta Pogliani, who had been Fine Arts Chairman since 1933. Both were guarded in their wording and said little more than hoping Madesin was well. They probably intended their messages to inform the International that they, at least, had come to no harm. When the U.S. signed a truce with Italy, at the surrender on September 8, 1943, Madesin quickly expressed her complete faith in the loyalty of the Italian Federation, adding: "I hope we can soon reach our members in Italy. At our next International Board Meeting we shall welcome the Italian women as always. Of this bitter war, and of its making, the honest must say that all have sinned and all have suffered. Let us begin again." A year later, in October 1944, the Outpost Service of the Office of War Information in Rome notified Madesin that a renewed Federation of Business and Professional Women had come into being in Italy, and had been designated the official organization charged with restoring democratic rights and ways of life to the Italian women. The new President, Dr. Ines de Guidi Insabato, was professor of Chinese History at the Oriental Institute in Naples. Her first letter to Madesin said: "We wish to work loyally under your leadership for our International Federation . . . The sorrows and the tears of these calamitous years have strengthened our faith . . . we are ready to serve our common ideals . . ."

The tide of war on the Eastern front had begun to turn in November 1942, when the Russians encircled the German armies at Stalingrad, forcing them to surrender by the end of January 1943. After six more months came D Day and the allied landing in Normandy, at dawn on June 6, 1944. All through the summer the terrible fighting continued, but when the Germans were forced out of Paris by a French armored division supported by American troops, bringing liberation to the city, the end was in sight. In a violent counter-attack the German divisions tried to reverse the trend again, but, even though it was at high cost to the Allies, they failed. The disintegration of the Nazi Empire was becoming inevitable, the Axis had snapped in the East and in the West. In the occupied countries the underground patriots were surfacing, eager to fight the enemy face to face. The lights were coming on again, bringing freedom—yes—but also the appalling vision of the destruction wrought from the air, and laying bare the inventory of poverty, need, hunger and sorrow which was all that millions of people could call their own. Soon the unparalleled outpouring of gifts in kind and in cash began all over the United States. Every existing organization and countless new ones were working around the clock to sort, pack and ship as soon as it was possible to send anything but arms and other military material overseas.

European Federations which had survived the war up to that hour, were used as distribution centers for the vast quantities of relief channeled to them through the International. As soon as the guns were really silenced, the reconstitution of Federations wiped out under Hitler would be a matter of importance, not merely to individual members trying to regroup themselves, but also to the liberated countries as a whole, for the invaluable services which clubs could quickly organize themselves to perform for their communities. This would take money. The first of it came in a generous and unexpected way.

Early in 1944, the New Zealand Federation had quietly started to collect a pound from each member, to be placed in what was imaginatively called *The Lights Up Rehabilitation Fund*. The British heard of the plan, at a time when the grim nightly blackout was a constant reminder of the hardships they were still enduring. The idea caught on and the British Federation, egged on by Gordon Holmes and Stella Phillips-Marder, announced its *Lights Up Fund*. The pounds came in from every part of Britain.

The year 1945 had barely entered upon its second month, when the need to define post-war plans brought Roosevelt, Churchill and Stalin to a secret meeting at Yalta, in the Crimea. The future of a defeated Germany and a division of powers among the victors were laid down, as were general plans for a United Nations Organization. The six months that followed were among the most dramatic in all of modern history. At the beginning of March, with General Eisenhower commanding the Allied forces, the Rhine was crossed and the thrust into Germany was under way. Suddenly, on April 12th, President Roosevelt died at Warm Springs, plunging the Allies into a state of shock, causing the enemies briefly to take heart. The United Nations Charter Conference on which he had worked so confidently, in which he so truly believed was only two weeks away.

Above the guns that roared in the last battles, FDR's words, spoken such a short time earlier, still echoed around the world: "For the second time in the lives of most of us, this generation is face to face with the objective of preventing wars. No plan is perfect. Whatever is adopted at San Francisco will doubtless have to be amended time and time again over the years. No one can say how long any plan will last. Peace can endure only so long as humanity really insists upon it, and is willing to work for it and sacrifice for it." The Charter Conference was in session when, on April 28th, Mussolini, caught by partisans on Lake Como trying to reach Switzerland, was summarily executed. Two days later Hitler committed suicide in the bunker beneath his bombed-out Chancellery in Berlin. On May 7th, the German armies surrendered unconditionally, at Rheims and in Berlin. The firing ceased at noon on May 9th. The war in Europe was over.

In May, the Emergency Committee of the International Federation, faced with requests from European members for help in rebuilding their clubs and federations, decided to send an International representative abroad. She would go to Paris, Brussels, Rome, London and perhaps other places, if possible. Margaret Hickey, then president of the U.S. Federation, immediately suggested that the trip be undertaken by Madesin who, she emphasized, would know what to do better than any other person. The Committee agreed, but Madesin's first reaction was that someone else should be chosen. Ever since her return from Sweden and Britain she had hardly had a breathing spell: speaking all over the country, organizing meetings of one sort or another in New York and in Connecticut, and trying to meet writing deadlines. Finally, she saw the logic of the Committee's choice and agreed to go.

Although the war was technically ended, overseas travel for civilians was still severely restricted to persons on government business. But, by now, Madesin knew the ropes. Again she was appointed Consultant to the Office of War Information, Outpost Service Bureau. Her orders read: "Assigned to a special mission on behalf of the International Federation of Business and Professional Women." This time, however, not to let her make the still difficult journey alone and in order to provide some help in the work that lay ahead, the OWI appointed Majory Lacey-Baker as her volunteer assistant. For Madesin this was the 26th time that she was crossing the ocean for the International and, as usual, at her own expense. She, and Marjory as well, always wished it to be that way, even when funds might have been available to cover their expenses. More often than not, this constituted a major sacrifice for both of them. But it was part of the idea of service which they shared.

Dr. Phillips at a Board Meeting of the National Federation of Business and Professional Women's Clubs of Great Britain and Northern Ireland, 1943. Seated, left to right: Miss M. Lappage (honorary treasurer), Miss Stella Phillips-Marder (finance chairman), Dr. Phillips, Miss Gordon Holmes (national president), Miss D. Lappage (secretary). Standing: Miss D. Foster (ex-chairman, employment planning committee) and Mrs. Nancy Anderson (organizer).

17.   The Lights Come On

The trip to Europe began from New York on June 11th and, as it turned out, was even more richly fraught with extraordinary experiences than Madesin herself, though seasoned in such travels could have imagined. She kept a record as best she could, from which to retell it later.

"Armed with: pre-embarkation Health Certificate for leaving our country, showing that we had no vermin and no communicable diseases; the permit to enter France; the priority certificate to travel on a military plane; a pass as representative for *Good Housekeeping Magazine,* we boarded the clipper bound for London. We stopped in Newfoundland and took off again at dawn. There were about 20 passengers on the plane, so each of us had a bed and I slept well into the next day. We made it to Foynes, Ireland, in less than eighteen hours flying time, a fact that, in those days, gave one a great sense of unreality.

"Our London billets, for which we were very grateful, consisted of two frowsy beds in a third floor room with panes shaken out of the windows, the cold damp winds always at home there, in a room drearier than either of us had ever occupied before. I can still hear a recording that broke into the silence of early morning and late evenings, with a young voice singing "I'll Be Thinking of you" and the sharp, insistant nasal tone of the House Manager, greeting each G.I. or WAC or civilian at the cafeteria for breakfast with the one monosyllable 'Juice'? There were also inconveniences and discomforts, and yet I would not lose the memory of any of it.

"I see again the Officers' Mess where we lunched and dined. The Great Room of the celebrated Grosvenor House, in Park Lane, had been christened Willow Run, for the colossal assembly line of the Ford plant in Detroit. The largest ball room in Europe, it had welcomed royalty, débutantes, labor leaders, diplomats and other celebrities from many parts of the world. General de Gaulle and King Haakon of Norway, fighting the war from the outside, and General Sikorski, the Polish Premier, had spoken here to their exiled countrymen. Queen Wilhelmina of the Netherlands and the Prime Minister of Belgium met their anxious people there. President Roosevelt's birthday had been celebrated there at the height of the bombing. Now, in 1945, the Great Room was a mess for the American officers and by the end of that year, five and a half million meals had been served.

"For us it was a cafeteria where we had good food which we could enjoy knowing that it came from American stores and not taken from the limited supplies of our British friends. In the course of many conferences with leading women I began to understand conditions in various countries. Prospects were good for going to Belgium and Italy. Norway was still closed.

"Gordon Holmes, with that old authoritative manner that made us call her the General, took us on a three-hour taxi ride through miles of destruction—not blocks, but miles—of vacant spaces where homes, stores, office buildings had been; and windowless houses—just fronts and a fragment of a stairway or a fireplace or a rear wall. We were sickened by it. But somehow, it was a great joy to be in London. There was an expansion of spirit and life, with the cessation of raids and the good news from the continent. Living was still very hard, although, of course, not for us. At least everyone could get about, even at night, with a total sense of security. And one could now begin to build for the future."

Arrangements had just been completed for the flight to Paris, when Madesin developed pneumonia. She spent some time in an Army hospital and it was not until July 7th that she was well enough to leave. Even with all the credentials, it was not easy to make arrangements to cross the Channel. Finally the friendship which had developed between Madesin and Ambassador Winant in the terrible winter of 1944, worked miracles, in the form of passage on an Army Transport, not merely to Paris but, also, to Rome, back to Paris and Brussels.

"In Paris," Madesin continues "there were no taxis or busses available, but the OWI had furnished a car to take us to the Hotel Astor, its headquarters. In Paris the OWI had become the U.S.I.S.—United States Information Service. The large, comfortable hotel was entirely taken over by U.S. Army personnel, American newspaper correspondents, etc. We were assigned two bedrooms, two baths and a large sitting room between, all at an incredibly low rate. It had its drawbacks, of course. You might be in the elevator, when the power was gone. There was nothing to do but sit on the elevator floor and wait half an hour, perhaps two or three hours, unless your head or feet were within pulling distance from the floor, above or below, and someone, hearing you call, would pull you out.

"Once more, we had Army food, sent from America. I remember those hearty meals chiefly because of the eagerness with which the one French guest a week which we were allowed, devoted herself to them. And there was the PX. We had our regular allowance of cigarettes, cheaper by far than in America. With these one could tip lavishly—one or two were enough to wreath any face in smiles. One day we had lunch with our dear Madame Laudner, and Captain Esther Corwin joined us, whom we knew well from New York. In her jeep she brought little gifts from the PX for our hostess, but she had also brought chewing gum. My surprise was quickly put down by Mme Laudner who exclaimed: "If you could see what my granddaughter can do with a package of chewing gum! She took one to school and traded it for a pound of honey!" From then on, we too, were appreciative of chewing gum.

"Oh, yes, there was plenty of everything for Americans—cars, jeeps, trucks, but not for the French. There was lavish food at the Hotel Astor, but the French were on the edge of starvation. I heard no complaints, but I was sick at heart.

"I met with most of the members of the Paris Club, others came from other towns and there were women I had not known before. Meetings were arranged with the women of the Resistance, a group of alert, active, socially conscious women with great latent power, unlike any group I had met before in France. They saw the need for organization, and were eager to get going. They told us we had not come a day too early for there was very much work to be done. What seemed to be their reason for furthering our Federation was that a newly organized *Union des Femmes Françaises,* had already enlisted some of the leading women of the resistance movement. It was well-financed, active and said to be under strong Communist leadership. In fact, that summer it sponsored an International Congress for the purpose of setting up an international organization to support the *Charte Internationale des Femmes,* the Women's International Charter. The objectives of the latter were equal pay for equal work, the end of exploitation, the right of women to work in all industries, etc. The International Federation could not cooperate closely with the presumably Communist-dominated UFF, but the strength of that organization made the other women all the more eager for some non-partisan body, such as our own.

"After many meetings and thorough analysis of conditions and needs, I selected, at their request, an organizing committee of six members, a President, a Treasurer, various other officers and with Mme. Laudner completed a slate for an Executive Committee. There was to be a larger committee to set up the federation, with top women from many other important groups, which would then form a National Committee. But this phase of the work was not to start until after the summer. However, the smaller group held its first meeting, and even agreed to substantial dues of which ten cents per capita was to go to the International Federation. In agreement with French temperament and tradition, the committee was strongly of the opinion that the early organization work should be done entirely by volunteers.

With new foundations laid for a renovated French Federation, Madesin was eager to go on to Rome. The red tape proved exasperating. Finally she was informed of the unwillingness of the Director of the European Theater of Operations to let her go, due to "transport, billeting and messing" difficulties. She finally persuaded him after a meeting in which she laid before him the international implications of her work among the women. He said arrangements would be made, if she would stay not more than a week and not mind the delay in departure. One day, in Paris, she received a letter from an old colleague from Utah, who asked her to call on her brother, Colonel Francis FitzGerald, stationed in Paris in charge of personnel. The visit led to an unexpected experience.

"Marjory went with me," writes Madesin "and presently the Colonel, who was most cordial, said 'Wouldn't you girls like to make a trip to Germany?' Of course the answer was 'We would.' He asked: 'Where would you like to go? Berchtesgaden? Munich? Hamburg?' I said that most of all I would like to see Berlin again. 'Berlin it shall be,' he replied. 'I have a WAC Captain on my staff recently transferred here from Berlin. Polly Spofford will make a good escort for you.'

"Within a week we were landing at Tempelhof Airport in Berlin. We were billeted in the U.S. occupation zone in the home of a German family, ordered to move out of their rooms to make place for three of us. We spent much time driving around in the army jeep, seeing the ravaged city.

"The contrast between the Berlin of 1936, when Hitler was host to the Olympic Games, and the desolation in 1945, was overwhelming. There were no words in which to describe the shock of it.

"The heart of the city, in a circle about five miles in diameter, was utter devastation. Yet walls still stood, like ghosts, gaping, remembering. The Reichstag, Opera House, University, Cathedral, Kaiserhof, the Adlon, all were completely or partially gone. The streets were cluttered with parts of planes, tanks, trucks, cars, ambulances, some upright, some overturned. The beautiful Tiergarten was totally ruined. And the curb markets were doing a flourishing business with young Russian soldiers who were paying five hundred dollars for a twenty dollar wrist watch, five dollars for five cent candy bars, one hundred dollars for a carton of cigarettes. There were few smiles in Berlin. Eyes were hard, filled with despair, a kind of deadness that was hideous to see. I cannot express the terrible feeling one had there like nothing in the world I had ever known or even imagined.

"Everywhere we saw brigades of women, from all walks of life, filling buckets with rubble and dumping it in waiting trucks. It was estimated that it would take sixteen years to cart it all away. We were not able to get in touch with any of our former members, but under the watchful eye of our Captain Spofford we were allowed to meet several of

Germany's one-time women leaders. We wanted to discuss with them, if we could, the future of their professional women, but they spoke so guardedly that the conversations had no value.

"In the Russian zone, with our interpreter, we stopped to talk with a group of Soviet women in military uniform. We asked them questions about their women in the military service, they asked many questions of the same kind from us. They wanted especially to know if American women took part in political life. We said they did, but refrained from adding, 'not as much as they should.' We saw Hitler's pride, his Chancellery. Escorted by a lieutenant we stumbled through it for hours. Russian guards stood at the entrance and practically anyone, except the Germans, could go in and help himself to anything he could carry away. In its hundreds of rooms rain pours in through bomb holes on the broken remnants of priceless chandeliers, alabaster wall brackets, ornate chairs, divans, cabinets. The upholstery had been ripped off the furniture, the brocade pulled from the walls of Hitler's spacious sanctum to be taken home by GIs as souvenirs. His great, beautiful writing table lay overturned. Files of papers, correspondence, books, photographs, yards of film were scattered across the floor in the rubble, room after room. The sense of degradation was tremendous. I was told that there were about 100,000 dead still buried in the wreckage of Berlin, 25,000 in the flooded subways. Water could not be used for any purpose until it was purified.

"After four days in Berlin I was glad to leave its dreadfulness—glad to get away from the hundreds of tragic faces we saw everywhere—the faces of those who had once been a proud people."

In Paris it was the fourteenth of August and the city was going wild over the news of the Japanese surrender. Cries of *'la guerre est finie'* echoed through the streets. Thousands upon thousands of French men and women, of American men and women in uniform, of children, streamed up and down the long, broad flight of steps of the Madeleine to say a prayer of thanksgiving. That was in the afternoon. Nightfall brought lights and music and dancing in the streets. There was drinking and dining and laughing and lovemaking. Who cared about tomorrow? Only today mattered—*'la guerre est finie.'*

"I too, was grateful," Madesin writes, "but I was very deeply troubled. Yes, the Japanese had surrendered, because the A-bomb had blasted Hiroshima and Nagasaki. This horrifying thing that we had done—was it right, was it wrong? I was very very troubled."

A week later the official order for the visit to Rome arrived, and Madesin and Marjory were put on a C47 that flew them across the Alps and down to the Eternal City. Space was at a premium and they were invited to stay at the American Academy of Art on the Janiculum, as guests of the acting Director, Dr. Charles Morey. A small group of men and women were also staying there. "The dinner hour in the company of this distinguished scholar from Princeton was an intellectual treat," Madesin comments, "and to be staying in that lovely building, hearing in the night the trickle of the little fountain in the cloistered courtyard was a lovely experience.

"It was an incredible Rome! On the streets very few automobiles, no busses, no streetcars. The only vehicle for transportation was a small open truck, a *camionetta*. Having climbed up into it by a short ladder, and paid the fare, one stood jammed in with the others. Food, of course, was strictly rationed. Prices on the black market were fantastic: chicken eighteen dollars apiece, horse-meat three dollars a pound, tea twelve dollars, coffee nonexistent. We gave our members everything we could buy at the PX—beef-tea cubes, candy bars, spools of thread and darning cotton, soap—anything to help.

"There were the usual, shocking contrasts. We attended a reception given by our Ambassador, Alexander Kirk, whom I had known since our first Goodwill Tour, in 1928. Despite the hardships, we were guests at several luncheons and at an unforgettable performance of *Carmen* under the stars in the ancient baths of Imperial Rome, the Baths of Caracalla. An invitation by the opera's conductor to come backstage, in the intermission, to meet the artists, added another prized experience to the many I had accumulated. Most important of all, of course, were the long talks with Maria Castellani, who was largely responsible for the rebirth of the Italian Federation. We spoke of the tragic years that had now come to an end. I met once more the many friends I had known and loved for many years."

The reconstituted Italian Federation was less than a year old, but the Rome Club, housed in a magnificent old palazzo, could already boast of close to five hundred active members. Clubs had been formed in Genoa and Milan and the Federation was issuing a bulletin, *Nuovi Orizzonti* (new horizons) bespeaking the purpose of its members. The Federation was eager to have Madesin's direction in setting up programs for social service, to work with the authorities for the return of the Italian prisoners of war, to arrange employment centers for women already experienced in business and the professions. They were eager to find means of participating in whatever special programs the International Federation had on hand. There was more liveliness, more readiness to work in order to serve the cause of the women in business and the professions, than Madesin had encountered elsewhere.

In Rome, as in every place she visited on that unforgettable post-war tour, Madesin came face to face with the dreadful aspects of the aftermath of war. She visited a huge encampment of refugees just outside the city where hundreds of homeless families and single people were waiting, with little hope, for resettlement and the possibility of beginning a new life. Another day the experience was so searing that it left a permanent scar in her mind.

"I was received at the Royal Palace, by Queen Marie José," she writes. "She was to be the last of the queens, for that was the sunset of the Italian monarchy. Italy became a republic within a year. She had wished to see me, she said, to tell me of her appreciation for my coming to Rome in this time of stress. We discussed organizations and the progress of Italian women, a subject in which she seemed to be truly interested. She spoke at length of her own and the King's concern for the people enduring such hardships and particularly the children some of whom, she added, I might see on the Palace grounds.

"In fact, after I left her, I was taken through the formal gardens to where scores of very small children were playing, all of them maimed in the war. One of the many lodges had been converted into a home for them. Blinded, or without hands, or arms, or legs, with serious, unchildlike faces marked by dreadful memories, they were an unendurable sight. Tears suddenly poured down my cheeks. When I tried to apologize, my escort said: 'When your Governor Lehman was here recently, in regard to your country's relief work he wept, just as you are doing.' I shall always remember the tender ways of the nuns who were caring for those tragic little victims of man's inhumanity to man and helping them to play."

Before leaving Rome, Madesin addressed a very large gathering of Club members and their friends. What she believed so completely in her heart, surfaced in her words as she spoke of her faith that Italy, with its great traditions, would come again into its own, of her vision of the future of the reborn Federation, of her belief in the value of its influence. A letter that reached her in London was a moving response to what she had wanted to convey: "You brought us the light of hope, the words of understanding, the flame of faith. Have you realized that listening to your words of good-by tears were in all eyes? Everybody is now anxious to help the organization. Success will certainly favor this new born child."

One of the nice things about traveling around in small uncomfortable army planes, Madesin found, was that at every airport there was a table piled high with paperback Armed Services Editions of books to fit in uniform pockets: current novels, plays, non-fiction, poetry, science. She would pick two or three at one airport and drop them off at another, and replenish her supply. At the Rome airport, she found a copy of John Steinbeck's *Cannery Row,* a story with such a depth of feeling for the mysteries of human existence, that she read it over more than once that summer.

"With John Steinbeck as my other traveling companion" she writes, "we flew to London in a C-47 army plane. After our only stop in Marseilles, we went through two terrific thunderstorms and hit a prodigious air pocket. We were all thrown violently to the floor. As we scrambled back into our seats, I saw that the young officer sitting opposite me was bent down and dripping blood from his forehead. I gave him the flask of brandy we always carried with us. He took it gratefully. Several of the other men also seemed to be hurt and an ambulance met us in Paris. We spent the night at the Astor, not hurt, but too badly shaken to go on to London until the next morning.

"In London, by chance, five members of the International's Board of Directors were there all at the same time, but for different reasons. Their presence, however, was the reason for my return to the British capital. We had a very productive all-day conference discussing, chiefly, the time, place and agenda for our first post-war Board meeting, which we decided to hold the following summer, and a model constitution to serve as guide for new federations. We took our first steps in regard to the United Nations and we agreed that, as spokesman for the International, I should request that our organization be granted early representation on the appropriate bodies of U.N. That our request was granted is, of course, a fact.

"We discussed the probable duties of our representative, confident that we would have one. She would formulate a program related to the U.N. for our Federations to adopt; she would be responsible for supplying the U.N. with such information about our Federations as it might request; she would recommend action to be taken by Federations in their own countries, and would have power to speak for the International at the U.N. The U.N. Charter Conference was then going on in San Francisco, and Miss Margaret Hickey would be attending it in a few days. We agreed that she should be the one to serve as our representative.

"We returned home by way of France, spending a few days in Brussels first, trying to make plans with members of our Belgian Federation. Badly disrupted by the invasion, its reorganization presented a number of problems in that brave small country that had suffered so greatly. There was very little that could be done to help them at that time and we went on to Paris, again staying at the Hotel Astor. I was anxious to get home, but planes and ships were overflowing with our returning military personnel who, of course, had priority. It was nearly the end of October before we could get a passage home."

Meanwhile, the weeks of delay became a well-earned vacation in a well-loved city. "The entire city only had one hundred taxicabs and there were no busses. Only the Metro. We learnt to walk for miles, enjoying it. We were sightseers and browsers along the Left Bank bookstalls, we went to the Opera and to the famous Flea Market, each day calling to see if there were any hope of transportation home. In our wanderings we tried to identify the vegetables that were growing in the once lovely flower beds in the Tuilleries gardens. We read the plaques on scarred walls, honoring those who fell in the courageous street fighting against the Nazis before the surrender.

"Came the day of the Municipal elections and women were voting for the first time. We were permitted to go into a polling place to watch the French procedures. Earlier, we had spent an afternoon at the Palais de Justice, during the trial of Maréchal Pétain who sat, hour after hour, immovable, looking straight ahead. The hated Pierre Laval was testifying. His face was hideous to see, worn and ravaged. But his voice, somehow, invited confidence and his quiet delivery was unexpected. The court room was crowded to suffocation and we stood, shoulder to shoulder, scarcely able to move, fascinated by the proceedings.

"We spent a harrowing day at the Hotel Lutetia where, in 1936, the International's second congress had been held, when our guest of honor had been Frances Perkins, Secretary of Labor. The huge hotel was now a house of mercy, in which hundreds of displaced persons were clothed, fed, given medical attention and housed until they could be started on a new way of life. In the lobby, which I had last seen filled with our members, getting their keys, chatting, going on to meetings, there was now a series of bulletin boards on which were posted thousands of small photographs of missing men and women, and crowds standing before them, looking for their own.

"Meals were no longer served in the dining room, but in the basement filled with long wooden tables and benches. Here we talked with a blond, good-looking young woman, a member of the Resistance, a survivor of imprisonment at Ravensbrueck. She told us of her underground activities before she was caught and of the concentration camp—the indignities, the tortures. I asked her how she could speak of these experiences—and so frankly. 'They live in the mind' she said, 'one cannot forget. It helps to talk about them.'

Shortly before we left Paris, Alva Myrdal came. As we dined together we sought a reassurance about the future that neither was able to give to the other."

At long last, passage was available on the E. B. Alexander, one of the older ships of the U.S. Lines. It had once accommodated 300 cabin passengers. Now, as a transport ship, it was carrying nearly 5000 officers and men, some 500 WACs, nurses, Red Cross personnel and a few wives of diplomats. "We were assigned a small stateroom with six bunks, three on either side, six clothes hooks, no closet. Sharing the cabin were the wife, teen-age daughter and young son of the Yugoslav Military and Air Attaché in Washington. The sixth occupant was the French-born wife of Norman Armour, the American Ambassador to Spain. For family reasons she had remained in Paris during the war. We had two meals a day, five sittings at a meal, and one joined whichever line was the shortest to the dining salon. All other space was used for sleeping quarters. Except at mealtime, you could only walk, stand, sit on the floor in a corridor or lie on your bunk. You could also lean over the rail to watch the GIs shooting craps on the deck below.

"Knowing I would have at least ten days at sea, I made a place of my own in which to 'relax.' There was a sizable corner outside the barbershop where one could safely sit on the floor without being in the way of passersby. Always after our five o'clock meal we sat there on our life-preservers, backs against the wall to read or write letters. I wanted to talk to some of the officers on our deck and I soon learned that a friendly glance or a smile as they passed was usually taken as an invitation to join us. I called this the Barbershop Club and as our group changed and expanded from night to night, it became a focus for many a provocative discussion.

"Many spoke of their disillusionment and hope that they would never have to fight another war. They told us of their wives, children, mothers, girl friends. They wondered how they would fit into the old life at home. But how eager they were to get there! Madame Récamier may have had a more elegant salon than mine. I doubt, however, if she could have valued her conversations more highly."

18. Foot Soldier for Peace

Madesin was still abroad when the atomic bombs were dropped on the Japanese cities of Hiroshima and Nagasaki. While the streets of Paris were teeming with people rejoicing that the war in the Pacific had also come to an end, Madesin's mind dwelt persistently on the dropping of those bombs, by her own country's orders. The great scientific achievement of those who, in the desert at Los Alamos, had proven man's ability to harness nuclear power for his needs, was forever blackened by its first use—to sow unparalleled death and destruction. Deeply impressed on her consciousness was the fact that this horrifying weapon, possessed then by only one country, her own, had been launched at the decision of one single government, representing only 160 million people, approximately fifteen and a half percent of mankind, and that this was the same government which, only a short time earlier, had welded together "a thousand million allies" under the promise of the Atlantic Charter in the name of Franklin Roosevelt's "Four Freedoms."

In her study in Westport, with her face away from the bare-branched beauty of the old apple trees outside the windows, she poured over the statements of the scientists who had access to the facts. She read and re-read the words of Einstein, the German, of Fermi, the Italian, and the words of leading physicists of her own country, and came quickly to envision the world as a tragically divided place in which the term goodwill already appeared to have lost its meaning. Her message in the next issue of *Widening Horizons* struck no comforting note though it was Christmas time. In January, speaking in many places, she was again the voice of conscience saying:

"We have emasculated the familiar term good will. It has come to mean an idle, effortless willingness on our part that all should be well with other people, other nations, provided nothing positive or of sacrifice is required of us . . . Millions are hungry and cold, sick and dying. I know that the needs are so colossal, the problems so complex that what one person can do seems to him little indeed. But, however great or small our part, we must do it and do it now. We shall be judged, and rightly, not by what we profess, but by what we do."

The United Nations Assembly and Security Council held their first meeting in London on January 20th and almost simultaneously a United States Conference on Women in World Affairs opened at the Waldorf Astoria in New York. A special committee appointed by Margaret Hickey organized the program to deal with: *Participation of Women in Public Life* led by Judge Sommerville Howarth, *Participation of Women in Economic Life* led by Mary Donlon and *Participation of Women in International Life* led by Josephine Schain. Madesin Phillips, at the luncheon session, told of her five-months experience overseas, pointing out that "the people of Europe have emerged ready to accept the sacrifices which are inevitable if we are to have a better world based on a more equitable distribution of both tangibles and intangibles. They have come to realize what we, in this country, are reluctant to acknowledge, namely that the old system will no longer work, and they are willing to try the new. They are not terrified of Socialism, Communism or any other ism. What they want is something simple, practical, workable that will mean a better life for all as the only foundation for a permanent peace."

But she was not done with her crusade. She set out on a lecture tour which took her 9000 miles around the United States. "It was a hard, fast trip of one night stands," she wrote Alva Myrdal. "In fact, I was gone nineteen days before sleeping two consecutive nights in the same bed."

By spring of 1946 communications had been established with all of Europe's business and professional women's federations: Norway, Denmark, Holland, Austria, Poland, Czechoslovakia and Finland had been heard from. Everywhere the news concerning the Federations was heartening: a nucleus remained, the women were ready and anxious to begin again, despite, the gradual realization that the extent of destruction and waste of human life was appalling. Austria had lost one fourth of her population. Five hundred thousand Jews in Hungary alone had been marched to their deaths in the last months of Nazi fighting. Russia had lost twenty million of her people and Germany was a shambles. The U.S. Federation's Food and Clothing Drives were stepped up as the cry of need came from more and more countries, even though this was obviously only a proverbial drop in the bucket.

Madesin's plans to hold the first post-war Board Meeting of the International in Brussels were taking shape without too much difficulty. The major problem of providing food for those who attended was solved by the generosity of the Minnesota Federation which volunteered to ship all that was needed. On the first day, however, consternation reigned because the food, having reached the port of Antwerp in good time, had not progressed as far as Brussels. Madame de Munther-Latinis came to the rescue, offering to lend her own packages received from friends to provide the first meal. When the large American cases were delivered, actually that same evening, another Belgian member who owned a café, offered to prepare and serve the meals. Her place was quickly re-named Minnesota Café and everyone involved in the Board meeting came for a share of the food. Some of the European women were tasting good food for the first time in years and all of them were having their first treat of a real cup of coffee since the invasion began! "This is a minor detail," Madesin observed, "but one which brought home to us from across the Atlantic, better than the recounting of many a tragic event, the hardships which most Europeans were still having to face."

Delegates from eleven countries answered the Board's roll call on July 30th, plus non-voting representatives from Belgium, Czechoslovakia and France whose federations had not yet been reconstituted. There were many observers, but it was not the glittering assemblage of earlier years. Most were shabbily dressed, many had only recently been saved from a Nazi prison camp, miraculously alive. But the radiance and warmth shining through their wan faces was like the return of spring after the hardest of winters. Most of the International Officers were on hand, but not all— Maria Castellani was teaching in the United States and Margery Toulson could not make the trip from the Far East. Absent, also, was the Treasurer, Isabelle Claridge Taylor, awaiting her first child in Philadelphia. Frantiska Plaminkova was present in every heart and mind, as were others who had not survived the war.

As each of the delegates reported for her Federation, relating what had become of it during the war, the tale that unfolded from simple words suddenly took on an epic quality. One saw a panorama of clubs going underground, of members protecting each other's homes or families, or finding shelter and jobs for refugees, of International Day observances in hundreds of communities, when members brought their own piece of bread just in order to break it with the others, and stare at unlit candles representing countries occupied like theirs, and in so doing finding comfort in the thought that they were not alone. However, the end of war had also brought unexpected advances for women's rights in many places and this, too, was reported.

Marie Wolfova, of Czechoslovakia, after paying a quiet and deeply stirring tribute to her countrywoman, Senator Plaminkòva, "the great leader of all Czech women," added that ten other members of the Executive Board of the Czech Federation had lost their lives, some executed, some persecuted till they died. She herself had survived two and a half years of concentration camp, but her husband, also a resistance fighter, had been beaten to death in his prison cell. She paused almost imperceptibly, then concluded saying: "There has been a restoration of women's rights now. Twenty-four are sitting in our Parliament among 300 mem-

214

bers and one of them has been elected Vice-President of the Chamber. The Deputy Mayor of Prague is a woman. We are making progress, and in freedom."

In Finland, reported Anni Voipio-Juvas, the struggle had been largely moral and psychological, but also against great shortages of every kind of food and fuel. Madame Vavasseur, praising the women of the French Resistance, emphasized that recognition of their courage had come, not merely when women were given the vote, but through the appointment of Madame Viennot as Secretary of State and Madame Lefaucheux as French Delegate to the United Nations. Thirty women had gained seats in the Constituent Assembly.

Britain had had seven and a half million women mobilized to serve. The number of those who had died in raids and elsewhere had not yet been ascertained. Poland had lost seven million people in the war. As in Austria, this was one quarter of the total population. In Holland, Mies Lanen recounted, the women's chief undertaking in the Resistance was to lead allied pilots, who had been downed but not caught by the Nazis, back to the coast where they could then return to Britain. This work was done at night and at incalculable risks. Some women had paid the price of death for their courage. It was by women such as those who had taken the risks that the new Dutch federation would now be fashioned, she said. Norway's tale of resistance was equally remarkable. Now, Bergliot Lie reported, there were eight women in Parliament, as against one before the war.

Madame Bodil Begtrup, Chairman of the Status of Women Commission of the U.N., who delivered the principal address, repeated once more the point so often made by feminists in the previous decades, saying: "In thousands of years of history, men have shown themselves incapable of establishing a lasting peace. Nobody knows what women can do, for they have never had the power to help to build the peace. Today they are still not in the Security Council of the U.N. or even in its Social and Economic Council. They are not in Foreign Offices nor in the Diplomatic Service and relatively few are in Parliaments. We have only one strong sphere of influence: the home, and that alone is not strong enough to change laws, education and public opinion or to repair social injustice. To accomplish this may cause inconveniences in the habits of the home, but mankind as a whole will benefit."

Margaret Hickey, having returned from San Francisco her mind alight with enthusiasm for the promise rekindled by the U.N. Conference, agreed to develop a United Nations program for the International Federation and the Board voted to "establish a United Nations Committee to coordinate the work of various national Federations in this area." She was appointed Chairman of that Committee and soon thereafter Madesin,

215

as International President, applied for and received from the Social and Economic Council of the U.N. recognition of the Federation as an organization qualified for Consultative Status. She was chosen to be the first Consultant and served most effectively for many years.

Reports heard and plans laid down at the Board Meeting in Brussels in 1946 were, in a sense, an integral part of the work done the following year at the first post-war International Congress, in Paris, in July 1947. Together their achievements constitute a summing up, a valedictory, for Lena Madesin Phillips' stewardship, for she did not intend to continue as president, even if asked to do so.

Since 1919, when she had so lightly told a YWCA executive in New York that she "would be interested in doing something for business and professional women," the two Federations she helped to found had been the paramount concern of her entire life. By training and capacity she had every opportunity to make a name for herself in the law, but when her legal practice interfered with her activities for the International Federation, she dissolved her law partnership and closed her office. Her four years as associate editor of *Pictorial Review* uncovered her gift for creative writing and editing, but she chose to pour her energies into the International Federation instead. She was not without political ambition, yet she put partisan politics aside whenever the welfare of the non-partisan International stood in the way. She was, in real fact, a leader: while she enjoyed praise, she abhorred adulation and valued work above all else.

In an editorial for *Pictorial Review* she once told a story about Susan B. Anthony which could easily have applied to her. Once, at a very large meeting, when tributes were being paid to the suffrage leader, a friend noticed that Miss Anthony herself was joining in the applause.

"Susan," the friend admonished, "you mustn't clap. They are talking about you." "No, my dear," replied the eighty-year old lady, "They are really talking not about me but about the cause."

For Madesin too the cause was all that mattered, in fact it was all she saw. Her magnetic personality drew to it women of vision and vigor similar to hers, women outstanding in their own fields and in their own countries, and she never pretended or let it be said, that the success of the Federation was due to her single efforts. The first time someone said this to her, intending it as a tribute, Madesin quickly answered: "If you really think that I did all this alone, then you are telling me that I am a failure, for I have striven all my life to bring about co-operation between people and, above all, between others and myself in order to promote a common cause into fruition."

From *Apple Acres* she wrote to Alva Myrdal, saying: "By the time this is in your hands, my earlier letter confirming my decision to not stand for reelection will have reached you. This should be no news to you, but one never knows with old girls like myself, whether or not they intend to go through with it. I do. My loyalty remains, of course, and such services as I can give will always be at the disposal of the International; but we need new leadership, more aggressive and energetic, for the future. I trust our members will use good judgment in their choice."

The eve of the formal opening of the Paris Congress, in July 1947, had been set aside for a gathering in memory of the many members who had been the victims of war. Madame Vavasseur, Congress Chairman, had planned a program of music, asking Madesin to pay the spoken tribute to the dead. The National Federation of every country invaded or attacked was asked to suggest a musical composition by an artist of that country for inclusion in the program, which was performed by a group of remarkable Polish and French musicians under the direction of Marguerite Canal of Paris. With the playing of each work, the International President lighted the candle of that country, in memory of Federation members whose lives had been sacrificed in the war. Then, paying them a tribute, Madesin said, in part: "Our only thoughts tonight are of our dead—those members of the International Federation who gave their lives in the struggle for homeland, for freedom, for humanity, and that the world might know enduring peace . . . As high symbol of them all we call the name of Frantiska Plaminkova, executed by the Nazis. Strong courageous, wise and just, with zeal for the right and compassion for all oppressed, Senator Plaminkova was a crusader of many causes, including our own. She died as she lived, fighting for those things in which she believed . . . The dead ask of us not tears, but deeds. Tonight we speak of them through that abiding beauty which is music, the international language, a bridge between the material and the spiritual, between a tangible and an intangible world. May we find them again in the spiritual qualities which are their immortality. For each we light a candle, symbol of the eternal flame." By request, the program was heard without applause and when the last notes had echoed away the audience dispersed silently, not hiding its emotion. No one, that evening, could have imagined that in less than two years the Communists would seize Czechoslovakia and that Marie Wolfova, who was in that silent audience, would pay the ultimate price for her belief in freedom. Like her compatriot Frantiska Plaminkova, she was sentenced to death and shot.

The Fourth International Congress convened the next day at UNESCO House, where quarters for the meeting had been generously offered by Julian Huxley, UNESCO's Director General. Of the eight Vice-Presidents only three had been able to attend. They were Anni Voipio-Juvas of Finland, Dorothy Heneker of Canada and Caroline Haslett of Great Britain, now Dame Caroline, for she had just been made Dame

Commander of the Order of the British Empire for her outstanding services to her country.

While Madesin listened to speeches of welcome and to gracious replies, she peered into the faces of delegates, observers and friends, many of them her friends of long standing. They were three hundred women, many from war-torn countries, many from nations that had remained officially neutral but had experienced much torment and anxiety nonetheless, many from countries that had fought but endured no real suffering at home. In Westport and at the Biltmore office she had thought a good deal about what she would say in her last speech as International President. She felt very deeply that the selfless spirit born of suffering and of constant peril must be kept alive in time of peace. Even more deeply she believed that a way had to be found to transmit this selflessness to those who, by an act of fate, had been spared the dangers and hardships. The gap created by the differences in experience could only be bridged, in the long run, by profound social changes which some countries were actively seeking while others were not even prepared to regard them as needed although they might find themselves unable to prevent them from taking place.

In her final address, Madesin sketched briefly what she had seen on her first visit to Europe during the war and again later, when the guns had just been silenced. She brought out, deftly and realistically, the role which women had played, the advances they had gained at war's end and, in the interest of peace and human welfare, the desperate need that these gains be further multiplied. The unifying force born of the common struggle was a positive side of war which, she insisted, must not be allowed to deteriorate. "I sometimes feel," she said, "that the last two years since V-J Day are even more tragic than those spent in a state of war. In war, nations were united for victory, they shared, reached agreements and understood the necessity of standing together. Individuals found deep satisfaction in sacrifice and service. If this was the price of victory and of the recovery of freedom, surely peace cannot be bought for less. I ask you, then, to be as great in building peace as you have been in achieving victory. We must now face the future with faith and with courage, realizing that the human race does go painfully forward, step by step, and that we are privileged to participate in this difficult but inevitable process.

"I do believe that what happens to any one of us matters little. It is the common welfare that counts. We are in a period of revolutionary striving. We are involved in a mammoth struggle between freedom and servitude, between equality and privilege, between too much for the few and too little for the many. Conditions have created questions which demand answers, regardless of the terms on which they may have to be exacted from those who are now reluctant even to seek such answers . . . As we resume our work together, I plead with you to try to see all that we do, or strive to do, as an integral part of a world-wide drive towards freedom, opportunity and security not merely for ourselves, but for all the people of the earth. It is a fight worth making. This is a time in which we must be as careless of self and as confident of victory as we were in war—because our goal is peace which deserves everything we have to give to it."

The work of the Congress proceeded smoothly, with much honest debating and many agreements reached, until the report of the Nominating Committee was called for. Margaret Hyndman, K.C., of Canada, Chairman, announced that her committee was unfortunately obliged to report that it had been unable to propose anyone for the Presidency or for any other office and that nominations would have to be made by the delegates. A murmur of surprise went through the assembly. Madesin, having received assurance that the Nominating Committee had investigated all avenues as fully as possible, discharged it, suspended the session temporarily and called for an immediate meeting of the Board of Directors.

The fact was that the members of the Nominating Committee had come to the unanimous conclusion that no European woman was ready, at that time, to take on the responsibility of the International presidency. Material conditions were very difficult all over Europe, the Federation's finances constituted a major problem and every woman who might have been qualified for the office was deeply committed to the necessity of rebuilding her own life and that of others around her. Recognizing the validity of these arguments, the Board agreed that the next president would have to be an American and Sally Butler, just ending her term as President of the U.S. Federation, appeared to everyone as the wise and logical choice. The new slate received the approval of the delegates and was voted upon by casting a single ballot. Sally Butler's first act was to move that Lena Madesin Phillips be named Founder-President with a permanent non-voting seat on the Board of Directors. The motion was passed by a loud round of applause.

A major chapter of Madesin's life was now concluded and the fruits of twenty-six years of unswerving and devoted effort were passing into new and younger hands, as she had wished. Earlier that Spring, planning the final details of the Paris Congress, Madesin had written her editorial for *Widening Horizons* foreshadowing something of what would lie ahead for her successor. She wrote: "I think most of us have underestimated the spiritual, mental and material rigors of this transition period between war and established peace. Dr. Williard Sperry, dean of Harvard Divinity School recently asked Professor Alfred North Whitehead how long it had been since the world had known as radical changes as were now taking place. 'If you are referring to the history of Europe,' replied Dr. Whitehead, 'the answer is "since the Thirty Years War (1618–1648)" but if you are referring to the life of mankind as a whole, the answer is "Never."

"If this is true, stability is not just ahead and we must accept suspense, conflict, shock, innovation, failure and change as the background against which our lives will be lived probably for many years. Can we find new techniques for such an unsettled life? Yes, if we are not too set in our ways to be flexible . . . Therefore, let us accept this time of transition for what it is and make the most of it. We shall need determination to push hard in what seems to us the right direction. In so doing we must exercise patience, tolerance and flexibility, and not demand immediate perfection. Moses saw but could not enter the Promised Land. To glimpse it and to help clear the path should at least bring us peace of mind."

Connecticut and *Apple Acres* were beautiful when Madesin returned there in early fall. The summer tenants had gone and the Italian orchard-man, having harvested the crop of apples in payment for his labor, had left a huge barrel of the best for Madesin and Marjory. Slacks, sweaters and country shoes were ready for use and the wood pile needed replenishing. The woods, where Madesin went wandering, armed with her faithful axe, were aflame with maples in their full autumnal glory. Indoors, the piano, the chess set, the books, stacks of papers to be sorted, and no end of souvenirs of Madesin's decades of service to the cause of woman's equality, welcomed her into an atmosphere of delicious serenity.

But Connecticut itself was far from serene. It bristled with controversy as, step by step, the country engulfed itself in the Cold War. Civilian control of atomic energy, so valiantly fought for the year before, had not stopped the manufacture of bombs. Debates were heated in the United Nations, but not more so than in the drawing rooms of America's suburbia, over Israel's establishment as an independent nation and the trouble brewing in Indonesia and Indochina. The Soviet Union retaliated for what it regarded as an anti-communist thrust by the Marshall Plan, by replacing the defunct Comintern with a new and ominously lively Cominform. "Now that we have defeated the common enemy," Madesin ruefully observed, "as in some madness bent on self-destruction, we are turning upon each other."

Speaking almost day in and day out to schools, service clubs, civic meetings and a host of other groups, Madesin was sharply aware of the general antagonism to the U.N. and of support for the Cold War. International action in the pursuit of peace was still the single most important effort to be made. Wherever she went, she made her plea: "I know that the needs everywhere in the world are colossal, that the problems are complex, but however great or small our own part, we must play it and play it now. Else, let us speak no more of goodwill."

The search for permanent headquarters for the U.N., and the vicissitudes surrounding it, had left a bitter taste in Madesin's mouth. A committee had traveled back and forth all over the United States, inspecting possible locations for accessibility, climate, cultural opportunities and the natural settings as well. Finally, Greenwich, Connecticut, seemed to fulfill all the requirements: New York, with its libraries and museums, its vast centers of communication, its international activity, was conveniently near, while Greenwich itself, in beautiful surroundings offered the vitally important distance from the metropolis and its inevitable drawbacks. Greenwich, however, with the greatest per capita measure of wealth in the country, would have none of the United Nations. The world organization, it was murmured, would bring unrest into that suburban Utopia as well as too many foreigners with slanted eyes or even black skins!

The Greenwich rejection was not very important in itself, but to anyone as sensitive to these things as Madesin, and there were many such in her circle, it was a symptom of the resurgence of a provincialism she had tried so long to liberalize. Sensational reports of controversies within the U.N. circulated on the air and in the press, fed misunderstandings and prejudice. It was easy to dramatize disagreements and quarrels in the Security Council or in the General Assembly, whereas the cooperation achieved in solving many problems affecting the welfare of human beings was being largely ignored or, at least, played down. Among facts which Madesin presented with her usual cool logic and eloquence were the brilliant work of the World Health Organization, of UNESCO, of UNICEF for children, of ILO for the working people, of the Trusteeship Council in preparing former colonies for nationhood, the studies conducted by some of the world's leading minds aiming to set standards for universal Human Rights and for the Status of Women all over the world.

Public opinion had a vital role to play, if it wished to, in enlightening the general population on these matters, while also challenging the opposition of any organized groups to any form of change in the old world order. The more than eighty Non-Governmental Organizations, known as NGOs, were particularly suited for this role. International in character and purpose, they had already embarked on programs which made Madesin feel that her own twenty-five years of concentrated effort, directed at international unity among such organizations, had not been entirely wasted. Thanks to her leadership, the International Federation of Business and Professional Women was among the first organizations to receive consultative status in the United Nations.

In 1947 the U.N. established a Bureau of Consultative Organizations, meeting alternately in New York and Geneva, to work out practical means of cooperation between them and the U.N. as well as among themselves. Madesin, a member of the Bureau, soon discovered that she could suggest solutions for certain of the problems confronting the members, that she had learned in working with women's organizations. Although the fields of activity often differed from those she knew so well, nonetheless she knew that 'human nature was very prevalent' in all areas of human endeavor, and its vagaries could be handled with a certain universal approach precisely because human nature was itself universal.

During the first winter of her retirement as president of the International, with the 1948 political campaign likely to become one of the most hotly contested in the nation's history, Madesin gave serious thought to what path she should follow, now that whatever political commitment she might undertake would involve no one other than herself. She had not forgotten what had happened in 1927 when a national controversy raged over the participation of the United States in the World Court and over a constitutional amendment, prohibiting child labor, inspired by the socially-conscious League of Nations. At that time she had been asked how she felt about having been so viciously attacked for her support of both issues. She had settled the doubt in the questioner's mind by her forthright reply: "I would rather be right with the radicals than wrong with the conservatives, or *vice versa*. If that is what is meant by being "a red," then I'm afraid you will have to count me in."

From the very start of 1948 political tension was evident all over the United States. Henry Wallace, who had been forced to resign as Secretary of Commerce in the Truman Cabinet because of his disagreement with White House policies in general and foreign policy in particular, sprang back into public view. Trying to salvage what was left of the bright hope of Roosevelt's program for post-war unity among the four major powers— the United States, the Soviet Union, China and Great Britain—became the spokesman for those who believed that seeds of suspicion and even hate being sown by the Cold War would inevitably bear a shooting war for their fruits. Soon a movement developed to advance his bid for the Presidency, in opposition to candidates of both major parties, and a third party was formed as The Progressive Party. Although only mildly socialist in philosophy and thoroughly equalitarian in respect to the status of all minorities including women, but especially blacks, it was immediately branded by its innumerable enemies as radical, pro-Communist or outright 'red.'

In February 1948, Madesin wrote to Alva Myrdal saying: "I have taken my stand with Henry Wallace and am presiding at the Wallace meeting here this week. Of course it is worth one's reputation to do so. A Communist is now being discovered under every bush and I am prepared to be smeared once more, along with plenty of other persons who have a social consciousness and a certain degree of courage. It is not pleasant, of course, but one must live with oneself. I can only do what seems right to me. Now, let me know what you think of this. If we are to avoid war, it seems to me that we must try to step back a year or so and begin

222

again. I have no faith in any other candidate being willing to do this except Henry Wallace. At present we are going in the wrong direction at an alarmingly rapid pace. Or so it seems to me. I do not relish being called "red" by much of Westport and being misunderstood by some of our friends. However, I cannot go against my conscience."

Her letter also made a reference to the term iron curtain, which had already found a place in the vocabulary of most countries outside the Communist sphere of influence. Alva Myrdal, in voicing her support for Madesin's decision to stand by the Wallace position, also spoke of the iron curtain saying: "It is neither a curtain nor made of iron, but just another of the irresponsible propaganda creations in the service of ill-will." She was then in Geneva where Gunnar had become Chief of the United Nations Economic Commission for Europe. Her letter added: "We have taken our stand on the bridge between East and West to defend it against both sides if needs be, to defend it even if the bridge crumbles. A bridge there must be . . ." Madesin, on her part, believed that such a bridge would hold: "Old roots of narrow selfish interests are hard to dislodge" she remarked, "but they will go. Tender shoots are fragile in cold ground, but enough of them will survive. The fair and peaceful world for which countless men and women have died may be delayed, but come it must."

By early September, Madesin had accepted the Progressive Party's nomination for Lieutenant Governor of the state of Connecticut and from then on she campaigned with her usual eloquence and fervor. When Chester Bowles, a forward-looking liberal, was nominated by the Democratic Party for the governorship of the State, the Yale professor running for that office on the Wallace ticket withdrew, leaving Madesin to run for the top position in his stead. Obviously, the Wallace forces had not expected to win the national election and the million or so votes cast for the Progressive Party were not sufficient to modify the nation's foreign policy. Nonetheless, the campaign highlighted a number of vital issues which might not have come to the fore without Wallace's prodding. One of these issues was the rights of black Americans.

At a time in American history when the racial issue was neither popular nor politically paramount, Madesin had arrived at some definite conclusions about it in her own mind, long before the Wallace campaign started. While it would have been alien to her nature to harbor any degree of racial bias, nonetheless the only blacks she had ever known belonged with her childhood and youth in Kentucky. They had been domestic workers in her home. For them and for their families she had always had a very real affection, but it was, perhaps unconciously, tinged with that certain condescension inherent in Southern mores. It was in New York, in the 1930's, that Madesin met and worked for the first time with black leaders, such as Mary McLeod Methune, involved in the Council of

Women and, consequently, also in the Chicago Congress of Women. Later, through the Myrdals, she met Ralph Bunche and other young black scholars on Gunnar's staff. Soon, these first contacts developed into friendships, enduring for years. In 1940, she had supported the membership of the first black in a Business and Professional Women's Club. Incidentally, that club, which had been newly formed in New York City, was at first refused a Charter because of the black member. Madesin's quiet but steadfast support of the member and of the club played no small part in the final change of position in those who had refused to charter the group.

However, it was not until 1948 that Madesin took a public stand for full integration. She then worked actively with the 'Committee of 100' to raise $100,000 for the National Association for the Advancement of Colored People. She found in Eunice Carter, a lawyer like herself, a friend and ally among American NGO representatives. They lunched together frequently at Lake Success—that remarkable microcosm of world civilizations—and Mrs. Carter was often at *Apple Acres*. A small thing in itself, this friendship, no doubt, but in Connecticut in the forties it placed Madesin Phillips, of Nicholasville, Kentucky, considerably ahead on the road which many of her associates and friends were not yet ready to follow.

With some trepidation and self-consciousness, two attitudes which rarely, if ever, manifested themselves in her, Madesin went to the Biennial Convention of the U.S. Federation in Fort Worth, in July, interrupting her campaign activities for a couple of weeks. She was anticipating open or implicit disapproval from many at the meeting for her support of the Progressive Party. She had geared herself to face it. "I held my breath" she wrote to Marjory in Westport, "but everyone was simply wonderful. A group of Connecticut delegates greeted me as Lieutenant Governor and when, at a luncheon with a fairly large group, I remarked that I had come to Fort Worth wondering if anyone would speak to me, one woman said: 'If I lived in Connecticut I would vote for you!' The rest, to my utter surprise, applauded. I hope they meant it. Not for the vote, but for what my stand was intended to signify."

That her popularity had not suffered because of her politics, was further borne out during the Convention when she once again proved her ability to shape a difficult decision while skirting its emotional overtones. The Federation had appointed a special committee to plan and propose a memorial to honor its past presidents. Believing it should "stand for a millemium at least," the committee, at the conclusion of an exceedingly long report, proposed that a stained-glass window be installed in the National Cathedral in Washington, D.C. to be known as 'The Women of the World' window. A colored reproduction of it would be framed in a suitable place in the Cathedral, and next to it were to be displayed two hand-made volumes, one a Book of Remembrance, containing data about

224

the Presidents, and the other a Book of Donors, listing the contributors. The cost of the entire project amounted to $75,000 to be raised from the Federation's membership. Madesin was horrified by the whole idea, especially at a time when human needs were mounting everywhere. She knew that her view was shared by several influential members present in the Convention Hall. When the motion to accept the report had been made and seconded, she asked for the floor. Two thousand pairs of eyes turned to where she was standing, sensing that something interesting was about to happen.

"As a past national president" she said, "and one of those being provided for today (laughter in the audience), I feel the same satisfaction that other past presidents must feel in seeing such appreciation on the part of our members . . . I think there is a question as to whether in this time of great need we want to put our money into a stained-glass window or into something for the living to meet the needs of the hour. There are many things that could be done for the living with $75,000. There isn't time to talk about them . . . (loud applause). The United Nations estimates it costs seven cents a day to keep a child alive. You can do your own arithmetic as to how many times seven cents will go into $75,000. . . ." She mentioned several other alternatives, praised the committee's work, drew laughter and applause alternatively and finally questioned the planning for a thousand years of presidents: "If we do our job well as we ought to, in a thousand years from now there will be no woman's organizations, but men and women united in common projects . . ." She questioned the use of an Episcopal church for presidents of different denominations and of spending $18,000 for the memorial books. Lastly, she spoke of the position of the window: "I think one should try to visualize. . . This ceiling is forty feet high and that window would begin twenty feet above this ceiling." A sea of faces turned up with a sudden simultaneous movement, all eyes focussed on the ceiling of the huge Will Rogers Memorial Auditorium of Fort Worth, Texas. A gasp went through the audience, then a sudden outburst of laughter. When silence was restored Madesin offered her amendment: that the matter be referred back to the committee for new recommendations, that each Club be sent these recommendations for study and that a vote be taken at the 1950 Convention. In rapid succession delegates popped up to speak, some for the amendment, some for the window, some merely to vent their own feelings. Finally the vote produced an overwhelming majority for Madesin's amendment. As it happens, in 1950 the motion to establish a memorial to presidents, of whatever nature, was defeated, 690 to 61.

Back in Westport, Madesin resumed her campaign believing, as did the overwhelming number of experts and pollsters, that Governor Dewey of New York would win the presidency. To the amazement of the American public, of the major candidates themselves, and of the rest of the world watching the election with profound concern, Harry S. Truman scored a personal triumph of unique proportions. When it was all over Madesin resigned from the Progressive Party. Henry Wallace thanked her in a letter which said: "I want you to know of my very deep respect and admiration for what you did, against bitter odds. . . ."

She summed up her own evaluation of the election writing to a friend in New Zealand, Daphne Chapman of Christchurch, president of the New Zealand BPW Federation. "Even New Zealand" she commented, "could hardly have been more surprised than the United States by Mr. Truman's victory. We did not expect Mr. Wallace to win, but we are convinced that his program and active campaign had an influence on the election. He forced Democratic Party candidates to take a stand on many vital issues, whereas Mr. Dewey took little stand on anything. . . It was not easy to come out publicly for the Progressive Party . . . but it was very satisfying to work with the serious-minded men—university professors, labor leaders, clergymen and public spirited citizens—who supported Mr. Wallace in this State. . . I was tired after the election, for the nervous strain was considerable, still, I believe it was worth doing, a good fight for our ideals and for our country. . ." The letter, published in the magazine of the New Zealand Federation, aroused wide interest and brought Madesin a letter which said: "We thought that after your long and strenuous term as International President you had retired for a well-earned rest!" Madesin, of course, had retired from a position, but never from the battlefield of ideas.

A major meeting of the NGOs was called by the United Nations in 1949. Eighty such organizations sent delegations totalling 850 outstanding men and women. The International Federation appointed its Founder-President to lead a delegation of seven, representing that many countries. Madesin was chosen to preside at this meeting and when the unique gathering came to order at her call she was unashamedly moved and thrilled. She had striven many long years to help bring about solidarity among the world's people. That day, as she recalled, "seated before me were the representatives of eighty international groups, without discrimination as to sex, race or creed, met together with one common purpose: to ensure the peace and well-being of mankind." The purpose of the NGOs was twofold: offer guidance to the United Nations experts in fields of activity and concern covered by these various organizations and, even more important, bring the work of the U.N. to public notice and thus gain public support for its efforts in the interest of world peace.

Not long after that meeting, which actually set a high tone for the work and the prestige of the NGOs, Madesin was honored by the United Nations. The Speakers Research Committee of the U.N. presented awards for Public Service to Madesin Phillips, Norman Corwin, for his radio programs presenting the United Nations, and to the editors of the *Christian Science Monitor*. In accepting the award Madesin called the non-governmental organizations "foot soldiers for peace," a phrase which fittingly defines the role which she herself played in the last years of her life.

Two more awards came to this "foot soldier" in 1950: The Order of the White Rose of Finland, First Class, for "humanitarian aid to the Finnish people" and a second Honorary Degree of Doctor of Laws awarded her by Cedar Crest College, of Allentown, Pennsylvania.

In 1949 Alva Myrdal came to New York, to fill a top-ranking post at the United Nations: Director of the Department of Social Affairs. This was the highest position ever accorded, so far, to a woman in the U.N. She immediately informed Madesin of the appointment in a letter in which she set forth some of her plans and expectations. She knew that no one could understand them better than Madesin:

"I need not tell you to what an extent I see the work slated for me there as a continuation of the strivings which have carried the movement of business and professional women forward. As a matter of fact, I take on the responsibility not only for myself, but very much for the international and national federations of BPW. I should feel very happy and confident if they shared that feeling. In so far as the appointment carries prestige, it is due them as well as me, in so far as it carries influence it concerns them as well as me. Of course, I cannot pledge such an allegiance which would appear too particularistic, but basically I mean that the aim of that woman movement is identical with the aim of getting a more harmonious modern society on the whole. I shall do my very best to earn the support of these great groups of women."

As Madesin, Alva and many other women knew only too well, women were still not "equal" and would not be so, while society granted them only an occasional stellar role. Out of 410 delegates to the U.N. Assembly at that time, only 18 were women and only one, Madame Pandit of India, headed a national delegation. Plainly, woman's struggle to participate fully in the social order was not yet won. Until that time the need for organizations such as Madesin had brought into being would continue. And Madesin, while becoming involved in other pursuits, such as writing or politics, continued to regard the International Federation as her primary concern, doing for it a number of things which she could not do when she was president of it. Her counsel was constantly sought, both by her successor Sally Butler and by other federations, and she gave it generously, but always conscious of the necessity of preventing anyone from receiving the impression—which would have been a false one—that she was still regarding herself as the leader of the International. She agreed, however, to attend the Board Meeting to be held in Finland, the first gathering since the Paris Congress of 1947. She and Marjory Lacey-Baker looked for and found suitable tenants for *Apple Acres* and went to what turned out to be the smallest gathering the Federation had ever had, but also one of the most meaningful.

It was small chiefly because, in many countries, the currency was still frozen and because the cost of traveling such a distance had kept many delegates from attending who might otherwise have been able to get there. It was meaningful because Finland was the first country in the world to grant suffrage to women, and a country which, in its forward-looking legislation, its arts and its enormous accomplishments in the post-war period, was really building a bridge to the future. Mrs. Phillips-Marder, of Great Britain, an industrialist in her own right and Chairman of the International Finance Committee, immediately sought a remedy to the situation which prevented delegates from attending because of the high cost of travel. She proposed the creation of a fund dedicated exclusively to the financing of delegates' travel to Board Meetings and Congresses. Her own country had already set up such a fund in preparation for the Triennial Congress to take place in London in 1950. Mrs. Phillips-Marder was authorized to solicit contributions to the fund from all National Federations.

Madesin loved Finland and the Finnish people took to her immediately wherever she went. After the meeting she and Marjory enjoyed a holiday exploring the country's northernmost reaches. It was a healthy change from the psychological heat of the Wallace campaign.

19. Looking Eastward

A tea-time guest at *Apple Acres* was a common occurrence, but one day in January, 1950, the visitor who braved a snow storm, was not paying a social call. Dr. Goodwin Watson, Director of World Study Tours of Columbia University Travel Service, was bent on persuading Madesin to lead the University's summer tour known as 'Citizen Activities for International Cooperation.' The proposed itinerary included Sweden, Denmark, England, Holland, Luxembourg, Germany, Switzerland and France and the tour would last two months. Its purpose was to stimulate international understanding by means of seminar programs combined with sightseeing.

Much as she agreed with the project, Madesin was totally unwilling, at that point, to consider taking even as few as ten or twelve persons on a foreign trip. However, she sent Dr. Watson off with the promise that she would give the matter some thought before turning it down. That evening it occurred to her that this tour might actually be a way of implementing a proposal she had made, that year, to the NGO Conference. Namely, that an NGO Study Committee be sent to hold conferences abroad to investigate ways of promoting rank and file support for the United Nations. Soon she was discussing the idea with James B. Orrick, U.N. Chief of the NGO section, who urged her to accept Columbia's invitation, offering to give the project official U.N. standing.

When she agreed to conduct the tour, however, she had not realized how much work would be involved on her part. Besides planning the conferences in each country and organizing the seminars, she found that she was expected to do some of the recruiting as well. It was now too late to withdraw and she began to write to friends she hoped would be interested in joining the tour. "Perhaps you had not thought of going to Europe this summer" her letters ran, "but neither had I. However, this one I could not resist, since it will give us an extraordinary opportunity to find out, first hand, how leading citizens in these various countries are working to develop international co-operation and how, in their view, the United Nations can be strengthened and the promise of peace brightened. . ." The itinerary included attending the Federation's Triennial

Congress in London. Getting all this lined up or, as Madesin said, "fitting the pieces together," overtaxed her physical resources. In mid-winter she suffered a grave recurrence of an earlier virus infection and her ulcer suddenly took a virulent turn. In April she was hospitalized for several weeks. The tolling of the bell had begun, but she seemed not to hear it or, if she did, she was not impressed.

In June, recovered and full of vigor, she went to Pennsylvania to receive her second Honorary Degree. Although the graduates and their families and friends gave her speech a standing ovation, they probably did not realize how prophetic it was. After providing considerable entertainment with her recollections of the girl's college to which she, too, had gone, she made her usual plea for understanding and peace, albeit in different terms from those she used with older audiences, adding: "Your generation has come in with the tide that is sweeping forward the egalitarian principle and you will, I believe, surpass your elders in recognizing your personal responsibility to humanity. We see the impact of modern science on those who are demanding not only freedom, but also the fruits of their hands and of their land. What part will their claims play in the future of the world? And what part the dark-skinned men and women who are determined to throw off the stigma of inferiority attached to the color of their skin? Fortunately, a modern education has prepared you to act in this dangerous, complex age in which mistakes can be costly. But your problems will no longer be academic. There is no book in which to find the answers. What do you ask of life? Unless you ask of it little that is personal and a good deal that is designed to make you a compassionate member of human society, you may receive little indeed from life. It is only from such compassion that you will derive the answers which the modern world so urgently needs."

Shortly before sailing for Europe with her group, she learned that three more members of the now disbanded Czech Federation had been tried for 'treason.' Milada Horakova had been sentenced to death, her two companions to life imprisonment. In an agonizing effort to stop the injustice, Madesin rushed to New York appealing to Trygve Lie, Secretary General of the U.N., to the President of the U.N.'s Economic and Social Council, to the International Red Cross, to the Chairmen of the Commission on Human Rights and on the Status of Women. All was fruitless. In the fall, she was in the vast crowd gathered in New York for a meeting in memory of the victims of that new episode of Communist repression.

Although Madesin had no sooner settled on board ship than she was taken to the infirmary where she spent the entire crossing,—'sciatica combined with severe exhaustion,' said the ship's doctor, recommending total rest for the entire summer—she lead the tour without faltering. The last day of July found them in London among the two thousand women who jammed the Great Hall in Westminster where the International Federation Congress was held. The speakers were outstanding: Lady Astor, Barbara Ward, the Hon. Harold Wilson, two women Members of Parliament, Irene Ward and Elaine Burton and, from the United States, Judge Florence Allen. Reports heard and action taken were of such significance as to have attracted the attention not only of the British government, but of the official representatives of many of the countries affiliated with the Federation. The press gave major coverage to the business sessions and to the many social events, one of which was especially worthy of note because it was without precedent: the closing banquet in the ancient Guildhall of the City of London, the use of which had never before been granted to a woman's organization.

As Founder-President, Madesin did her part, presiding at meetings assigned to her, supporting motions, giving counsel when requested, which was frequently, and relishing the feeling that no responsibilities for the Congress rested on her shoulders. She rejoiced in its success for Sally Butler and in the warmth with which Dame Caroline Haslett was elected as the International's Third President.

Madesin shared the commonly held view that no one, at that moment, was better fitted than Dame Caroline to guide the International Federation. She was one of those rare individuals able to direct their energies into many fields concurrently and with equal skill. One of the foremost electrical engineers in England, the uncontested leader of women in her profession, author of the resolution on peaceful use of atomic energy, top ranking official in the Labor Government's town-planning program, she was still the gay "saucy girl" she had once been called by the Lord of the Manor of the Sussex village in which she lived. Unlike most of the Federation leaders, she knew what it was to be a poor girl with no training. She liked to tell the story of her youth to illustrate the progress of women in England in her lifetime. As a girl, Caroline went to ask a favor of the lord of the local Manor. In those arrogant days shortly after the turn of the century, she had reason to tremble in her boots. Although she came of a very respectable middle-class family, she was crossing class lines and defying the local customs in calling on His Lordship. Having been shown into his library, although the old baronet scowled at her, she managed to make her request: would His Lordship allow a small portion of his acreages to be used as a playing field for the village girls? He gave his answer without hesitation: "You're a saucy girl" he fairly roared, "What do girls want with playing fields. If they're good girls, let them go into service, as they should!"

Margaret Culking Banning, writing about Caroline Haslett in the *Independent Woman* said: "Forty years later, the saucy girl had earned a title of her own: Dame Commander of the Order of the British Empire, the highest honor the Crown bestows on women for distinguished achievement. She is also a member of the Crowley New Town Corporation which, by government authority, is planning and building a city of fifty thousand people on a site where two thousand now live, forty-five miles outside of London. It will be a model city, surrounded by beauty, an example of housing that is at once scientific and attractive. But the irony of it is that the Corporation controls some of the land once owned by the old Baronet who turned down Caroline's request for playing fields. He may turn over in his grave, but there *will be* playing fields there now and some of those girls will have many choices of occupations other than going into service."

After the Congress, Madesin and Caroline talked at length about the Federation's future. Federations were coming up in such distant places as South Africa and Rhodesia, but they touched only the European women living there, evidence of the old colonial powers. They did not reach out to the native women whose problems and aspirations were an unknown quantity. To know and understand these, not merely in Africa, but all over the once-subjected world, was a new challenge on which Madesin Phillips, Caroline Haslett, Alva Myrdal and Margaret Hickey decided they should focus some attention.

In 1945 Caroline Haslett had returned from a trip to Egypt with a dream. The Middle East was a land beckoning explorers in human relations. Sixteen years earlier, Madesin had returned from her visit to Turkey, Lebanon and Syria with the same thought in her mind. The women of the Arab world were beginning to emerge. They needed real support without having a Western program imposed upon them. This would require a particular study of conditions in their countries that would be costly in terms of money and involving the direction of someone already familiar with those lands. It was a dream to be kept alive, knowing that its realization was distant at best, but Madesin clung to it steadfastly.

Madesin and her Columbia tour returned to the United States on a student ship. "There were some physical hardships because of overcrowded conditions" Madesin wrote, "but I, for one, was richly repaid by the contact with American students. Dozens of them, curious about what the United Nations ladies were discussing on deck, attended, uninvited but always welcome, the conferences we held to evaluate our tour. Their comments were enlightening and gave me great hope for a true international spirit among the rising generation in America."

Mingling with the inquisitive students had brought back to Madesin's mind memories of her own college days at Goucher. Half a century had passed since she had broken off her college education to give herself up to music, which was to be her career until the fateful fall on an icy street had wrecked her dream. But her interest in the college had remained

232

constant and she had served as Chairman of its Building Fund campaign until the war brought the drive to a halt. Among the first letters she read, from the pile awaiting her return, was one from Goucher's president, announcing the resumption of the fund-raising campaign, requesting her help in reaching alumnae in the East and asking her to deliver the keynote address at the dinner which was to launch the campaign in New York, the following January.

"It was a thoughtful and stirring speech" commented Goucher's President at the close of very succeful banquet, after which he used the theme she had developed—The College, Custodian of Ideas—for a new campaign brochure. The response to her personal appeals for funds was so remarkable that she was asked to join a professional fund–raising team at a substantial salary. "Much as I want to help Goucher, I literally have no free time in which to undertake so important a piece of work" was her reply, although, as usual, she could well have used the earnings. Her schedule was filled with speaking engagements and her various commitments to the United Nations took up almost every hour she felt she could spend away from *Apple Acres*. What made her want to stay in Westport for the unbroken stretches of time she never seemed able to set aside, was the determination to write a full history of the International Federation, as well as her autobiography. Both were not even in their first-draft stage, four years later, at the time of her death.

The year 1951 brought with it two anniversary celebrations: the twenty-first birthday of the International Federation, to be highlighted at the June Board Meeting in Holland, and her own seventieth which came on September 15th. For that occasion, of course, she would be in Westport after the trip to the Netherlands. The Board had invited her as the guest of honor, asking her to review the Federation's history in her banquet speech. The meeting, held in Scheveningen, the celebrated seaside resort very near The Hague, proved to be memorable for many reasons, including the stupendous setting,—Holland with the tulips in full bloom—the reports from eighteen affiliated federations giving unquestioned evidence of the organization's acknowledged influence in bringing vast improvement to the status of women, an hour-long visit with Queen Juliana for the International Officers, the presence of high government officials and members of the diplomatic corps at the public sessions and the coverage by the press, but most memorable of all was Madesin's address. A large number of those present had often heard her speak on a variety of subjects and in many different and sometimes taxing circumstances, but they all seemed to feel that, at Scheveningen, Madesin had indeed surpassed herself.

The legal mind was in charge when she reviewed the Federation's mistakes and false starts, as well as its successes, assessing the residual value of each with absolute fairness. The dreamer took over in pointing to the still distant goals, but the organizer emerged in outlining the steps that, taken one by one, would bring the goals within reach, even as the little group of 200 women who had met in Geneva in 1930 had now become a quarter of a million in eighteen countries. The poet evoked the night of the war years and the memory of those who had not survived, at the end it was the crusader who prevailed, the soldier with a faith who concluded, saying: "Now you, on this our twenty-first birthday, are the inheritors of the past, the leaders of the present, the guardians of the future. The dream of peace and social justice will come to pass. It matters little whether you or I live to see that day. It is only important that each of us struggle towards it. And so, until we reach that future, let us keep our foot on the firing line."

From Holland, Madesin flew to London hoping to see Gordon Holmes, who had been ill. She found her in the hospital, much too sick to receive any visitors. At the end of November the General died. Madesin's tribute to her in the December issue of *Widening Horizons* was an eloquent reminder of how much the International was indebted to that remarkable English woman, who was a tough financier yet aptly described herself as one "always in love, always caught by some star on the horizon."

On the 15th of September, on her seventieth birthday, at *Apple Acres* Madesin received a flood of messages and gifts, but one that must have secretly pleased her in a particular way was the beautifully lettered text of Anni Voipio-Juvas' brief thanks to her in behalf of the International, after her speech in Holland: "We thank you, Lena Madesin Phillips, for these wonderful twenty-one years you have given us. We want to tell you that in our eyes you, yourself, are as young as twenty-one, and we hope to meet you again and again and always in the splendid youthfulness of your spirit." Anni's words had confirmed what Madesin herself firmly believed: "Youth is entirely a matter of the spirit."

At Scheveningen, Agda Rössel, speaking for the Swedish Federation, had invited the International to hold its 1953 Congress in Stockholm and Judge Sarah Hughes, President of the United States Federation, quite unexpectedly, had delighted the Board by announcing that the U.S. Federation was happy to offer full hospitality to all members of the Board who would attend the Board Meeting, to be held in New York in 1952.

This Board Meeting, as Madesin saw it, would be different from all those that had preceded it because, for the first time, some of Europe's leading women would be able to meet and mingle with good, sound, everyday American women. They had met leaders in one field or another, but she wanted them to sense the sterling quality of the followers as well, without which no federation could ever have come into being. But before she could dedicate herself to giving as much help to its planners as she was being asked for, all sorts of other matters came her way in the early months of 1952.

For one thing she was nominated to represent the state of Connecticut on a newly organized National Board of the Woman's Medical College of Pennsylvania, which had celebrated 100 years of achievement in 1950. It was still the first and only college in the Western Hemisphere chartered to educate women in medicine. She hesitated a long while before accepting. "I am unable to make generous contributions" she explained to the President, "and, since my retirement, I am less in touch with women of great means." But the College wanted her prestige and her counsel. When she had accepted, both were called upon frequently and Madesin was glad of it.

Suddenly, at about that time, she received a frantic appeal for assistance in helping to free Ezra Pound from confinement in a mental institution. Ruled insane in 1945 in the United States, he had thus been saved from standing trial for treason. For six years and more, the arguments over his case had never ceased. Some held that, being a great poet at one time expected to receive the Nobel Prize, he should be released. Others, claiming that he had been treated with outrageous favoritism, wanted him declared sane and tried. Madesin, knowing very little about Ezra Pound's broadcasts from fascist Italy, which were the basis for the allegation of treason, sought counsel from a distinguished writer, well acquainted with Pound and whose sense of fairness she valued greatly. His reply to Madesin was little comfort to the poet's supporters. Nonetheless, Madesin shared it with them, emphasizing the reliability but not disclosing the identity of its source. Although Madesin felt she had done all that was within her reach, the case began to interest her and the uncertainties connected with it to trouble her. But she never had occasion to be involved in it again.

During the Board Meeting in New York, that summer, Madesin and Caroline Haslett resumed their conversation about studying the women of the Middle East. Feeling certain that the time was ripe to lay down concrete plans, they presented the Board with a resolution setting up a planning committee to study the means of initiating the project. Chaired by Madesin, the members were Caroline, Lisa Sergio, a news commentator and since 1948 editor of *Widening Horizons* and member of the Board and Dr. Yvonne Soudan of Belgium, acquainted with the Middle East countries. The Resolution authorized them "to co-opt anyone with specialized knowledge of the subject, who could assist them." "We'll do as much we can at our end" Madesin told Caroline before she returned to England, "and we'll talk again about it in Stockholm. It will come about, because it must come about." Eventually it did, but the talk in Stockholm never took place nor did Madesin and Caroline ever meet again. Madesin was ill in July 1953, missing a Congress for the first time. Caroline Haslett, who was present, was re-elected President for another three year term. Not many months later she developed nephritis, disfiguring, painful and incurable. Knowing that she would never recover, she secluded herself at her home in Suffolk, cared for by her devoted sister, Rosalind Messenger. Only by letter and cable could she keep in touch with the outside world and, for a considerable length of time, carry on some of her activities.

In New York, during the Board Meeting, Dame Caroline had made a great impression on the vast number of Americans who attended as observers and, likewise, later, on the twenty-two hundred who were at the U.S. Federation Convention in Boston at which Caroline was the guest of honor. American interest in the International had never flagged, but now that the President was across an ocean, Caroline's presence gave them a unique opportunity to strengthen their bond with her, face to face. Nearly all the foreign members of the Board and observers were also guests of the U.S. Federation Convention, the generous hospitality having been meant to include the trip to Boston as well.

The New York meeting had satisfied Madesin because it had come to grips with matters that needed attention and had animated the Middle East study plan, by giving the project official acceptance and standing. But, above all, she had been delighted by the welcome which the American members had given to the foreign women, and to the genuinely warm side of the American way of doing things that had so marvelously come to the fore. Her pride in her own country had been flattered by it all and, once again, she felt rewarded for her past efforts.

The Boston Convention was followed immediately by a long Fourth of July week-end. There was open house at *Apple Acres* as many American as well as European friends stopped in on their way back to New York. Some came for a cup of tea or a meal, others for a day or two, some stayed a week. Madesin's brand of hospitality, totally informal, was a reflection of her ability to handle people in general, creating friendships among those who had barely met before. Knowing that a stop-over in Connecticut would be on the itinerary of scores of Federation members that week-end, thoughtful members from Iowa and Wisconsin had sent Madesin gifts of ham and cheese from their respective states to keep her larder well stocked no matter how large a crowd descended upon her, or how long they stayed.

A few of the Europeans remained long enough in America to sense what a lively presidential campaign was like. Adlai Stevenson was running against General Eisenhower. They were both exceptional men and, for once, political discussion centered around the question of who to vote for, rather than merely against. Madesin supported Adlai Stevenson, less because he was a Democrat like herself, than because she admired and respected his sophisticated mind. In Boston the U.S. Federation had stepped firmly into the political arena by endorsing two members for Vice-President of the United States: Senator Margaret Chase Smith on the Republican ticket and Judge Sarah Hughes on the Democratic ticket. The resolution was carried by a standing vote and both would-be candidates accepted the endorsement, knowing, of course, that they were certain of defeat. But, as Judge Hughes observed, "I am not so naive as to believe that this year we will have a woman for Vice-President of the United States, but we do have to get into the arena and fight." Like Madesin, she believed "in keeping a foot on the firing line."

After the campaign was over, which General Eisenhower won overwhelmingly, Lisa Sergio made a first attempt to request funds for the Middle East project from two large American Foundations. That particular field of study failed to interest either of them, and Madesin agreed with her that it might be well to wait a while and revise the approach before appealing to a third one.

Meanwhile Madesin, too, had been keeping her foot on the firing line, and had helped to create an organization called Committee of Correspondence with the purpose of establishing direct communication with women leaders all over the free world to exchange information and ideas on the major issues of concern to women. The Committee consisted of twelve women, each of them involved in an international organization, yet each distinguished in her own right. Mrs. William Barclay Parsons chaired the Committee in whose work the U.S. Department of State immediately expressed active interest. Within two years the Committee was in communication with 1400 women leaders in seventy-five countries, had received substantial grants, had an office and a staff and was issuing a monthly News Bulletin as well as sending out reprints of significant articles. Madesin devoted considerable time to the Committee of Correspondence to which, among other contributions, she was able to provide the names of some of the most important women in Europe active in the feminist movement.

Through much of 1953 Madesin had been feeling under the weather, and one morning towards the end of June, she was at the Baltimore office of the International trying to decide if she should go to Stockholm. The symptoms of the attack which finally prevented her from going were already making themselves felt and she was in one of her rare moods of depression. In idle fashion she was reading the morning's *New York Times* when her eye noticed a small item occupying an insignificant place on one of the middle pages. It merely stated that the Ford Foundation's grants made to Americans carrying out various research projects in Asia and the Near and Middle East, had amounted to $488,150.

Quickly she clipped the item and suddenly forgot her age, forgot that she was feeling poorly, forgot that she had retired from active duty on the world's perpetual battlefields where her causes were being fought out. Her mind leapt to the possibility of a grant to the International for her cherished Middle East study project. She picked up the telephone and talked to Mr. Gordon Gray, Chairman of the Ford Foundation Board on overseas training and research. Other calls followed. A week later a conference at the Ford Foundation had been arranged. From this point on, the plan moved forward, slowly but steadily. The Special Committee of the International was enlarged to include Isabelle Claridge Taylor and Margaret Hickey. With the assistance of Dr. Ruth Woodsmall and Mrs. Mary Tenison-Woods, Director of the U.N.'s Commission on the Status of Women, a nine-page proposal was drawn up covering every phase of the projected study. The purpose of the project was defined as "research on the fundamental issues that have held from further advance the women of the Near or Far East."

It was May 1954 before Madesin heard from the Ford Foundation. The letter said:

"Dear Dr. Phillips,

I am pleased to inform you that the payment of a sum not to exceed $47,500 to the International Federation of Business and Professional Women to support a study of the role of women, their activities and organizations in Egypt, Iraq, Jordan and Syria, has been authorized by the Ford Foundation, on the following terms and conditions . . ."

As soon as the grant had been received, Ruth Woodsmall was appointed Director of the Project, Isabelle Claridge Taylor was made Administrator of the funds, research workers were interviewed in order to find an assistant for Dr. Woodsmall. The unique aspect of this study had to be made clear. While many sociologists and economists had gone to the Arab countries in the last few years to carry on research, they had reported on the social changes in the Middle East always from the outsider's standpoint. The project of the International was the first comprehensive study to be conducted under the leadership of the women of the area. Miss Charlotte Johnson, chosen as assistant was in full agreement with this approach, as of course was Ruth Woodsmall who had already published a significant book on the women of the Arab world many years before. She knew the field and was eager to see the changes she knew had taken place. If all went according to the Committee's plans the field work should have been completed by May 1955. A conference in early June to evaluate the findings, would allow sufficient time for the report to be written and presented in August to the International Board, meeting in Switzerland to celebrate the Federation's Silver Jubilee—twenty five years since the founding in Geneva.

Through the spring of 1954 Madesin and her committee worked incessantly to do the necessary ground work in consultation with the U.N.

and with the embassies of the countries covered by the project. Finally on their way to the Middle East, Dr. Woodsmall and Miss Johnson stopped in London to establish a personal contact with the official Headquarters of the International Federation. They went on to Paris to consult with UNESCO, to Geneva to get data from the World Health Organization and by October 24th, they had set up working headquarters in Beirut.

As reports came in from the field, it became increasingly evident that one of the most significant parts of the project would be the consultation in the Middle East prior to the writing of the final report. It was decided that the members of the Project Committee would attend as well as a representative from UNESCO. Madesin was delighted when she heard that Alva Myrdal was to be that representative. She remembered clearly how, five or six years earlier, Alva had once written to her on the subject of the Middle East, saying: "That is where the big job is that must be done for and with women. But how? And by who? I am modest enough to say that I don't think we have the entrance ticket to these cultures."

As Madesin visualized the consultation, the participants would meet in the village of Bhamdoun, on the outskirts of Beirut where, around a table, the Arab members of the study's Advisory Committee could discuss the findings with the International Federation group. Ruth Woodsmall had written to Madesin that "the idea of a joint study met with very favorable response from the women leaders from each country who had been invited to participate. It appealed to them as a different approach from that of the usual surveys of Eastern life made so often without reference to the people of the country. This study, instead, considered timely, was on a sound basis of partnership which enabled the Arab leaders to share in the analysis and interpretation of their own situation."

Around that table, in the Lebanon, there was to be cooperation and not dictation by anyone. Isabelle, Alva and Madesin, together with Ruth Woodsmall and Charlotte Johnson would contribute what they could out of their own experience, but would not try to force conclusions. The meeting was to be a new adventure in friendship, as well as a serious evaluation of the research. It was to be a bridge, however modest, between civilizations. Mark Twain once said that a thousand great novels could reveal the soul of mankind. Madesin felt that a thousand studies carried out in this way might finally develop a framework in which the peoples of the world could live together.

The Ford Foundation grant had included a generous allowance to cover the costs of the consultation which was scheduled for the end of May 1955. In January of that year, Isabelle Claridge Taylor's husband died, after a short but fatal illness, leaving her with two small children. Madesin was at her side in Philadelphia, herself heartbroken over the loss of such a cherished friend as Elbert Taylor had been to her since his marriage to Isabelle. Naturally Isabelle's presence at the consultation was now out of the question, a fact which saddened Madesin and also troubled her because her reliance on Isabelle's financial skill and good judgment had increased over the years.

As the month of May approached, Madesin began to give serious thought to the idea that she and Marjory should sell *Apple Acres*. The care of the grounds had become too great a demand on Madesin's strength. The house, though beautiful, was also very old and therefore difficult and very costly to heat in Connecticut's cold winters. Much as Madesin enjoyed working outdoors, chopping wood and bringing in logs to burn in the big fireplace, she was being forced to admit that she was no longer as young as she used to be and that her reserve of energy was dwindling. They would sell *Apple Acres* before going abroad, if possible, arrange to not have to vacate until, say, October, and buy a smaller place still in Connecticut but, hopefully, of easier access to the town of Westport, if that was where they would eventually remain. Several friends with whom Madesin and Marjory discussed their plan tried to dissuade them from trying to sell the place in such haste, before going abroad. Marjory might possibly have been brought over to this point of view, but Madesin was adamant about making the sale as soon as possible, as if she had had a premonition that, unless they did it now, Marjory would have to face the situation alone later.

Quickly *Apple Acres* had the right purchaser: one who did not wish to use the house until the fall. Therefore the only packing to be done was for the trip to Lebanon and Switzerland while all the rest would wait until their return. April flew by as rapidly as a gust of wind, with Madesin representing the International Federation at a session of the U.N. Commission on the Status of Women during practically the entire month. This proved useful to the Middle East project, however, in the sense that she could conveniently discuss some of its aspects with people she otherwise rarely saw, who were attending meetings that month in the towering, still unlandscaped U.N. Headquarters on Manhattan's East River. The Project Committee, meanwhile, had agreed with her suggestion that one member of the Advisory Committee from each of the Middle East countries under study should attend the Jubilee Board Meeting and spend a month in Europe as a guest of Federation members in Britain, Norway, Sweden, Holland or elsewhere, as the interest aroused might dictate.

The presence in Berne, where the Board was meeting, of some of the outstanding Arab women, thanks to whose support the project would, by then, have moved well along, was certain to lay foundations for the better understanding which Madesin still so ardently sought. Moreover, the visitors from the Middle East would also go on the one-day pilgrimage to Geneva to revisit the old Salle Centrale where, twenty-five years before, the dream had finally emerged into tangible reality.

Madesin, grieved by the thought of Caroline Haslett's absence, had been deeply touched by a letter from Agda Rössel, the Acting President, informing her that the day in Geneva was designed "as a day to honor you, dear Dr. Phillips." Twenty-five countries had announced that they would be sending delegates. Their list included a remarkable number who had been in the founding group. "Some, alas, will be present only in spirit" Madesin wrote a friend. "The pioneers are slipping away very fast now, but that is to be expected. Those of us who are left awhile must keep the faith both for the past and the future."

Answering Agda Rössel's letter she said once more, as she had so often pointed out during that quarter century, that the honor of the day in Geneva was not for any one person alone. It was "for the heritage that belongs to the young. Working alone, nothing could have been accomplished. Together—three hundred thousand now and millions reaching out for our friendship—together, that is the secret of all success." On board ship, Madesin told herself while she packed her papers, she would have ample time to marshal her thoughts and map out the message she would take to Geneva, reiterating the absolute necessity of cooperation.

A gay party boarded the *S. S. Excambion,* with many to see them off on their leisurely cruise through the Mediterranean on the way to Beirut. A neighbor from Westport, Mrs. Dudley Wadsworth, Madesin's niece, Mrs. Lang Wharton and Marjory, ever faithful and always competently helpful, were going with Madesin to Lebanon and, afterwards, to the Jubilee Meeting as duly registered observers from the United States. Once all the business activity was over, they planned to spend a few more weeks in Europe. For Madesin it would be a true vacation without any commitments. While her traveling companions were sightseeing or doing whatever else might strike their fancy, she would be installed in some comfortable corner with a view, free to begin to revise the first sketchy draft of the autobiography she had been dictating, in somewhat desultory fashion, for the past several months. The bundle of typewritten sheets was at the bottom of her satchel, to be exhumed only after all Federation business had been dispensed with.

Marianne Beth and her husband appearing unexpectedly at the pier made her particularly happy. Their own happiness was a contagious thing, a reassuring testimony that 'love overcometh all obstacles.' At the last minute she handed them a note for Caroline Haslett which she had forgotten to mail. She hoped Caroline might be able to read it herself, or at least have it read to her. Madesin told her how much she would be missed at Beirut as well as in Switzerland, and how encouraged Madesin felt about the prospects offered by the Middle East Consultation. She never knew how greatly appreciated her note had been.

Madesin's love for the outdoors and the healing effect of the open air on her mind and body were always intensified by the nearness of the

241

sea. The water's endless changes of form and color soothed her nerves yet fired her imagination, filling the daily routine of life on board a cruising ship with no end of adventure. None of these sensations had ever failed her, or even declined, in the twenty-six times she had crossed the ocean. Every crossing had yielded its own special little moments of delight—some so gossamer of substance that she could not even describe them—which she collected as other people collect seashells, postage stamps or any other precious item.

However, on the second day out, Madesin began to wonder if the sea had lost its magic. She barely felt its call and she could respond but barely. Her accumulated fatigue, this time, was not yielding to the spell, nor did it seem willing to be transformed by the gifts of rest which each day brought in its wake. At last, by the time the coast of Spain came into view, her old eager self had been recovered and Madesin was ready to go ashore at Barcelona, see the sights and have lunch at some picturesque spot in the old seaport. She enjoyed every minute of that day, and kept her party constantly entertained with her own unending curiosity and her lively comments. At dinner on board, that evening, they talked eagerly of how they would make the most of the next day's stop-over at Marseilles.

During the night Madesin was awakened by an excruciating abdominal pain. Never had her old ulcer flared up so violently before, but she recognized the cause of the sudden agonizing seizure. The ship's doctor gave her some relief, but when they docked at Marseilles, early the next morning, the ambulance he had ordered was already waiting to rush her to a leading hospital—*La Clinique Juge*. Tests and X-rays revealed a perforated ulcer and the need for immediate surgery. Marjory chose to wait alone through the ordeal, while her two companions took their belongings off the ship and arranged for a hotel. At last the doctors joined her, reporting that they had intervened in time for the operation to be successful. Dr. Phillips, they assured her, had an excellent chance for complete recovery, though her condition was still serious.

Within forty-eight hours, suddenly, the chance was lost. Uremic poisoning had set in, inducing a state of coma from which, peacefully and quietly, Madesin slipped away from life, while the night was still young, on the twentieth of May, 1955.

Marjory wrote to her sister in Connecticut: "The hospital's Catholic Chaplain was twice at Madesin's bedside, praying for her, just before she died. I had not realized how near the end was, but I had wanted the Chaplain anyway. And now, this afternoon, at the English Church in Marseilles, it is Church of England, we had the Burial Service. It was very simple and very beautiful. Just the three of us, the Consul General and his wife, three or four French women who had know she was coming and had gone to greet her at the pier, and some members of the Church.

Wednesday we sail and I am taking her to Kentucky, to the town where she was born, to rest beside her father and mother."

Lena Madesin Phillips' last journey home was on the *SS Constitution*, a ship symbolic of the ideal she had served all her life with reverence and faith. Had the choice been hers, it could have been no other.

Dr. Phillips at Scheveningen, the Netherlands, July, 1951

20. "That You Love One Another . . ."

The news of Lena Madesin Phillips' death, carried by *The New York Times,* was picked up by the press in many countries and, of course, by newspapers all over the United States. Cables, telegrams, letters and cards piled up in the office at the Biltmore in New York, at *Apple Acres,* in Nicholasville, Kentucky and at the London headquarters of the International Federation.

The report was hard to believe. Madesin was one of the most vital and vibrant persons most of her friends and associates had ever known. After the first shock had subsided, her closest collaborators, as by one accord, took her going as she would have wished them to—a challenge to action.

Agda Rössel hastened from Stockholm to preside at the Beirut consultation so that the work so dear to Madesin's heart and already bidding fair to become very significant to the Federation, might suffer no interruption or delay. The Silver Jubilee Meeting, planned "to rejoice in her presence and honor her achievements," became a memorial to the ideals she had raised high on her banner. On August 22, five hundred women gathered in Berne from twenty-five countries, some of them to learn of their loss only after their arrival.

That morning, at eleven o'clock, the great bells of the Cathedral at Berne echoed through the ancient city and down into the valley of the Aar, when women from five continents, whom the vision of Lena Madesin Phillips had brought together, began to take their place in the nave under the tall gothic arches. The sprays of white flowers on the altar caught the glow of the sun streaming in from the stained glass windows, while the organ filled the church with the strains of Bach's *Fantasia* which Madesin loved so well.

The passages from Scripture, chosen among those she had preferred in her lifetime, became even more meaningful after her death: from the Psalms, the 121st, with which she could indeed say "I have lifted up mine eyes unto the hills . . . ," from the Book of Wisdom, words of comfort for those who mourned "In the sight of the unwise they seemed to die and their departure is taken for misery, but they are in peace," and from

244

the Gospel of John the assurance "I go and prepare a place for you . . . that where I am there you may be also."

The hymns, too, were her favorites. Sung in unison, the words of *Abide with Me* and *Love Divine, All Love Excelling,* rose to a majestic swell all through the nave. Then the five hundred women recited Madesin's *International Prayer,* knowing that her plea had now become their pledge: "Make effective, O Lord, our efforts for a better world. Show us the path to peace and in it help us to walk steadfastly and with courage."

From the pulpit, Dr. Bernard Gray noted the high points of Madesin's career then, with equal conciseness and understanding, brought out the essence of her personality saying: "If we were to try to express the aims and achievements of Lena Madesin Phillips, we could not find more fitting words than those of her Lord and Master, Jesus Christ—*I am amongst you as one that serves.* She believed with the utmost conviction that no nation or people can rise higher than the standard set by its womanhood. She had given the best of her life in unstinting support of this conviction. But there was a price to pay. The very manner of her passing placed the seal upon that splendid record. It was in no small measure hastened by the ceaseless drain upon her physical powers, given without thought for herself, in selfless service."

Those who, on the morrow, would be picking up the threads, would be encouraged by what the very early report of the Middle East Study could already say about the women of the Arab countries: 'One is impressed with the fact that, in each of these five countries, there is to be found great latent as well as active woman power of which the leaders of the area are conscious, but which could more fully be developed through the cooperation of groups having already passed through their own country's struggle for equality.'

What Madesin had looked for and found, first among the working women of her own country then among those of Europe and elsewhere, she also sought and found in the Middle East, that unique portion of the globe so aptly defined by England's Sir Halford MacKinder as "the heartland of the world," the place where three continents meet. Her unending quest was for an opportunity to waken a particular segment of womanhood, the women working in business and the professions, groping in isolation and confusion, to a sense of solidarity and obligation to themselves and to the community.

A bridge was needed between the early feminist movement that freed the individual until then denied the basic rights of citizenship, and the later need to achieve full partnership with men, in the fundamental effort of bringing the entire human race to the full use of its power and riches. Madesin Phillips set out to build such a bridge and she grounded its pillars on a solid foundation of work. Her concept spanned five continents, link-ing individuals in many countries. Because she had the gift of eloquence and an unswerving purpose she was able to move thousands of people—men as well as women—to give of their best in a world in which second-best often passes for good.

With scant material resources, but rich in the quality of her co-workers, she created in the International Federation of Business and Professional Women, indeed in every organization whose course she undertook to steer, a living organism with power to grow. Thus far, their growth has not been stemmed, neither has it been stunted. Her vision, however, ranged far beyond her own time in history, where women were still waging a struggle for equal place in society still failing to benefit from the fully realized potentialities of men as well as women. She foresaw and believed that such a society, equal, just and at peace, would some day be a reality.

"The fair and peaceful world for which countless men and women have died can be delayed," she wrote, "but come it must. . . It matters little whether or not we live to see it. It is only important that each struggle for it."

On the Celtic cross which marks Lena Madesin Phillips' place of rest is engraved the bidding of Christ which she most faithfully strove to obey: *"A new commandment I give unto you, that you love one another."*